Ralph McKay

Risk Mechanics

Financial derivatives - finding and fixing risk holes

Risk holes *are unidentified or unwanted exposures to market forces.*

Copyright

Publisher

The publisher is Risk Technology Pty Limited.
A.C.N. 051 645 526.
Suite 302, 3 Smail Street, Broadway Sydney
NSW 2007 Australia.

Telephone	+612 9281 0533
Facsimile	+612 9281 6393
E-mail	ristek@ristek.com
Internet	http://www.ristek.com/~ristek/

Disclaimer

ISBN 0 646 30803 3

Print date July 1997

Cover design by Suzanne Boccalatte

Printed by Bridge Printery Pty Ltd

For my parents, Alan and Norma, and Claire.

Warning

This book may perplex or even irritate those entrapped by the dismal "science" of economic forecasting. It may also disturb some conscientious risk managers. But it may also enlighten.

Perplex, because forecasters do not need risk management – all risk vanishes the moment they "see" the economic future.

Irritate, because it provides no clues on how to anticipate markets and is based on techniques that assume forecasting is futile.

Disturb, because knowledge may bring to light previously unseen *risk holes*.

Enlighten, because *Risk Mechanics* shows how to find and fix *risk holes.*

Ralph McKay

Risk Mechanics
Financial derivatives - finding and fixing risk holes

Ralph McKay is founder and Managing Director of Sydney-based Risk Technology Pty Limited (Ristek). He is also the author of the related book *Dimensionless Risk.*

McKay spearheaded development of the Ristek *Universal Risk Engine* – a risk management technology based on innovative risk-keeping, multirisk processes. He created the Internet risk intuition competition known as *First Risk Olympics.*

He holds a Bachelor's degree in Mechanical Engineering from the University of Melbourne.

Acknowledgements

Van Thu Thi Le has worked tirelessly towards the production of this publication. She demonstrated great intelligence, tenacity and a motivation that can only come from within.

Francis Pacey provided generous and valuable support on many levels. He demonstrated unbounded patience and kindness and an erudite mind full of good humour. He is also the best spell checker I know – but I am not to tell anyone. His wife, Sue, has also been a great help putting up with untold phone calls at all hours. She also provided some editing assistance.

All other Ristek people have helped one way or another in particular Tuan and Mykel who were always there when needed.

Paul Noone, a very competent banker with both derivatives and balance sheet management experience reviewed many aspects of this material with enthusiasm – asking no reward. He provided many good suggestions. I regret that time did not allow all his ideas to be implemented in this edition.

Richard Collins, the best editor I know and a good friend, was a great help. He has been trying to prove to me for many years that even engineers can write – he persists but *has* taught me not to spare that ha'p'orth of tar whose omission could sink the ship.

T. Erle Keefer from consulting group Glendan Ltd outside Washington DC – specialising in non-apparent risk – provided numerous valuable comments. He was the first to appreciate fully the significance of *Multirisk* and *Dimensionless Risk* and flew half way around the world to investigate.

Dr Ian Hoffman, a mathematician from the University of Technology, Sydney (UTS) provided thoughtful and diligent comments and was quick to see the significant educational potential of this volume.

Dr John Price of the Maharishi University of Management Iowa and Intergrated Energy Systems Inc., has been a willing and generous teacher of financial maths to me for many years. But I will of course never be a mathematician. His contribution to this publication, although mostly indirect, is significant.

Kevin Tant, National Australia Bank Fellow in Treasury Operations, Department of Accounting and Finance, Monash University has been an influential source of encouragement.

None of these people is responsible for any errors in this publication – these remain the fault of unseen *risk holes.*

I sincerely thank all these people. I also thank my supportive family and friends particularly my parents, Alan, Andrew, Stuart, Bud, Ojha, Bill, John and Anne, Peter and of course Claire.

R*isk***: the possibility of meeting danger or suffering harm or loss; exposure to this. (The Australian Oxford Dictionary)

It is an expression of dynamic balance between opposing natural forces. Without risk there would be no activity, no markets, no life.

Risk management is the process of achieving a risk equilibrium – remaining in the field of risk without being touched by it.

The perfect hedge – the key to creative risk manufacturing – is a state of equanimity or harmony between opposing market forces. A permanent state of risk transcendence.

Contents

About this book

Style and content

Risk Mechanics is a "how to" book. It deals with how to analyse, measure and reshape financial market risk exposure using financial derivatives.

It says nothing about economic forecasting, except to say that forecasting, or speculation, creates *risk holes*. Risk management is the activity of detecting and sealing *risk holes*.

The book unfolds as a collection of risk principles and techniques complemented by exercises in the form of worked examples.

The objective is not to cover all possible situations that risk managers may encounter. Rather, the intention is to lead the reader to discover many fundamental laws of market risk management. Particularly those encounted when using financial derivatives. The risk techniques explored provide a "risk tool box" from which solutions to a vast number of practical everyday risk problems can be devised.

The early chapters introduce basic risk measurement, hedging and replication techniques. We introduce an innovative technique, known as *Dimensionless Risk,*[1] used for reducing the number of risk variables and collapsing vast amounts of data into reliable and readily accessible forms. Elementary dynamic replication is explored along with more sophisticated techniques for improving accuracy known as *Multirisk*[1], *AAA hedge*[1] and *Risklock*[1]. These provide the intuitive basis for many hedging or risk reshaping activities. Cashflow risk exposure is analysed in detail and provides the foundation for understanding bonds, mortgages, swaps, FRAs, annuities and complex cashflow related exposures.

The fundamental differences between symmetric and asymmetric instruments are explored and related to the ability to form reliable, forecast-independent performance benchmarks.

Exotic forms of derivatives with path-dependent payoffs are not discussed. However, we do provide many basic skills required for using plain vanilla instruments such as forwards, swaps, futures and call and put options in a creative manner.

Risk steering

Only the more basic, commonly used option pricing variants of the Black-Scholes formula are used here. Inaccuracies in pricing algorithms, known as model risk, do represent a source of *risk holes*. However, we are more concerned with the way pricing algorithms are used. The author believes that, in general, the most serious *risk holes* are created by misuse of pricing models rather than inaccuraties in the pricing models themselves. Attempting to refine the pricing model without sealing the obvious *risk holes* caused by misuse is like attempting to balance a car's tyre pressure when the steering mechanism is broken. We focus on "risk steering".

Assumed knowledge

We assume readers have a basic understanding of forwards, futures, swaps, options and bonds. Where appropriate, mathematical formulae and derivations are provided. However, frequently it is not essential for readers to understand the details of these derivations in order to use the techniques presented. Emphasis is given to understanding the inputs and knowing how to use the formulae.

Constructing the examples

All our examples were constructed using Ristek's *Universal Risk Manager*[1] (*URM*) software system. The Windows 95 and NT versions of *URM* are being tested as we go to print.

However the screen images appearing in this publication used the DOS version of *URM* operating under Windows 3.11.

URM's kernel is a sophisticated *Universal Risk Engine*[1] which processes and solves risk problems in terms of pure risk elements. It incorporates the *AAA hedge*, *Multirisk* and *Risklock* techniques. "*AAA*" means the ability to hedge Anything with Anything to achieve Anything within natural mathematical limits. "Achieve Anything" means anything that does not defy arbitrage laws. "*Multirisk*" means the ability to control many market risks simultaneously. "*Risklock*" means the ability to stabilise the hedge to minimise market gap risks. These three features alone make *URM* a unique management as well as teaching tool.

We do not assume readers have access to the *URM* software, however for those who do, we rework many of the exercises, separately, using the software.

Most exercises are based on Australian market data published in the Australian Financial Review on 19 May 1995. However, the currency or date of the data is not considered important.

Market scope

Risk principles and techniques are demonstrated using money market and fixed interest rate instruments. However, most concepts and techniques discussed are applicable to other markets such as equities, foreign exchange and commodities.

Abbreviations

The following abbreviations are used in this book:

bp	Basis points – 1bp is .0001 or .01 per cent
PVbp	Present value basis points
dur_{mac}	Macaulay duration
dur_{mod}	Modified duration
PV	Present value
FV	Future value
FRA	Forward Rate Agreement

Notes

1 *Dimensionless Risk*, *Multirisk*, *AAA hedge*, *Risklock*, *Universal Risk Engine* and *Universal Risk Hub* are trademarks used by Risk Technology Systems Pty Limited.

Derivatives and risk

Many different forms of derivatives exist. Derivatives are so named because they "derive" their properties and names from pricing links to one or more physical assets or economic parameters. Assets may include foreign currencies, commodities, equities or interest rate instruments such as bank bills or government bonds.

Derivatives can be used to break down naturally occurring risks into tradeable, fungible parcels. This enables companies exposed to market forces to transfer risk to other parties willing to accept it or to those experiencing the opposite risk.

Used correctly, derivatives are risk management instruments that hedge or reshape balance sheet risks related to price movements in underlying assets or economic parameters. Used incorrectly, derivatives may actually increase exposure to their underlying markets.

A carefully designed hedging program includes:

- a detailed analysis of all underlying or native balance sheet market risk exposures;
- a thorough analysis of the payoff characteristics of any derivatives used to reshape or hedge native risks, and
- a sensible risk reshaping benchmark.

Oversights in any one of these three tasks can introduce "*risk holes*" by which through the vagaries of chance, a company's wealth can leak into the financial markets. The existence of very large *risk holes* is the common link in all the reported derivatives debacles in recent years[2]. Undoubtedly, smaller *risk holes*, with less devastating consequences, are much more common. Poor quality hedging becomes inadvertent speculation.

Arbitrage pricing algorithms

High quality hedging requires a thorough understanding of risk mechanics. Risk mechanics is based on arbitrage pricing models. Pricing models provide a scientific basis for all aspects of risk management, including fair market and mark-to-market valuation, transaction cost analysis, market sensitivity analysis, risk measurement and benchmark formulation.

What determines a derivative's price? As with all traded assets and financial instruments, a derivative is worth whatever it can be traded for. But, unlike markets in the underlying physical assets which reflect supply and demand, derivative prices are constrained by their link to the physical markets. Therefore, their traded prices do not merely reflect supply and demand for the derivative in isolation.

By the same token, it is not just the underlying asset price that affects derivative prices. Prior to expiry, other market parameters, such as interest rates, dividend yields, volatilities, as well as time constraints, may affect derivative prices, depending on the type of derivative.

How are the relevant market parameters determined and what is the exact relationship between these parameters and a derivative's price? Modern derivative pricing theory is based on arbitrage models. Arbitrage means the existence of risk free returns higher than the risk free rate. Arbitrage pricing models are built on the assumption that arbitrage opportunities do not exist. The arbitrage model assumes that risk free investments yield close to the risk free rate of return, such as that available from a government-issued bond. The key to a pricing model is discovered by identifying an alternative parcel of instruments that replicates the price payoff of the derivative.

If a replicating portfolio can be identified, it follows that it can also be used to hedge the derivative and effectively lock in its current value. Such a portfolio would have no market risk exposure – it is riskless – and therefore is expected to yield close to the riskless rate of return. It follows that the price of the derivative can be expressed in terms of the prices of the instruments comprising the replicating portfolio. This pricing relationship is the derivative arbitrage based pricing algorithm.

For example, the forward purchase price of a foreign currency can be locked in using a derivative called a currency forward contract which sets the rate, in advance, for the exchange of two currencies. Alternatively, the forward exchange rate can be locked in by borrowing for a term equal to the forward date in the base currency, converting the proceeds to the foreign currency at the spot exchange rate and lending the funds to the forward date. This financial structure is a form of synthetic FX forward. However, this replicating mechanism also reveals the logic behind the arbitrage based currency forward-pricing algorithm. The market value of the various instruments making up the synthetic or replicating portfolio determines the market price of the FX forward. Thus, the price of a currency forward has a precise mathematical relationship to the spot exchange rate, interest rates in both currencies and the term of the instrument. This is known as the interest rate parity relationship.

Similarly, an arbitrage relationship exists between an interest rate forward, such as a FRA, and two pure discount bonds straddling the FRA's expiry and maturity dates. Importantly, arbitrage based pricing formulae are independent of currency forecasts. Forecasting is not a part of the pricing mechanism. This is a characteristic of all arbitrage based pricing formulae.

The arbitrage pricing algorithm reveals the fair market value of the instrument based on observable or derived market parameters. This method of pricing is elegant, powerful and scientific. Significant deviations from the arbitrage price represent opportunities to capture safe rates of return above the prevailing risk free rate.

Astute traders exploit or harvest these situations, and, in the process, force prices towards the arbitrage based price. Hence, such opportunities are not expected to last for extended periods of time. For this reason the arbitrage based price is considered reliable.

Notes

2 Many of these *risk holes* may be classified as operational, nevertheless the traders involved failed to identify the true nature of their market risks – invariably tricked by a risk illusion.

Greek Letters, PV risk measures and VaR

Arbitrage pricing algorithms are used to produce risk measures that represent a portfolio's price sensitivity to changes in one or more economic market parameter. At least one risk measure can be produced for each market parameter. Risk measures should be discounted to a consistent date, such as the current date, to produce present value risk measures. Commonly, three types of risk measures are used:

- *Greek Letters* – mathematical derivatives of calculus such as the rate of change of a portfolio's price with respect to a market parameter;
- *PV risk measures* – actual changes in the present value of a portfolio resulting from a defined shift, or nudge, in one or more market parameter, and
- *Value at risk (VaR)* – the change in value, such as the maximum loss a portfolio may incur within a defined probability and time lapse .

Greek Letters

Greek Letters indicate a portfolio's sensitivities to very small range movements in market parameters. First order Greek Letters are the slope of the tangent of the price/parameter curve at prevailing market rates. Therefore, if the portfolio's price payoff with respect to the chosen market parameter is linear, the change in portfolio value resulting from a given shift in the relevant market parameter is produced by multiplying the shift by the Greek Letter. However, portfolios often show non-linear price behaviour. In this case, multiplying the Greek Letter by the shift produces approximate changes in value only. Usually, this error increases as the nudge size increases or the non-linearity increases. However, this non-linear risk can be modelled, with some success, using higher order derivatives.

PV risk measures

PV risk measures express portfolio risk directly as the change in present value of the instrument caused by a defined change in the market parameters. We refer to these as PV risk measures. PV risk measures are formed by changing, or nudging directly the market parameters in an arbitrage model simulation. However, a vast number of combinations and sizes of possible market changes are possible. Hence, it is sensible, at first, to adopt a sampling method such as the nudging of only one market parameter at a time. This method isolates the price sensitivity to each market parameter. Each nudge produces a separate risk measure or risk component. Also, it is useful to examine the effect of nudging each parameter – except time – in both directions. This highlights any asymmetry in the portfolio. Small nudges in the market parameters indicate immediate market sensitivities. Larger nudges indicate more extreme exposure and highlight non-linear tendencies.

The simple exercise of nudging only one market parameter at a time is unlikely to reflect actual behaviour since, in reality, several market parameters may change simultaneously. Nevertheless, used sensibly, PV risk measures do in general provide a reasonable picture of the overall market risk exposure. It is not necessary to limit PV risk measures to isolated market nudges – that is, moving only one market parameter at a time. In fact, several market parameters can be moved simultaneously perhaps making use of correlations between the different market parameters. However, conservative combination risk measures are produced by ignoring correlation factors and simply selecting the most adverse PV risk measures based on isolated nudges in both directions.

Also, it is useful to produce a set of risk measures reflecting consistent probabilities implied in the nudge sizes used for the different market parameters. For example, it may be desirable to test the change in a derivative's value associated with a movement encompassing say 99 per cent of the likely daily changes in each market parameter. This assists a more accurate comparison between one risk component and another.

Compared with the Greek Letter approach, PV risk measures tend to be more easily interpreted and do not require understanding of special terminology.

Value at risk

VaR measures represent risk as a single statistic – such as the maximum loss within a defined probability and time lapse.

Typically, a VaR measure is produced using techniques such as historic modelling, variance/covariance or Monte Carlo simulation. While a VaR style risk measure is convenient for risk reporting, such single statistic risk measures do not, in general, provide a detailed picture of the form of risks involved. Consequently, necessary risk minimisation transactions cannot be determined from the VaR. Also, valuable information about risk asymmetry may not be known. Further, portfolios with small VaRs may be more risky than portfolios with higher VaRs – both in terms of wealth at risk and complexity of risk reshaping.

A common approach is to define the VaR as the maximum loss over a 10 day period within a 99 per cent confidence level. This means that the 10 day loss will on average exceed the VaR approximately three times in a year. Reliance on this form of exposure management can produce serious *risk holes* particularly as financial markets often exhibit leptokurtosis meaning that the frequency of very large shifts is greater than expected from a normal distribution.

When a risk Tunguska[3] strikes, massive market shifts can occur almost instantaneously. At such times 99 per cent confidence levels may be of little value. Also some derivatives may actually produce accelerating losses beyond the 99 per cent level.

Risk management is 90 per cent dealing with the unexpected and 10 per cent dealing the expected. Viewed in this light VaR is at most a 10 per cent solution.

In summary, Greek Letters and PV risk measures indicate actual changes in portfolio value for defined changes in market parameters yet they say little about the probability of the event occurring. This is not a problem if market risk is reshaped to eliminate all unacceptable outcomes, regardless of how remote the possibility of each outcome may seem. This is the objective of sensible risk management. On the other hand, VaR measures indicate the probability of the loss exceeding a defined limit but do not provide sensitivity to specific changes in market parameters. Risk reshaping transactions can be formulated using either Greek Letters or PV risk measures but not conventional VaR measures. Further, PV measures provide a direct measure of wealth at risk and can model accurately non-linearity or asymmetry. Therefore, throughout this book we focus on PV and Greek Letter risk measures.

Notes

3 The Tunguska event was a large mysterious aerial explosion in Siberia at 7.40 am on June 30, 1908. It devastated 500,000 acres. It is thought to have been caused by a comet. June 30 remains the financial day of reckoning for many companies.

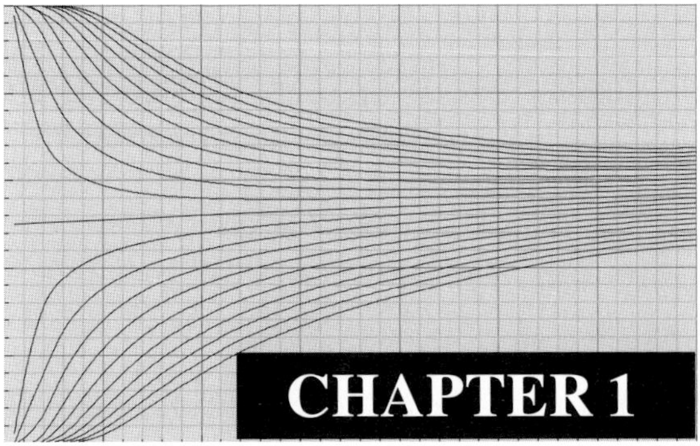

PV Risk Components

This chapter focuses on present value risk measurement techniques, with particular attention given to:

- FRA and option on FRAs;
- risk measurement formulae;
- the differences between symmetric and asymmetric instruments;
- netting of PV risk components, and
- risk scaling.

FRA PV and risk components

The market risk of a Forward Rate Agreement (FRA) is determined by expressing the FRA's unrealised settlement value in present value terms and then analysing the sensitivity of the present value to changes in the various economic parameters affecting it.

FRA settlement values are based on the difference between the value of an underlying short term security priced using the contract or strike rate and the market interest rate. Typically, interest rates may be quoted using either the yield or discount formulae.

Using yield quotes:

$$PV = \frac{FV}{1 + rt}$$

Equation 1.1 Yield quote, interest in arrears

and using discount quotes:

$$PV = FV(1 - rt)$$

Equation 1.2 Discount quote, interest in advance

where:

PV = present value of the underlying instrument

FV = future value of the underlying instrument

r = current or market FRA rate

t = FRA term in days divided by 360 or 365.

Also, depending on convention, either PV or FV may be referred to as the face value – that is, either the discounted or the full amount may be called the face value.

Assuming yield quotes are used and the full value is called the face value, the future or settlement value of a borrower's FRA, FV_{FRA} can be expressed as:

$$FV_{FRA} = FV\left[\frac{1}{1 + r_1 t} - \frac{1}{1 + rt}\right]$$

Equation 1.2.1 Borrower's FRA future value, yield quote

and for discount quotes:

$$FV_{FRA} = FV[(1 - r_1 t) - (1 - rt)]$$

Therefore:

$$FV_{FRA} = FV(rt - r_1 t)$$

Equation 1.2.2 Borrower's FRA future value, discount quote

and in present value terms:

$$PV_{FRA} = d_f FV\left[\frac{1}{1 + r_1 t} - \frac{1}{1 + rt}\right]$$

Equation 1.2.3 Borrower's FRA present value, yield quote

$$PV_{FRA} = d_f FV(rt - r_1 t)$$

Equation 1.2.4 Borrower's FRA present value, discount quote

where:

r_1 = FRA contract or entry rate, and

d_f = current discount factor from the FRA cashflow settlement date to today.

Note the signs are reversed for a lender's FRA.

Thus, in the case of the yield quote, the future value $FV_{FRA.\Delta r}$ after a yield nudge, Δr is:

$$FV_{FRA.\Delta r} = FV[1/(1 + r_1 t) - 1/(1 + (r + \Delta r)t)]$$

The change in the future value of a borrower's FRA, $\Delta FV_{FRA.\Delta r}$ is equal to the difference between the future value after the rate nudge, $FV_{FRA.\Delta r}$ and the current FRA future value, FV_{FRA}. That is:

$$\Delta FV_{FRA.\Delta r} = FV_{FRA.\Delta r} - FV_{FRA}$$

$$= FV[1/(1 + r_1 t) - 1/(1 + (r + \Delta r)t)]$$
$$- FV[1/(1 + r_1 t) -1/(1 + rt)]$$

Therefore:

$$\Delta FV_{FRA.\Delta r} = FV\left[\frac{1}{1+rt} - \frac{1}{1+(r+\Delta r)t}\right]$$

Equation 1.3 Borrower's FRA change in future value, yield quote

and if the discount quote, *equation 1.2* is used:

$$\Delta FV_{FRA.\Delta r} = FV \times \Delta rt$$

Equation 1.3.1 Borrower's FRA change in future value, discount quote

and the change in the FRA present value assuming a yield quote is used:

$$\Delta PV_{FRA.\Delta r} = d_{f\Delta} FV[1/(1+r_1 t) - 1/(1+(r+\Delta r)t)] - d_f FV[1/(1+r_1 t) - 1/(1+rt)]$$

Equation 1.4 Borrower's FRA change in present value, yield quote

and the change in present value assuming discount quotes are used:

$$\Delta PV_{FRA.\Delta r} = FVt[d_{f\Delta}(r - r_1 + \Delta r) - d_f(r - r_1)]$$

Equation 1.4.1 Borrower's FRA change in present value, discount quote

where:

$d_{f\Delta}$ = discount factor from the FRA settlement date to present after yields are nudged by Δr.

Hence:

ΔFV = fn(FV, r, Δr, t), and

ΔPV = fn(FV, r, r_1, Δr, t, d_f)

Also, d_f is a function of the interest rate Y to the settlement date and the term to settlement date T, hence:

ΔPV = fn(FV, r, r_1, Δr, t, T, Y)

Note that the FRA present value *equations 1.4 and 1.4.1*

include the FRA entry of contract rate r_1. This is because it is important to account for the sensitivity of the unrealised FRA settlement or future value to changes in the discount factor. Notice that if $r_1 = r$ *equation 1.4* becomes the same as *equation 1.3* and *equation 1.4.1* becomes the same as *equation 1.3.1* but adjusted by $d_{f\Delta}$.

If we assume Y is expressed as a semi-annual yield quote then the discount factors are given by:

$$d_f = \frac{1}{(1+Y/2)^{2T}}$$

Equation 1.5 Discount factor in terms of semi-annual yield

and:

$$d_{f\Delta} = \frac{1}{(1+(Y+\Delta Y)/2)^{2T}}$$

Equation 1.6 Nudge adjusted discount factor

Forming the nudge

Notice we allow the discount factor to change when the FRA rate r changes, allowing for the possibility that the entire yield curve moves.

If we assume the entire yield curve moves we must also nudge Y by, say, ΔY. However, since Y and r are likely to be based on different compounding frequencies we cannot assume that Δr is equal to ΔY.

It is necessary to decide which interest rate is being moved by the specified shift – or nudge. For example, if the simple interest rate r is moved 10bp, then the equivalent movement in Y, which may be, say, a semi-annual rate, will not be exactly 10bp.

We will assume the nudge is defined in terms of Y. Therefore we require the equivalent nudge for a FRA priced using the simple yield rate expressed by *equation 1.1*.

It is convenient to choose a base rate to move, such as a semi-annual interest rate rather than use the FRA rate because a portfolio may contain FRAs of different terms or even other types of instruments with differing quote types.

First, we need to convert the FRA rate r to a semi-annual rate R. This semi-annual rate is then nudged and the new rate converted back to the FRA rate. Thus we begin by expressing the simple rate r in terms of the compound R and vice versa:

Starting with the PV expressions:

$PV = FV/(1 + rt)$ – simple yield quote

$PV = FV(1 - rt)$ – simple discount quote

$PV = FV/(1 + R/n)^{nt}$ – compound yield quote

By rearranging and using yield quotes for the FRA:

$$R = n(1+rt)^{1/nt} - n$$

Equation 1.7 Compound yield in terms of simple yield rate

$$r = \frac{(1+R/n)^{nt} - 1}{t}$$

Equation 1.7.1 Simple yield rate in terms of compound yield

And using discount quotes for the FRA:

$$R = n(1 - rt)^{-1/nt} - n$$

Equation 1.8 Compound yield in terms of simple discount rate

$$r = \frac{1}{t[1-(1+R/n)^{-nt}]}$$

Equation 1.8.1 Simple discount rate in terms of compound yield

Exercise 1a – FRA yield risk

Consider a borrower's 12 month×90 day interest forward rate agreement (FRA) with face value $10 million. Assume the FRA market rate is 8.33 per cent per annum and that the contract rate is the same as the market rate. Also assume the FRA is priced using the simple interest yield formula – *Equation 1.1* and that the 12 month interest rate is 8.004 per cent per annum using semi-annual compounding. Determine the present value yield risk component based on a 10bp uniform yield shift in the semi-annual yield.

We need to determine the FRA rate, $r_{FRA+\Delta}$, after the yield shift.

First, we use an approximate method to produce $r_{FRA+\Delta}$, then we use the precise method.

Approximate:
We express the FRA rate as a semi-annual rate using *equation 1.7*:

$$R = n(1 + rt)^{1/nt} - n$$

$$= 2(1+(.0833 \times 90/365))^{365/(2 \times 90)} - 2$$

$$= .08417940932 \text{ per annum}$$

Thus the FRA rate expressed as a semi-annual rate is 8.417940932 per cent per annum. As expected, the semi-annual equivalent rate is slightly larger than the simple rate of 8.33 per cent per annum.

This interest rate of .08417940932 is now nudged by 10bp to .08517940932 and then converted back to a simple rate using *equation 1.7.1:*

$$r_{FRA+\Delta} = [(1 + R/n)^{nt} - 1]/t$$

$$= [(1 + .08517940932/2)^{2 \times 90/365} - 1]365/90$$

$$= .0842792014$$

Thus,

$$\Delta r_{FRA} = .0842792 - .0833$$

$$= .0009792$$

In fact, this method of calculating Δr_{FRA} only produces an approximate result.

Precise:
The true change in the FRA rate, consistent with a uniform shift in the semi-annual zero coupon rate, is produced by nudging the semi-annual zero rate to the FRA settlement date and nudging, separately, the semi-annual zero rate to the FRA maturity. This second zero rate is implied from the first zero rate and the FRA rate. In this case the first semi-annual zero rate is 8.004 per cent per annum and the FRA rate is 8.33 per cent per annum. The nudged FRA rate is then implied from the two nudged semi-annual rates. Using this method $r_{FRA+\Delta}$ is 8.42791998 instead of the approximate result of 8.42792014 produced above. In this case, the approximate method produces a very accurate result.

Next we determine the discount factor based on the 12 month semi-annual rate of 8.004 per cent per annum, using *equation 1.6*:

$$d_{f\Delta} = 1/(1 + (Y + \Delta Y)\ /2)^{2T}$$

$$= 1/(1 + (.08004 + .001)/2)^{2(366/365)}$$

$$= 1/(1 + (.08104)/2)^{2(366/365)}$$

$$d_{f\Delta} = .923431$$

Note that in this case we assumed a leap year with 366 days.

Now we use *equation 1.3* to produce the change in the FRA future value:

$$\Delta FV_{FRA.\Delta r\ yld} = FV[1/(1 + rt) - 1/(1 + (r + \Delta r)t)]$$

$$\Delta FV_{FRA.+10bp\ yld} = 10{,}000{,}000[1/(1 + .0833 \times 90/365) - 1/(1 + .0842792 \times 90/365)]$$

$$= \$2{,}317$$

Therefore the FRA produces a future value profit of $2,317 when the semi-annual rate jumps instantaneously by 10bp.

However the future value change is not a consistent measure of risk. We must discount the exposure to present value using the discount factor.

The present value risk component is:

$$\Delta PV_{FRA.+10bp\ yld} = d_{f\Delta} \times 2{,}317$$

$$= .923432 \times 2{,}317$$

Hence:

$$\Delta PV_{FRA.+10bp\ yld} = \$2{,}140 \qquad \textbf{Record 1.1}$$

See *window 1.1.*

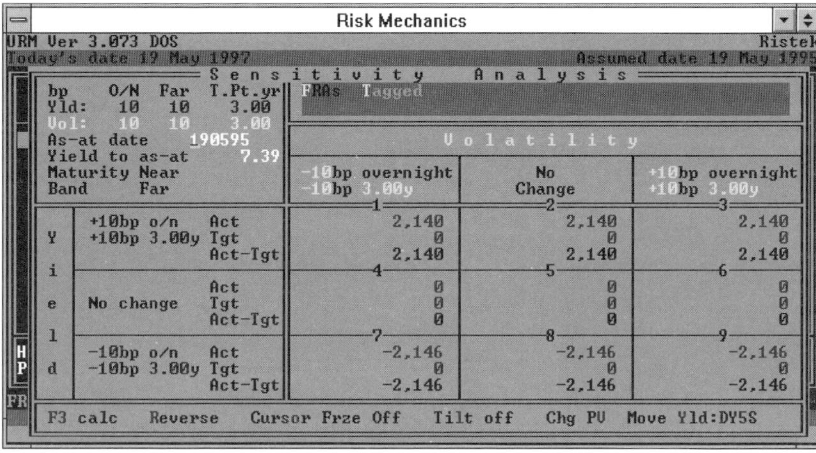

Window 1.1
FRA sensitivity – no time lapse

Different uniform shifts

In *exercise 1a* we moved uniformly the semi-annual yield based on a 365 day count. However, different sensitivity results are produced if different interest rates are moved uniformly.

Table 1.0 illustrates the variation in results for *exercise 1a* when different interest rate types are moved uniformly. It provides a comparison between yield and discount quotes, 360 and 365 day counts, different compounding frequencies and also forward rate shifts instead of zero rate shifts.

Uniform shift	Day count	Yield quote	Discount quote
Semi-annual	365	2140	2325
Semi-annual	360	2171	2356
Quarterly	365	2185	2278
Quarterly	360	2216	2308
90 day Fwd	365	2186	2277
90 day Fwd	360	2216	2308
180 day Fwd	365	2141	2324
180 day Fwd	360	2171	2356
Continuous	365	2231	
Continuous	360	2262	

Table 1.0
Illustrating different PV changes – depending on which interest rate is moved uniformly using 10bp yield increase, and a $10 million 12/15 months borrower's FRA

Exercise 1b – FRA time risk

Repeat *exercise 1a* assuming 14 days have lapsed but the forward remains unchanged.

The discount factor changes as time lapses, otherwise this calculation is identical to *exercise 1a.*

The new discount factor is:

$$d_{f\Delta} = 1/(1 + (Y + \Delta Y)/2)^{2T}$$

$$= 1/(1 + .08104/2)^{2(352/365)}$$

$$= .9262$$

and as determined in *exercise 1a:*

$$\Delta FV_{FRA.+10bp\ yld.14day} = \$2{,}317$$

Therefore:

$$\Delta PV_{FRA.+10bp\ yld.14day} = .9262 \times 2317$$

$$\Delta PV_{FRA.+10bp\ yld.14day} = \$2{,}146$$

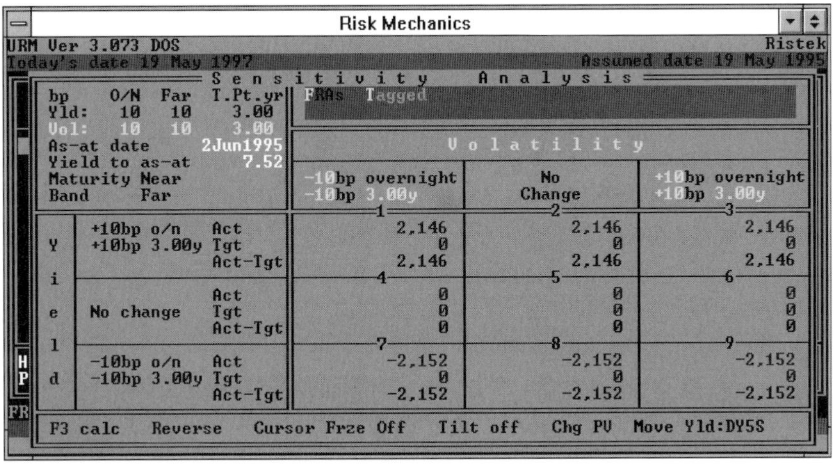

Window 1.2
FRA sensitivity with 14 day time lapse

Exercise 1c – FRA strike rate risk

Repeat *exercise 1a* but assume the FRA strike or entry rate is 7.00 per cent rather than the market rate of 8.33 per cent. This calculation is similar to *exercise 1a* except r_1 is 7.0 instead of 8.33.

Therefore, instead of *equation 1.3*, we use *equation 1.4*:

$$\Delta PV_{\Delta r\ yld.r1} = d_{f\Delta}FV[1/(1 + r_1t) - 1/(1 + (r + \Delta r)t)] - d_fFV[1/(1 + r_1t) - 1/(1 + rt)]$$

$$\Delta PV_{+10bp\ yld.r1} = d_{f\Delta}10{,}000{,}000[1/(1+.07\times 90/365) - 1/(1+.0842792\times 90/365)] - d_f 10{,}000{,}000[1/(1+.07\times 90/365) - 1/(1+.0833\times 90/365)]$$

$$= d_{f\Delta}\times 3{,}906.07 - d_f\times 1{,}588.37$$

From *exercise 1a*:

$$d_{f\Delta} = .923431$$

and,

$$d_f = 1/(1+Y/2)^{2T}$$

$$= 1/(1+.08004/2)^{2\times 366/365}$$

$$= .924322$$

Hence:

$$\Delta PV_{FRA.+10bp\ yld.r1} = \$2{,}112$$

Compare this with *record 1.1* – $2,140. Notice the PV risk depends on the FRA strike rate.

Question 1a

Why is the FRA sensitive to time lapse when the entry rate is different from the market rate?

Answer

When the market moves from the entry rate the FRA shows an unrealised profit or loss. This can be viewed as a cashflow that occurs at the FRA settlement date. The cashflow's present value is produced by multiplying the unrealised value by its discount factor. Even if rates remain unchanged the discount factor diminishes as time lapses. Therefore the

FRA present value changes with time.

FRA risk – 10 point check list

- Is the discounted or full amount used as the face value?
- Is the discount or yield quote used?
- Is the day count 360 or 365?
- Which type of base interest rate is nudged?
- Is the FRA rate nudge normalised to be consistent with the base rate shift?
- Is the nudge normalisation process precise or approximate?
- Is the FRA value change discounted to the present?
- Is the discounting rate also nudged?
- Is the nudge for the discounting rate also normalised to the base rate shift?
- Is the change in the unrealised FRA profit included?

Option PV and risk components

As with FRAs, option risk is determined by expressing the option value in present value terms and then analysing the sensitivity of the present value to changes in the various market parameters affecting it.

We will restrict our present value risk component analysis to European options – that is, options that can only be exercised on expiry. However, the PV risk component technique is basically the same for American and exotic options only that the pricing algorithm is different.

European option pricing formula

A convenient variant of the Black-Scholes[1] formula known as the Garman-Kohlhagen[2]/Grabbe[3] formula appears as *equation 1.9.* This formula is commonly used for foreign exchange option pricing. It can also be used to estimate the price of interest rate options.

$$C = e^{-r_f T} S N(x+\sigma\sqrt{T}) - e^{-r_d T} K N(x) \geq 0$$

$$P = e^{-r_f t} S[N(x+\sigma\sqrt{T})-1] - e^{-r_d t} K[N(x)-1] \geq 0$$

where:

$$x = \frac{\ln(S/K) + r_d T - r_f T - \sigma^2 T/2}{\sigma\sqrt{T}}$$

Equation 1.9 Garman Kohlhagen/Grabbe option pricing formula, a Black-Scholes variant

where:

C	=	call price
P	=	put price
S	=	spot rate
K	=	strike
σ	=	annualised standard deviation of daily returns
T	=	years to maturity
r_d	=	base interest rate – risk free continuous rate
r_f	=	dividend yield of underlying asset, or foreign currency – risk free continuous rate

N = cumulative standard normal distribution function.

Approximate values for the cumulative standard normal distribution function are determined with the following expression:

$$N_1(x) = \begin{cases} 0 & \text{if } x < -6 \\ p(-x) & \text{if } -6 \leq x < 0 \\ 1/2 & \text{if } x = 0 \\ 1-p(x) & \text{if } 0 < x \leq 6 \\ 1 & \text{if } x > 6 \end{cases}$$

where:

$$p(x) = \frac{e^{-x^2/2}}{\sqrt{2\pi}}(a_1 y + a_2 y^2 + a_3 y^3 + a_4 y^4 + a_5 y^5)$$

and:

$y = 1/(1 + a_0 x)$
$a_0 = 0.2316419$
$a_1 = 0.31938153$
$a_2 = -0.356563782$
$a_3 = 1.781477937$
$a_4 = -1.821255978$
$a_5 = 1.330274429$
$\sqrt{2\pi} = 2.50662827463100050242$

The Black formula and pricing interest rate options

A common technique for producing approximate arbitrage based interest rate options prices as well as options on futures is to set r_f equal to r_d. This is known as the Black formula. Alternatively, setting both r_f and r_d to zero produces the future value of the option – that is, the option premium paid at the option's expiry.

Either the price or the yield of the underlying instrument can be used as the pricing variable. Frequently, the two methods produce similar values. However, significant differences tend to arise for out-of-the-money options, particularly when interest rates are low.

The different option pricing outcomes relate to the different assumptions regarding the underlying nature of the price or yield distributions. For example, if the price of the underlying instrument is used, the Black formula result is based on the assumption that the price of the underlying instrument is open ended – when in fact in the case of a discount instrument price cannot be higher than the face value assuming interest rates cannot be negative. On the other hand, if the yield is used the Black formula result is based on the assumption that yields are open ended. The latter seems to be a more realistic assumption, although clearly neither method models reality perfectly.

When performing sensitivity analyses it is important to realise that if yield volatility is assumed to remain constant, then as yields change, the price volatility must change. Likewise if the price volatility is held constant, as yields change then the yield volatility similarly must change.

Intuitively, option pricing based on yields appears more accurate. However, when performing a stress test – that is, a sensitivity analysis – with the assumption of constant volatility, it appears more realistic to hold the price volatility constant rather than the yield volatility. Oversights here are known to have caused surprises – *risk holes.*

Option valuation using yield

When using the Black formula to value options based on yields rather than price use:

S = market rate of underlying instrument's yield

K = strike rate in terms of the instrument's yield

σ = assumed volatility of the instrument's yield

Note: In this case, call options profit from rising interest rates and put options profit from falling interest rates.

The formulae produce option values expressed as basis points which are converted to dollars using:

$$\text{Dollar value} = \frac{FV}{1 + rt}\left[\frac{bp}{10{,}000}\right]$$

Equation 1.10 Converts basis points to dollars-yield quote

FV = instrument face value assuming the face value is the discounted or smaller amount. Alternatively, if the face value is the full amount replace FV with FV/(1 + Kt)

r = forward rate assuming simple yield quote

t = term, in years, of the underlying FRA based on 360 or 365 day count

Option valuation using price

When using the Black formula to value options based on price rather than yields use:

S = market rate of underlying instrument's price

K = strike rate in terms of the instrument's price

σ = assumed volatility of the instrument's price

Note: In this case, put options profit from rising interest rates – price falling – and call options profit from falling rates.

Unlike option valuation based on yield, the price method produces premiums expressed directly in dollars.

Option on FRA – PV risk components

We will assume option valuations are based on yield rather than price.

The present value of the option PV_{opt} is a function of seven variables:

$$PV_{opt.} = fn(FV, r, K, T, t, \sigma, Y)$$

where r is used as S. However, for a given option on a FRA the face value FV, strike K and forward projection term t are constants. Therefore, the option is exposed to changes in r, T, σ and Y. Thus an option on a FRA has four market risk components.

Price and yield volatility conversion

We can convert from yield volatility to price volatility and vice versa using the following approximation:

$$Vol_{price} \approx -\frac{\frac{\partial PV}{\partial r}\left[r \times Vol_{yld}\right]}{PV}$$

Equation 1.11 Price volatility in terms of yield volatility – approximation

Therefore, for a FRA based on yield quotes:

$$Vol_{price.FRA} \approx Vol_{yld.FRA}\left[\frac{rt}{1+rt}\right]$$

Equation 1.11.1 FRA yield quote – price volatility in terms of yield volatility – approximation

Exercise 1d – Option on FRA risk components

Consider an at-the-money European option on the FRA studied in *exercises 1a, 1b* and *1c*. Analyse the option sensitivity to small changes in yield, volatility and time to maturity. Assume the annualised yield volatility of 17.01 per cent.

For convenience the details of the FRA used in the previous exercises are repeated:

Consider a borrower's 12 month × 90 day interest forward rate agreement (FRA) with face value \$10 million. Assume that the FRA market rate is 8.33 per cent per annum and the strike rate is the same as the market rate. Also assume that the FRA is priced using simple yield quotes – *Equation 1.1* and the 12 month interest rate is 8.004 per cent per annum using semi-annual compounding.

First we determine the present value of the option on the FRA. Then we determine the option present value sensitivity to small changes in yields, volatility and time to maturity.

The option pricing variables are FV, r, Y, K, T, t, σ. At current rates the value of these variables are:

S	=	.0833	
K	=	.0833	
T	=	366/365	– assumes leap year
t	=	90/365	– assumes 365 day basis
σ	=	.1701	
Y	=	.08004	

We substitute these values into the Black formula – *Equation 1.9* with the variables r_d and r_f set to zero to give the future value of the option premium. The variable Y is not used at this point.

We begin by determining *x:*

$$x = \frac{\ln(S/K) + r_d T - r_f T - \sigma^2 T/2}{\sigma\sqrt{T}}$$

$$= \frac{\ln(1) - \sigma^2 T/2}{\sigma\sqrt{T}} \qquad \text{recall } \ln(1) = 0$$

$$= \frac{-\sigma\sqrt{T}}{2}$$

$$= \frac{-.1701\sqrt{366/365}}{2}$$

$$= -.085166427$$

Therefore the call option future value FV_{opt} is:

$$FV_{opt} = e^{-r_f T} SN(x+\sigma\sqrt{T}) - e^{-r_d T} KN(x)$$

$$= SN((\sigma\sqrt{T})/2) - KN(-(\sigma\sqrt{T})/2)$$

$$= .0833\,[N(.085166) - N(-.085166)]$$

$$= .0833[.533936 - .466064]$$

$$= .00565374 \text{ or}$$

$$= 56.537\text{bp}$$

The basis points expression is converted to dollars using *equation 1.10:*

$$FV_{opt} = [FV/(1 + Kt)]bp/10{,}000\; t/(1 + r\,t)$$

Therefore:

$$FV_{opt} = \frac{10{,}000{,}000(56.537/10{,}000)90/365}{(1+.0833 \times 90/365)^2}$$

$$= \$13{,}385$$

To form the present value PV_{opt} we multiply the future value by the discount factor d_f as determined in *exercise 1c.*

$$d_f = .924322$$

Therefore:

PV_{opt}	=	\$12,372	**Record 1.2**

Option yield risk

As with *exercise 1a – FRA yield risk* we will assume that the semi-annual zero rate is increased 10bp. Also from *exercise 1a* we know that a 10bp nudge in the semi-annual rate is equivalent to a 9.792bp nudge in the 90 day FRA rate.

The option 10bp yield risk, $\Delta PV_{opt+10bp\ yld}$ is produced by recalculating the option price with S increased by 9.792bp – that is, S is increased from .0833 to .0842792 – and subtracting the current value shown in *record 1.2*. We use the Black formula again to produce the option future value with the yield nudged. This gives:

$$FV_{opt.+10bp\ yld} = \$14{,}651$$

Also from *exercise 1a* we know that the discount factor after the nudge is:

$$d_{f\Delta} = .923431$$

Therefore, the option present value after the yield nudge is:

$$PV_{opt.+10bp\ yld} = .923431 \times 14{,}651$$

Therefore:

$$PV_{opt.+10bp\ yld} = \$13{,}529$$

Thus, the change in present value is:

$$\Delta PV_{opt.+10bp\ yld} = 13{,}529 - 12{,}372$$

$$= \$1{,}157$$

See *window 1.3*.

Option volatility risk

Volatility risk is determined by pricing the option with volatility nudged while holding all other parameters constant and subtracting the current present value.

Again we use the Black formula to price the option but nudge yield volatility by +10bp. Thus we change σ from .01701 to .01711.

This gives:

$$PV_{opt.+10bp\ vol} = \$12{,}445$$

Therefore:

$$PV_{opt.+10bp\ vol} = \$12{,}445$$

Therefore:

$$\Delta PV_{opt.+10bp\ vol} = 12{,}445 - 12{,}372$$

$$= \$73$$

See *window 1.3.*

Option time risk

Time risk is determined by pricing the option with a reduced term to expiry while holding all other parameters constant and subtracting the current present value.

We will use a time lapse of 14 days. Again we use the Black formula to produce the value of the option after 14 days lapse. Thus using T = 351/366 gives:

$$PV_{opt.14day} = \$12{,}168$$

Therefore:

$$\Delta PV_{opt.14day} = 12{,}168 - 12{,}372$$

$$= -\$204$$

See *window 1.4.*

FRA linear price behaviour

FRA present value risk tends to be close to linear. This means that usually the magnitude of the present value change of an FRA is almost directly proportional to the size of the yield shift or time lapse. Therefore, one set of risk components can be used to produce risk components for larger or smaller shifts. Also, when linear instruments are hedged correctly with other linear instruments the hedge is stable – meaning it will be effective for large shifts without requiring adjustment. This is an extremely important feature of linear instruments.

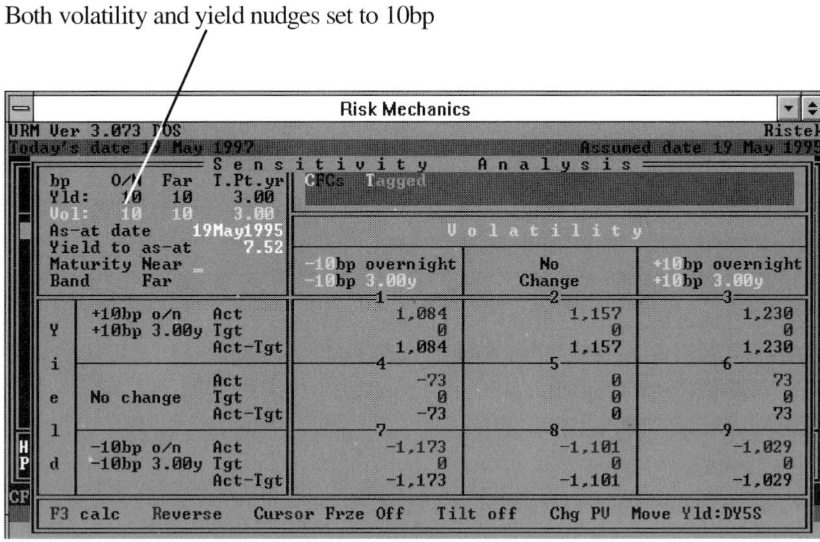

Window 1.3
Option sensitivity – no time lapse

Notice the option is sensitive to both yield and volatility shifts.

Exercise 1e – FRA linear risk components

Show that the present value risk components of the FRA studied in *exercise 1a* are close to linear.

For convenience the FRA details from *exercise 1a* are repeated: Consider a borrower's 12 month × 90 day interest forward rate agreement (FRA) with face value \$10 million. Assume the FRA market rate is 8.33 per cent per annum and that the contract rate is the same as the market rate. Also assume the FRA is priced using the simple yield formula and that the 12 month interest rate is 8.004 per cent per annum using semi-annual compounding.

The as-at date is moved 14 days forward

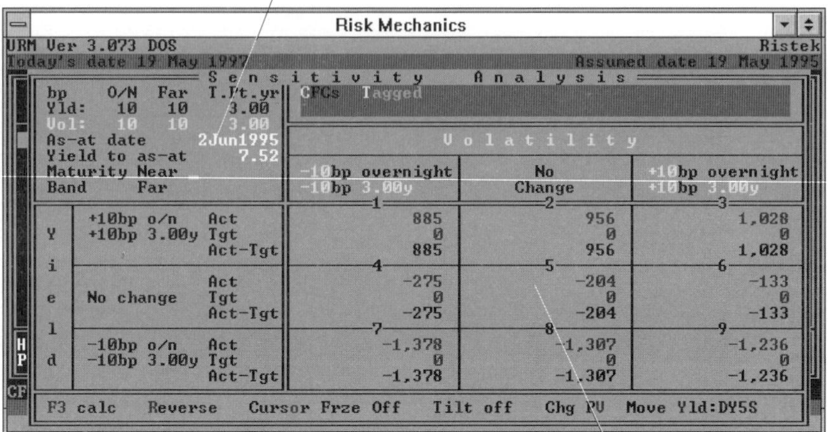

Notice the option is also sensitive to time lapse - cell 5

Window 1.4
Option sensitivity – with 14 days time lapse

FRA yield risk – near linear

As with *exercise 1a,* we use *equation 1.3* and discount to present value to produce the FRA yield PV changes. Except this time we test a range of yield shifts in 10bp increments, as illustrated in the first row of *table 1.1*. The second row labelled delta provides the difference in the FRA present value from one yield shift to the next. If this difference is constant the yield price risk is linear. The variation from pure linear behaviour is provided in the third row labelled gamma. Notice the FRA PV yield risk is very close to linear.

Yield Chg	10bp	20bp	30bp	200bp	210bp	220bp
ΔPV_{FRA}	2,140	2,135	6,404	41,748	43,778	45,803
Delta	2,140	2,135	2,129		2,030	2,025
Gamma		-6	-6			-5

Table 1.1
FRA – yield PV risk

FRA time risk - near linear

Now study the effect of time lapse. We have already observed that the FRA is insensitive to time lapse whenever the market rate is the same as the contract rate. Therefore change the contract rate to, say, 7.00. The results are recorded in *table 1.2.*

Notice the relationship between time lapse and the FRA value is also close to linear.

Yield Chg	7 days	14 days	21 days	180 days	187 days	194 days
ΔPV_{FRA}	41	83	125	1,121	1,167	1,212
Diff		42	42		46	46

Table 1.2
FRA – time PV risk

Question 1b

Why is the FRA payoff slightly non-linear?

Hint:

Study the FRA pricing *equations 1.4, 1.4.1* and the discount factor *equation 1.5,* repeated below:

Using yield quotes:

$$\Delta PV_{FRA.\Delta r} = d_{f\Delta}FV[1/(1 + r_1t) - 1/(1 + (r + \Delta r)t)] - d_fFV[1/(1 + r_1t) - 1/(1 + rt)]$$

or using discount quotes:

$$\Delta PV_{FRA.\Delta r} = FVt[d_{f\Delta}(r - r_1+\Delta r) - d_f(r - r_1)]$$

and the discount factor:

$$d_f = 1/(1 + Y/2)^{2T}$$

Notice, there are two sources of non-linear behaviour in the yield quote formula and one source of non-linear behaviour in the discount formula.

Option non-linear and local linear price behaviour

Unlike FRAs and other forwards, option present value risk is often strongly non-linear. That is, the magnitude of an option's present value is not necessarily directly proportional to the size of the yield shift or time lapse. Therefore one set of risk components cannot be used to extrapolate or interpolate risk components for larger or smaller shifts. However option price behaviour is often close to linear for small range market shifts. This means options can be hedged or replicated using linear instruments but the hedge will be effective for small range shifts only.

Exercise 1f – Options and asymmetry

Demonstrate the non-linear nature of the yield, volatility and time lapse PV risk components of the option studied in *exercise 1d*. Also show that, for small parameter shifts, the PV risk components are approximately linear.

For convenience the option details from *exercise 1d* are repeated:

Consider an at-the-money European option on a borrower's 12 month × 90 day interest forward rate agreement (FRA) with face value \$10 million. The option strike rate is 8.33. The 12 month interest rate is 8.004 per cent per annum using semi-annual compounding and the yield volatility is 17.01 per cent.

Option yield risk – near linear and non-linear

As with *exercise 1d,* we use *equations 1.9* and *1.10* to produce the option yield shift PV changes, except this time we test a range of 10bp yield shifts, as provided in the first row of *table 1.3*. The second row, labelled delta, provides the difference in the option present value from one yield shift to the next. If this difference is constant, the yield price risk is linear.

The variation from pure linear behaviour is provided in the third row, labelled gamma. Notice that the option PV yield risk is close to linear for small yield shifts. However as the size of the nudge increases, a strong non-linear relationship becomes apparent.

The rate of change of the price change as yield varies is a measure of gamma risk. When gamma is high the local linear approximation is less effective.

Option time lapse and volatility – near linear and non-linear

Similarly, *equations 1.9* and *1.10* are used to test the change in option present value by varying the time to maturity and volatility as recorded in *tables 1.4* and *1.5*. Notice from *table 1.4* that for small time lapses the PV change is close to linear but the non-linear behaviour is evident with larger time lapses.

The option volatility risk appears to be perfectly linear in *table 1.5*. It is, in fact, very close to linear and the non-linearity is not evident in this case.

Yield Chg	10bp	20bp	30bp	200bp	210bp	220bp
ΔPV_{opt}	1,157	2,368	3,633	31,122	32,966	34,822
Delta	1,157	1,211	1,265		1,844	1,856
Gamma		54	54			12

Table 1.3
Option – yield PV risk

Yield Chg	7 days	14 days	21 days	180 days	187 days	194 days
ΔPV_{opt}	-101	-204	-308	-3,208	-3,369	-3,533
Diff		-103	-104		-161	-164

Table 1.4
Option – time PV risk

Yield Chg	10bp	20bp	30bp	200bp	210bp	220bp
ΔPV_{opt}	73	145	218	1,451	1,523	1,596
Diff		73	73		73	73

Table 1.5
Option – volatility PV risk

Netting PV risk components

Fortunately, risk measures relating to exactly the same market parameter can be netted. This means the PV risk measures of each derivative in a portfolio of derivatives can be added in a linear fashion to produce net portfolio risk measures. Moreover, this rule applies to different types of derivatives with common market parameters. For example, the interest rate risk components in a portfolio of currency forwards could be added linearly to the interest rate risk components in, say, a money market or bond portfolio.

Furthermore, risk components related to any underlying exposures hedged with derivatives can be netted with the derivative portfolio risks to produce a set of net portfolio risk measures. This produces the overall or aggregate risk measures.

Care must be taken to net like with like. That is, the risk measures from each instrument included in the risk netting process must be based on exactly the same nudge sizes and discounted to the same reference date. Discounting oversights commonly occur when forwards and futures are mixed.

Option/FRA convergence

The price sensitivity of a call option becomes similar to the price sensitivity of a borrower's FRA as the option moves further in the money (S/K increases) – particularly as volatility and time to expiry decreases. Or using the terminology of *Chapter 4 – Dimensionless Risk*, call option price sensitivity approaches the FRA behaviour as spotik increases and voltime decreases. Conversely a put option approaches a lender's FRA as both spotik and voltime decrease.

Volatility: symmetric and asymmetric derivatives

Market volatility of an asset is a measure of dispersion about its mean or average return. Volatility has no effect on the fair market price of instruments with linear payoffs but it does effect the price of instruments with non-linear or asymmetric payoffs.

For example, volatility is not an input in the pricing of interest rate or currency forwards. However, volatility may affect market bid ask spreads which tend to widen in times of high volatility. Yet changes in volatility have no effect on the arbitrage based price! Of course, market volatility does influence the tendency of the price to change and, in this sense, it increases the risk of holding an instrument whether it is linear or non-linear.

Linear means that present value changes in the instrument are proportional to the size of movement in the underlying market parameter. Instruments that are usually considered to have linear, symmetric payoffs include currency forwards, forward rate agreements, interest rate and currency swaps and futures. In fact, interest rate swaps and forwards exhibit slight asymmetry but this is usually ignored in the pricing algorithms and the effect is often minor.

On the other hand, the price of a non-linear or asymmetric instrument is sensitive to market volatility. Call and put options are common examples of highly asymmetric instruments. A long option has limited potential for loss but open ended potential for profit. In line with arbitrage based pricing this payoff advantage must be paid for in the form of an option premium. The fair market value of this premium is known from the foundational Black-Scholes option pricing formula or one of its variants. The greater the market volatility the greater the potential for profit and therefore the higher the option premium.

Risk scaling

We have analysed risk in terms of components. Each component relates to a separate market parameter. It is important to scale these risks in order of significance. In particular, we might like to know which is the dominant risk component. That is, which market parameter is most likely to cause the largest tracking error – yield shifts, volatility shifts or time lapse?

In the case of the FRA sensitivities recorded in *windows 1.1* and *1.2*, yield shift appears to be the dominant risk and time decay risk seems to be minor in comparison. There is no volatility risk. In the case of the option sensitivities recorded in *windows 1.3* and *1.4,* the dominant market risk appears to be yield shift followed by time lapse, then volatility. However, for the option/FRA delta portfolio sensitivities recorded in *windows 3.1* and *3.2*, the risk order appears to be quite different, namely time lapse then volatility with yield the smallest risk.

Have we overlooked something? Yes; inappropriate nudge sizes will exaggerate or understate the relative importance of the various risk components. For consistency, the nudges must be normalised. This process involves a probability assessment.

The yield and volatility nudges must be consistent with the specified time lapse. In this case we used a 14 day time lapse.

Therefore, the yield and volatility nudge bands should encompass the likely range of both yield and volatility shifts over the chosen time span.

Ideally, the probability of the yield remaining within its nudge band should be exactly the same as the probability of the volatility remaining within its nudge band. For example, the nudge ranges may be chosen to include say 95 per cent of all outcomes for both the yield and volatility shifts within the span of the time nudge.

Check using URM – Exercise 1a

Load file RMW1A. A message appears asking if you want the selected file to merge with or replace the current file. Select <R> for replace. The FRA appears in the FRA window <F>.

Go to sensitivity analysis <F6> and set the yield and volatility movements to 10bp. Check that the as-at date is the same as the assumed date; if not, type <0 Enter> in this field. Confirm the records of the PV variations in the analysis *window 1.1.*

Notice the result appearing in cell 2 is the same as the result from *exercise 1a* – appearing in *record 1.1.* Note that *URM* moves the semi-annual rate by the specified nudge, as with *exercise 1a.*

Check using URM – Exercise 1b

Continuing with file RMW1A, from the sensitivity analysis <F6> move the as-at date 14 days ahead of the assumed date by typing <14 Enter> in the as-at field.

Confirm the records of the PV variations in the *window 1.2.*

Notice this FRA is also insensitive to pure time lapse – cell 5 – but the impact of yield shift is slightly affected by time lapse. Compare cells 2 and 8 with *window 1.1.*

Check using URM – Exercise 1c

Exit sensitivity analysis <Esc> and go to the FRA portfolio window <F>. Change the FRA contract rate field to 7.00 <7 Enter>. Return to sensitivity analysis <F6> ensure that the as-at date is reset to <0> and compare the sensitivity result with *window 1.1.*

Notice the value in cell 2 is 2,112 as expected from the calculation performed in this exercise. Reset the as-at date to <14>. Notice the value in cell 2 now changes to 2,201 and that the middle cell, representing pure time lapse, is now 82.

Reset the FRA entry rate to the same as the market rate for use in later exercises. <Esc> <F> <8.33 Enter>.

Check using URM – Exercise 1d

Load file RMW1B. The option on the FRA appears in the cap/floor window <C>. Calculate the premium <F3>. Notice the premium appears to the right, expressed both in terms of basis points and future value dollars. Also the present value premium is produced by pressing <V>. Go to the sensitivity analysis <F6>. Set both the yield and volatility nudges to 10bp. Confirm the records in the option sensitivity *window 1.3*. The isolated +10bp yield risk appears in cell 2 and the isolated +10bp volatility risk appears in cell 6. Notice that the other cells provide risk measures with reversed sign nudges as well as combined yield, volatility and time lapse nudges.

Now go to sensitivity analysis <F6> and reduce the options life 14 days by typing <14 Enter> into the as-at field. Notice the value appearing in cell 5 is -204 as expected.

See *window 1.4.*

Check using URM – Exercise 1e

We can use the sensitivity analysis to check the values in *table 1.1*.

Load file RMW1A. Go to sensitivity analysis <F6>. Set the yield shift to 10bp. Check that the as-at date is the same as the assumed date 19 May 1995. The value appearing in cell 2 should be 2,140 – the same as the first cell of *table 1.1*.

Now start to change the yield nudge. It will be convenient to freeze the cursor on this field. Move the cursor to the yield field and press <R> to freeze the cursor. Repeat for yield nudges of 20, 30bp and then 200, 210 and 220bp. Confirm the values appearing in cell 2 with the first row in *table 1.1*.

The values appearing in *table 1.2* can also be checked by changing the as-at field and observing cell 5.

Check using URM – Exercise 1f

Load file RMW1B. Go to sensitivity <F6>. Now try to replicate the results recorded in *tables 1.3* by changing the yield shift field and observing the value appearing in cell 2.

Similarly, the sensitivity as-at and volatility input fields can be used to check the values appearing in *tables 1.4* and *1.5* by observing cells 5 and 6 respectively.

Summary

- In general, arbitrage based forward prices are sensitive to both yield shifts and time lapse but not volatility.
- Options are sensitive to both yield and volatility shifts, as well as time lapse.
- The FRA price relationship with both yield and time is close to linear.
- The option price change relationship with yield, time and volatility is non-linear but approximates linear behaviour for small changes in market parameters – particularly for volatility shifts.
- The option payoff with yield change is asymmetric and this asymmetry tends to increase as time to expiry diminishes.
- In general, an option on a FRA is less sensitive than the underlying FRA to yield curve shifts.
- PV Risk components, discounted to a consistent date and based on identical market nudges, are additive even when related to different instrument types.
- Market nudges used to produce risk components should be normalised relative to a chosen base rate such as a semi-annual zero rate.

Notes

1 F.Black and M. Scholes. The Pricing of Options and Corporate Liabilities. *Journal of Political Economy*. 81:637-659, May-June 1973.

2 M. B. Garman and S. W. Kohlhagen. Foreign Currency Option Values. *Journal of International Money and Finance*. 2:231-237, Dec. 1983

3 J. O. Grabbe. The Pricing of Call and Put Options on Foreign Exchange. *Journal of International Money and Finance*. 2:239-253, Dec. 1983

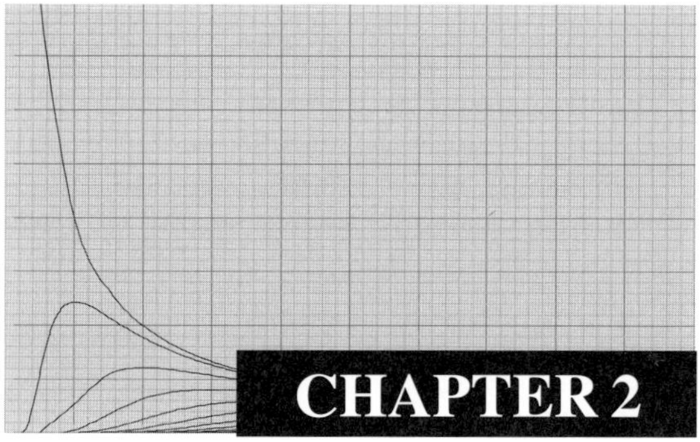

CHAPTER 2

Greek Letter Risk Components

In this chapter we explore Greek Letters with emphasis on:

- FRA and option Greek Letters;
- the relationship between PV risk measures and Greek Letters, and
- netting of Greek Letters.

Mathematical Greek Letters

In *Chapter 1*, we expressed risk in terms of PV risk measures. We now explore the mathematical derivatives – known by Greek Letter names – of interest rate forwards and the Garman-Kohlhagen[1] (Grabbe[2]) European option pricing formula.

Greek Letter definitions

Traditional Greek Letter names for each risk type are:

***Delta*:** rate of change of the PV of the instrument with respect to the price of the underlying asset.

***Gamma*:** rate of change of delta with respect to the price of the underlying asset.

***Vega*:** also known as Kappa, rate of change of the PV of the instrument with respect to the volatility of the underlying asset.

***Rho*:** rate of change of the PV of the instrument with respect to the riskless interest rate to the instrument's maturity.

***Theta*:** rate of change of the PV of the instrument with respect to time lapse.

Mathematically, these are all first derivatives with respect to the various market parameters except for gamma which is a second derivative with respect to asset price.

FRA Greek Letters

We will call the derivative of PV_{FRA} with respect to r $delta_{FRA}\,\delta$, the derivative of $delta_{FRA}$ with respect to r $gamma_{FRA.r}\,\gamma$, the derivative of PV_{FRA} with respect to T $theta_{FRA}\,\tau$, the derivative of PV_{FRA} with respect to Y $rho_{FRA}\,\rho$ and the derivative of rho_{FRA} with respect to Y $gamma_{FRA.Y}\,\gamma$.

The present value of a borrower's FRA assuming yield quotes is, as defined in *equation 1.2.3*:

$$PV_{FRA} = d_f FV[1/(1 + r_1 t) - 1/(1 + rt)]$$

Therefore:

$$delta_{FRA}\ \delta = t d_f FV(1 + rt)^{-2}$$

$$\text{If } d_f = 1/(1 + Y/n)^{nT}, \text{ and}$$

$$K = 1 + Y/n$$

then:

$$Delta_{FRA}\,\delta = \frac{\partial PV_{FRA}}{\partial r} = tFVK^{-nT}(1+rt)^{-2}$$

Equation 2.1 Borrower's FRA delta, yield quote

$$\text{Gamma}_{FRA.r}\,\gamma = \frac{\partial^2 PV_{FRA}}{\partial r^2} = -2t^2 FVK^{-nT}(1+rt)^{-3}$$

Equation 2.1.1 Borrower's FRA gamma$_r$, yield quote

$$\text{Theta}_{FRA}\,\tau = \frac{\partial PV_{FRA}}{\partial T} = -nFVK^{-nT}\ln K\left[\frac{1}{1+r_1t} - \frac{1}{1+rt}\right]$$

Equation 2.1.2 Borrower's FRA theta, yield quote

$$\text{Rho}_{FRA}\,\rho = \frac{\partial PV_{FRA}}{\partial Y} = -TFVK^{(-nT-1)}\left[\frac{1}{1+r_1t} - \frac{1}{1+rt}\right]$$

Equation 2.1.3 Borrower's FRA rho, yield quote

$$\text{Gamma}_{FRA.Y}\,\gamma = \frac{\partial^2 PV_{FRA}}{\partial Y^2}$$
$$= \frac{T(nT+1)}{n}FVK^{(-nT-2)}\left[\frac{1}{1+r_1t} - \frac{1}{1+rt}\right]$$

Equation 2.1.4 Borrower's FRA gamma$_Y$, yield quote

Note: in forming gamma$_{FRA.r}$ we have assumed that when r moves Y is constant and when forming gamma$_{FRA.Y}$ we have assumed that when Y moves r is constant.

And if discount quotes are used, from *equation 1.2.4*:

$$PV_{FRA} = d_f FV(rt - r_1 t)$$

Therefore:

$$\text{Delta}_{FRA}\ \delta = \frac{\partial PV_{FRA}}{\partial r} = d_f FVt$$

Equation 2.2 Borrower's FRA delta, discount quote

$$\text{Theta}_{FRA}\ \tau = \frac{\partial PV_{FRA}}{\partial T} = -nFVK^{-nT}\ln K(rt - r_1 t)$$

Equation 2.2.1 Borrower's FRA theta, discount quote

$$\text{Rho}_{FRA}\ \rho = \frac{\partial PV_{FRA}}{\partial Y} = -TFVK^{(-nT-1)}(rt - r_1 t)$$

Equation 2.2.2 Borrower's FRA rho, discount quote

$$\text{Gamma}_{FRA.Y}\ \gamma = \frac{\partial^2 PV_{FRA}}{\partial Y^2} = \frac{T(nT+1)}{n} FVK^{(-nT-2)}(rt - r_1 t)$$

Equation 2.2.3 Borrower's FRA gamma$_Y$, discount quote

Notice that in the case of the discount FRA the $gamma_r$ is zero.

And for the sake of completeness – in terms of continuously compounded rates:

$$PV_{FRA} = e^{-YT} FV[e^{-r_1 t} - e^{-rt}]$$

Equation 2.3 Borrower's FRA present value, continuous quote

$$Delta_{FRA}\,\delta = \frac{\partial PV_{FRA}}{\partial r} = te^{-YT} FVe^{-rt}$$

Equation 2.3.1 Borrower's FRA delta, continuous quote

$$Gamma_{FRA.r}\,\gamma = \frac{\partial^2 PV_{FRA}}{\partial r^2} = -t^2 e^{-YT} FVe^{-rt}$$

Equation 2.3.2 Borrower's FRA $gamma_r$, continuous quote

$$Theta_{FRA}\,\tau = \frac{\partial PV_{FRA}}{\partial T} = -Ye^{-YT} FV[e^{-r_1 t} - e^{-rt}]$$

Equation 2.3.3 Borrower's FRA theta, continuous quote

$$\text{Rho}_{\text{FRA}}\,\rho \;=\; \frac{\partial PV_{FRA}}{\partial Y} \;=\; -\,Te^{-YT}FV[e^{-r_l t} - e^{-rt}]$$

Equation 2.3.4 Borrower's FRA rho, continuous quote

$$\text{Gamma}_{\text{FRA.Y}}\,\gamma \;=\; \frac{\partial^2 PV_{FRA}}{\partial Y^2} \;=\; T^2e^{-YT}FV[e^{-r_l t} - e^{-rt}]$$

Equation 2.3.5 Borrower's FRA gamma$_Y$, continuous quote

Option Greek Letters

We will call the derivative of PV_{opt} with respect to S delta$_{opt}$ δ, the derivative of delta$_{opt}$ with respect to S gamma$_{opt}$ γ, the derivative of PV_{opt} with respect to σ vega$_{opt}$ λ, the derivative of PV_{opt} with respect to r_d rho$_{opt.r_d}$ ρ_{r_d}, the derivative of PV_{opt} with respect to r_f rho$_{opt.r_f}$ ρ_{r_f} and the derivative of PV_{opt} with respect to T theta$_{opt}$ τ.

For simplicity we assume that all interest rates are expressed as continuously compounded rates.

Thus from the Garman-Kohlhagen[1]/Grabbe[2] *equation 1.9:*

$$\begin{aligned}\text{Delta}_{\text{opt}}\,\delta &= \frac{\partial C}{\partial S} = e^{-r_f T}N_1(x + \sigma\sqrt{T}) \geq 0\\ &= \frac{\partial P}{\partial S} = e^{-r_f T}[N_1(x + \sigma\sqrt{T}) - 1] \leq 0\end{aligned}$$

Equation 2.4 Option delta, continuous interest rates

$$\text{Gamma}_{opt}\ \gamma$$

$$\frac{\partial\delta}{\partial S} = \frac{\partial^2 C}{\partial S^2} = \frac{\partial^2 P}{\partial S^2} = \frac{e^{-r_f T}[N'_1(x+\sigma\sqrt{T})]}{S\sigma\sqrt{T}} \geq 0$$

Equation 2.4.1 Option gamma, continuous interest rates

$$\text{Vega}_{opt}\ \lambda = \frac{\partial C}{\partial\sigma} = \frac{\partial P}{\partial\sigma} = e^{-r_d T} K\sqrt{T} N'_1(x) \geq 0$$

Equation 2.4.2 Option vega, continuous interest rates

$$\text{Rho}_{FXopt.r_d}\ \rho_{r_d} = \frac{\partial C}{\partial r_d} = Te^{-r_d T} K N_1(x) \geq 0$$

$$= \frac{\partial P}{\partial r_d} = Te^{-r_d T} K[N_1(x) - 1] \leq 0$$

Equation 2.4.3 FX Option rho$_{r_d}$, continuous interest rates

$$\text{Rho}_{opt.r_d}\ \rho_{r_d}$$

$$\frac{\partial C}{\partial r_f} = Te^{-r_f T}[KN_1(x) - SN_1(x+\sigma\sqrt{T}) \geq 0$$

$$\frac{\partial P}{\partial r_f} = Te^{-r_f T}[KN_1(x) - K\text{-}SN_1(x+\sigma\sqrt{T}) + S] \leq 0$$

Equation 2.4.3a Option rho$_{r_d}$, r_d=r_f continuous interest rates

$$\text{Rho}_{\text{FXopt.r}_f}\ \rho_{r_f} = \frac{\partial C}{\partial r_f} = -Te^{-r_fT}SN_1(x+\sigma\sqrt{T}) \le 0$$
$$= \frac{\partial P}{\partial r_f} = -Te^{-r_fT}S[N_1(x+\sigma\sqrt{T})-1] \ge 0$$

Equation 2.4.4 FX Option rho$_{r_f}$, continuous interest rates

$\text{Theta}_{\text{opt}}\ \tau$

$$\frac{\partial C}{\partial T} = -r_f e^{-r_fT}SN_1(x+\sigma\sqrt{T}) + r_d e^{-r_dT}KN_1(x) + \frac{e^{-r_dT}\sigma KN'_1(x)}{\sigma\sqrt{T}}$$
$$\frac{\partial P}{\partial T} = -r_f e^{-r_fT}S\left[N_1(x+\sigma\sqrt{T})-1\right] + r_d e^{-r_dT}K\left[N_1(x)-1\right] + \frac{e^{-r_dT}\sigma KN'_1(x)}{\sigma\sqrt{T}}$$

Equation 2.4.5 Option theta, continuous interest rates

where:

$N_1(x)$ is defined to be the cumulative standard normal distribution function and is denoted mathematically by:

$$N_1(x) = \frac{1}{\sqrt{2\pi}}\int_{-\infty}^{x} e^{-z^2/2}dz$$

and the derivative of $N_1(x)$ with respect to x is:

$$N'_1(x) = \frac{e^{-x^2/2}}{\sqrt{2\pi}}$$

Notice that *equation 2.4.3* – $\text{rho}_{\text{FXopt.r}_d}$ and *equation 2.4.4* – $\text{rho}_{\text{FXopt.r}_f}$ are labelled as FX option. These derivatives are not valid for interest rate options because r_d and r_f must be equal when pricing interest rate options.

The Greek Letter derivative produced using the constraint r_d equal to r_f appears as *equation 2.4.3a*. Also note that $theta_{opt}\ \tau$ from *equation 2.4.5* can be positive or negative.

Forming approximate Greek Letter derivatives

Price changes recorded in sensitivity results can be used to form Greek Letters – without needing to use or understand the complex Greek Letter formulae.

A Greek Letter is the rate of change of an instrument's price, or that of another Greek Letter, with respect to a small change in one of the market parameters. It can be produced by dividing the price change, or Greek Letter change, by the size of the nudge in the market parameter. If the price or Greek Letter behaviour is linear with respect to the parameter it does not matter what size market nudge is used. However if the price or Greek Letter behaviour is non-linear this method produces approximate Greek Letter values. Accuracy increases as the nudge size decreases providing the sensitivity results are accurate.

Greek Letters can be used to determine the price change for any size market shift without the need to perform a new sensitivity analysis, providing we remain within a range that is close to linear.

Exercise 2a – Greek Letter estimates using sensitivity values

Use the FRA and option sensitivity results recorded in *tables 1.1, 1.2, 1.3, 1.4* and *1.5* to form approximate Greek Letter derivatives for both the FRA and option.

We will use the 10bp nudge changes to calculate delta and vega, the 10bp and 20bp price changes for gamma and the 7 day lapse risk measure to calculate theta. Also, the sensitivity results were formed with FRA and option face values of $10 million. Therefore, we will divide the Greek Letter approximations by 10,000,000 to produce unit Greek Letter derivatives.

Therefore, the Greek Letters are produced using the formula:

$$\text{Greek Letter} \approx \frac{\Delta PV \times 10^{-7}}{\Delta(\text{parameter})}$$

Equation 2.5 Approximate Greek Letter

In this case, when forming delta, gamma and vega Δ(parameter) is set to .001 – that is, 10bp and for theta Δ(parameter) is set to 7/365 years.

The results of this analysis appear in *table 2.1.*

Greek Letter Type	nudge	FRA		Option	
		ΔPV	App Grk Letter	ΔPV	App Grk Letter
Delta	10 bp	2,140	.2140	1,157	.1157
Gamma	10 bp	-6	-0.0006	55	.0055
Vega	10 bp	0	0	73	.0073
Theta	7 days	0	0	-101	-.1443

Table 2.1
PV risk measures and approximate Greek Letters

Exercise 2b – Using Greek Letters to estimate PV change

Use the delta recorded in *table 2.1* to determine the approximate option present value price change expected from a sudden 20bp and 30bp yield shift. Then use *table 1.3* to check the accuracy of these results.

In *table 2.1* the option unit delta is .1157. This was determined using only the 10bp nudge result recorded in *table 1.3.*

Re-arranging *equation 2.5* gives: $\Delta PV \times 10^{-7} \approx$ Greek Letter by Δ(parameter) or nudge.

Therefore, ΔPV resulting from a 20bp yield nudge is:

$\Delta PV_{opt.20bp\ yld}$	$\approx$	$.1157 \times .0020$
	$\approx$	\$.00023140 per \$
or	$\approx$	\$2,314 per \$10 million

and, ΔPV resulting from a 30bp yield nudge is:

$\Delta PV_{opt.20bp\ yld}$	$\approx$	$.1157 \times .0030$
	$\approx$	.00034710 per \$
or	$\approx$	\$3,471 per \$10 million

Notice the accurate results appearing in *table 1.3* are \$2,368 and \$3,633 for the 20bp and 30bp shifts respectively. The 20bp estimate is \$54 lower than actual and the 30bp estimate is \$162 lower than actual. This inaccuracy is caused by the non-linear nature of options. We should expect this error to increase for larger yield nudges as the option has a positive gamma. This means the delta increases as the yield increases and this is what we see in this example.

Conversely, the delta decreases as the yield decreases. This is why the option's profit potential is open ended but its loss potential is limited – an asymmetric payoff. In the case of more symmetric instruments such as FRAs, swaps and futures, the Greek Letters can be used to estimate price changes with greater accuracy over larger yield shifts. High symmetry means low gamma.

Question 2a

Why is there not a row for the rho Greek Letter risk measure in *table 2.1*? Rho is the Greek Letter name for the interest rate exposure. Therefore its absence in *table 2.1* may be surprising since FRAs and options are both interest rate-sensitive instruments!

Answer

The market rate of the underlying FRA is treated as the spot rate and therefore the delta and gamma represent the price exposure to interest rate shifts.

Question 2b

In general, are FRAs and options on FRAs really exposed to only one interest rate? How could a rho risk measure be introduced?

Answer

A more complete representation of the option and FRA risks recognises two components to the interest rate risk. The second component is the discount factor. The market rate of the FRA may move differently to the discount factor. The discount factor is determined by the interest rate (Y) to the expiry of the option or FRA.

The rho Greek Letter for FRAs and options on FRAs

In the risk analysis performed in earlier exercises of this chapter both the Y and FRA rates were moved together. A more thorough analysis would nudge the Y and FRA rates separately. The Y nudge is used to form the rho risk measure. *Table 2.2* is the same as *table 2.1* except the rho risk measure has been included. Notice the option delta is slightly higher now because the option's Rho is negative. The FRA rho is zero in this case because its unrealised profit is zero.

A further refinement could be achieved by nudging the market parameters in both directions and taking the average.

Greek Letter Type	nudge	FRA		Option	
		ΔPV	App Grk Letter	ΔPV	App Grk Letter
Delta	10bp	2,140	.2140	1,169	.1169
Gamma	10bp	-6	-.0006	55	.0056
Vega	10bp	0	0	73	.0073
Rho	10bp	0	0	-12	-.0012
Theta	7 days	0	0	-101	-.1443

Table 2.2
PV risk measures and approximate Greek Letters, including rho

Note that the Greek Letters formed in *table 2.1* and *table 2.2* are based on unit present values divided by the relevant market nudge. This means the option Greek Letter values are not in the same form produced by *equations 2.4* and *2.4.5*. For example in *equation 2.4* $delta_{opt}$ is a dimensionless number. However, the dimension of delta in *tables 2.1* and *2.2* is \$years, that is price/interest rate.

Exercise 2c – Comparing FRA Greek estimates with actual

Produce FRA Greek Letter estimates in a form that can be compared directly with the FRA delta and gamma *equations 2.1, 2.1.1* and *2.1.4.* Also produce the actual FRA Greeks.

We nudge the FRA rate, r and the discounting rate,Y, separately. Also, when forming $delta_{FRA}$ and $gamma_{FRA}$ we divide by the change in the FRA rate rather than the semi-annual rate as used in *table 2.2*.

FRA delta

$Delta_{FRA}$ is produced by dividing the change in the FRA value by the change in the FRA rate. Also it is useful to express the delta in future value terms, $delta_{FV.FRA}$.

Thus:

$$delta_{FV.FRA} \approx \Delta FV/\Delta r$$

$$\approx .00023177/.0009792$$

$$\approx .23669$$

The actual value for $delta_{FV.FRA}$ produced using *equation 2.1* with d_f equal to 1 is .23675.

The dimension of $delta_{FRA}$ is \$years.

FRA gamma

FRA gamma with respect to r, $gamma_{FRA.r}$, is calculated

by determining the delta after a 20bp shift and subtracting the delta from a 10bp shift and dividing by Δr. In this case Δr for the first 10bp semi-annual shift is 9.792bp and for the second 10bp semi-annual yield shift Δr is 9.795bp – both being equivalent to a 10bp shift in the semi-annual rate.

The FRA delta produced using the second 10bp yield shift is .23658. Therefore:

$$\text{gamma}_{FRA.r} \approx (.23658 - .23669)/.00097935$$

$$\approx -.1123$$

The actual $\text{gamma}_{FRA.r}$ produced using *equation 2.1.1* with d_f equal to 1 is -.1144.

The dimension of gamma_{FRA} is $\$(\text{years})^2$.

Exercise 2d – Comparing option on FRA Greek estimates with actual

Produce option on FRA Greek Letter estimates in a form that can be compared directly with *equations 2.4* and *2.4.5*. Also, produce the actual option Greeks.

We express the change in the option value in terms of basis points rather than present value dollars. When using basis points we do not need to divide by the face value, therefore *equation 2.5* becomes:

$$\text{Greek Letter} \approx \frac{\Delta(\text{basis point}) \times 10^{-4}}{\Delta(\text{parameter})}$$

Also when producing delta and gamma we divide the change in option value by the change in the FRA rate rather than the semi-annual rate as used in *table 2.2*.

Option delta

It is useful to produce a future value delta because the future value delta indicates directly the FRA position that hedges or replicates the option for small yield shifts. The option future value before the yield nudge is 56.54bp and after the 10bp semi-annual shift ($\Delta r = 9.792$bp) the option price is 62.02bp.

Therefore:

$$\text{delta}_{opt} \approx (.006202 - .005654)/ .0009792$$

$$\approx .5596$$

The actual delta_{opt} produced using *equation 2.4* is .5339 – a dimensionless number.

Note this option delta is dimensionless whereas the FRA delta in *equation 2.1* - yield quote or *equation 2.2* – discount quote, is $years. It is useful to express the option delta in the same dimensions as the FRA delta so they can be compared directly and used to form FRA/option hedge ratios.

To do this we make use of *equations 1.10* and *1.10.1* – dollar value of premium in terms of basis points for yield and discount quotes respectively and the Quotient rule:

$$\frac{\partial(u/v)}{\partial x} = \frac{u\frac{\partial v}{\partial x} - v\frac{\partial u}{\partial x}}{v^2}$$

Thus, assuming yield quotes:

$$\frac{\partial P_\$}{\partial r} = \frac{(1+rt)\frac{\partial P_{bp}}{\partial r} - tP_{bp}}{10{,}000}\left[\frac{FVt}{(1+rt)^2}\right]$$

Equation 2.6 Option $years delta in terms of dimensionless delta - yield quote

where:

P_{bp} = option future value in terms of basis points

$\frac{\partial P_\$}{\partial r}$ = option $years delta

$\frac{\partial P_{bp}}{\partial r}$ = option dimensionless delta

Option gamma

$Gamma_{opt}$ is produced by determining $delta_{opt}$ using a 10bp and 20bp yield shift and subtracting the $delta_{opt}$ produced using a 10bp yield shift and dividing by Δr.

Now,

$delta_{opt\ 20bp} \approx (.006777 - .006202)/.0009795$

$\approx .5870$

Therefore:

$gamma_{opt} \approx (.5870 - .5596)/.00097935$

≈ 27.98 years

The actual $gamma_{opt}$ produced using *equation 2.4.1* is 28.001.

The dimension of $gamma_{opt}$ as defined, is years.

Option vega

$Vega_{opt}$ is produced by determining the option price in basis points after a 10bp increases in the volatility, subtracting the initial option price and dividing by 10bp.

$$vega_{opt} \approx (.0052564 - .0052258)/.001$$

$$\approx .0306$$

The actual $vega_{opt}$ produced using *equation 2.4.2* is .0332.

The dimension of $vega_{opt}$ is $1/\sqrt{(years)}$

Option rho

Rho_{opt} is produced by determining the change in the option price in terms of basis points from an increase ΔY in the interest rate to expiry Y and dividing by the option basis point change by ΔY. However as the actual rho is produced using *equation 2.4.3a,* which assumes continuous rates, we will express ΔY as a continuous rate. Also rho_{opt} indicates the sensitivity of the option value to the discounting interest rate Y. Therefore, rho_{opt} necessarily relates to the present value of the option.

When using the option pricing *equation 1.9* with r_d equal to r_f the option premium is 52.258bp and when both r_d and r_f are increased by 10bp semi-annual the premium is 52.253bp. Note that here r_d and r_f is the same as Y expressed in continuous form. Also the change in Y expressed as a continuous rate is determined using the formula:

$$r_{cont} = 2\ln(1 + R_{SA}/2)$$

Hence:

at R_{SA} = .08004 r_{cont} = .07848 ,

and:

at R_{SA} = .08104 r_{cont} = .07944

Therefore:

$$rho_{opt} \approx (.0052208 - .0052253)/(.07944 - .07848)$$

$$\approx -.00469$$

The actual rho_{opt} produced using *equation 2.4.3a* is -.00521.

Rho_{opt} as defined, is a dimensionless number.

Option theta

$Theta_{opt}$ is produced by determining option prices in terms of basis point after a seven day time lapse, subtracting the initial price and dividing by 7/365.

$$theta_{opt} \approx (.0051786 - .0052208)365/7$$

$$\approx - 0.00200$$

The actual $theta_{opt}$ produced using *equation 2.4.5* is -.00216. Note that *equation 2.4.5* actually produces a positive value but we have reversed the sign – that is, in this case the option losses value as time lapses.

$Theta_{opt}$ as defined, is a dimensionless number.

Table 2.3 summarises the FRA and option Greek Letters, approximate and actual.

Greek Letter Type	nudge	FRA Greek		Option Greek	
		Approx.	Actual	Approx.	Actual
Delta$_{FV}$	10bp	.23669	.23675	.5596	.5339
Gamma$_{FV}$	10bp	-.1123	-.1144	27.98	28.02
Vega$_{PV}$	10bp	0	0	.0306	.0332
Rho$_{PV}$	10bp	0	0	-.00469	-.00521
Theta$_{PV}$	7 days	0	0	.00200	-.00216

Table 2.3
Approximate Greek Letters against actual Greek Letters

Summary

- Greek Letters indicate the rate of change of an instrument's value, or one of its other Greek Letters, in reaction to an infinitesimal change in a specific market parameter.
- PV risk measures can be obtained from Greek Letters and vice versa but the accuracy diminishes as non-linear characteristics develop.
- Greek Letters, discounted to a consistent date, are additive provided the same interest rate is used for the infinitesimal shift in all cases.

Notes

1 M. B. Garman and S. W. Kohlhagen. Foreign Currency Option Values. *Journal of International Money and Finance.* 2:231-237, Dec. 1983

2 J. O. Grabbe. The Pricing of Call and Put Options on Foreign Exchange. *Journal of International Money and Finance.* 2:239-253, Dec. 1983

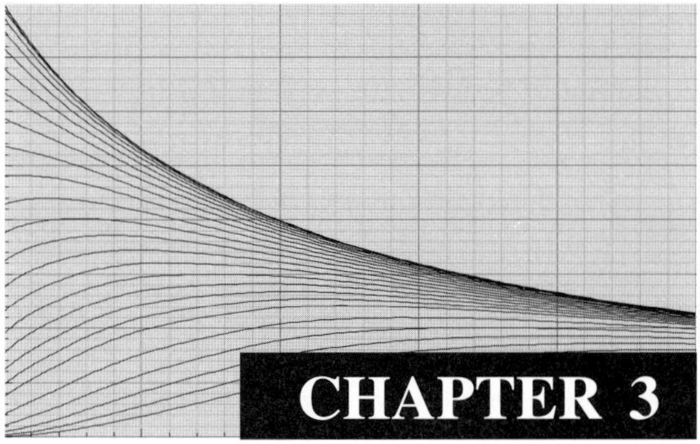

Delta Hedging

This chapter introduces the technique known as dynamic delta hedging. To illustrate the technique we:

- determine a FRA position that hedges an option on a FRA for small yield shifts, and
- use a FRA to replicate an option on a FRA for small range yield shifts and then formulate a rebalancing FRA transaction to improve the option replicating process over larger range yield shifts.

Option delta hedging

As demonstrated in *Chapter 1 – PV Risk Components,* the change in the present value of an option is, in general, non-linear with respect to market changes while the change in the present value of a forward tends to be close to linear. Therefore in general, a static forward position cannot be used to hedge an option safely. However, as discussed in *exercise 1f*, options exhibit local linear price behaviour, so forwards can be used, quite effectively, to hedge option exposure to small yield shifts.

An option's delta indicates the position in its underlying asset required to replicate the option's price change for small instantaneous changes in the price of the underlying asset. The reverse position hedges the option's price change.

Exercise 3a – Option/FRA delta hedge

Use the present value sensitivities recorded in *table 2.1 to* determine the FRA position which hedges, for small instantaneous yield shifts, the option studied in *exercise 1a.*

The delta approximations recorded in *table 2.1* were formed by dividing change in present value by change in yield. Therefore the FRA hedge position based on a 10bp increase in the semi-annual rate $FRA_{opt.hdg + 10bp}$, is the negative of the option's delta divided by the FRA delta multiplied by the option's face value, thus:

$$FRA_{opt.hdg+10bp} \approx -10{,}000{,}000 \frac{delta_{opt}}{delta_{FRA}}$$

$$\approx -10{,}000{,}000\,(.1157/.2140)$$

$$\approx -\$5.41 \text{ million} \qquad (a)$$

This means the option can be hedged, for small yield shifts, with a synchronous lender's FRA with face value of $5.41 million. Note that a lender's FRA has a negative delta.

A slightly more accurate hedge is produced using the average delta produced from both up and down yield nudges. Thus, using the results recorded in cells 2 and 8 of *windows 1.1* and *1.3*:

$$FRA_{opt.hdg-10bp} \approx 10{,}000{,}000\,(.1101/.2146)$$

$$\approx \$5.13 \text{ million} \qquad (b)$$

Therefore, the average is:

$$FRA_{opt.hdg.ave} \approx (a + b)/2$$

$$\approx \$5.27 \text{ million}$$

Note that this method of calculating the FRA hedge assumes that the FRA hedges the present value of the option. This is because *table 2.1* and *windows 1.1* and *1.3* are based on present value changes. The FRA hedge position of $5.27million produced above implies a unit option delta of .527. Notice this is less than the option's actual delta of .5339 recorded in *table 2.8*. This is because the option's true delta of .5339 indicates the option's future value sensitivity to small changes in its underlying FRA rate. It does not represent the option's sensitivity to changes in the option's discount factor. Also, the true dimensionless delta does not indicate directly the precise FRA delta hedge position. The accurate FRA position is produced by forming the ratio of the $years deltas. See *exercise 3c – Option Replication, Tracking and Rebalancing.*

In the FRA hedge position of $5.27 million, the option's underlying FRA is also used to hedge the option's exposure to changes in its discount factor, represented by the rho Greek Letter in *table 2.3*. This introduces a small *risk hole* because this method of hedging the rho risk is based on the naive assumption of uniform yield curve shifts. The *risk hole* is small because in this case the rho risk is minor. However, rho risk can be significant for long-dated or deep-in-the-money options. A safer hedge does not assume uniform shifts and manages the rho risk or discount factor directly using, for example, a strip of FRAs – refer to *Chapter 7 – Cashflow Risk and Hedging*.

Hedge gamma risk

We know from *Chapter 1 – PV Risk Components* that the FRA payoff is slightly asymmetric and the option payoff is strongly asymmetric. Therefore, a mis-match between the FRA delta and option delta develops when yields shift and this mis-match increases as the yield shift increases. This is known as gamma or non-linear risk. As yields increase the option becomes more sensitive to yield shifts. Consequently, a sudden yield jump causes the option value to increase in value faster than the FRA loses value and a net profit is produced. Also, if yields decrease the option becomes less sensitive to yield shifts and the FRA increases in value faster than the option loses value and again a net profit is produced.

So, through simple intuitive reasoning it is apparent that a long option position delta hedged with a low gamma instrument, such as a FRA, profits from market jumps *regardless* of the direction of the yield shift. This is a general characteristic of zero delta, positive gamma portfolios.

For example, in the case of the option/FRA hedge constructed in *exercise 3a,* a 10bp jump in the semi-annual yield produces a $29 profit and a 10bp fall produces a $30 profit. A 100bp jump produces a $2,646 profit and a 100bp fall produces a $3,036 profit. A 200bp jump produces a $9,121 profit and a 200bp fall produces a profit of $11,503. *window 3.1* illustrates the positive gamma profit "smile" for the option/FRA position over a 100bp range of yield shifts.

A long option that is carefully delta hedged might appear to be an attractive portfolio – particularly if volatility is expected to increase. But can such a portfolio lose? Is this a risk-free profit opportunity? No. This portfolio is exposed to a decrease in both volatility and time to maturity – a voltime risk in the terminology of *Chapter 4 – Dimensionless Risk.*

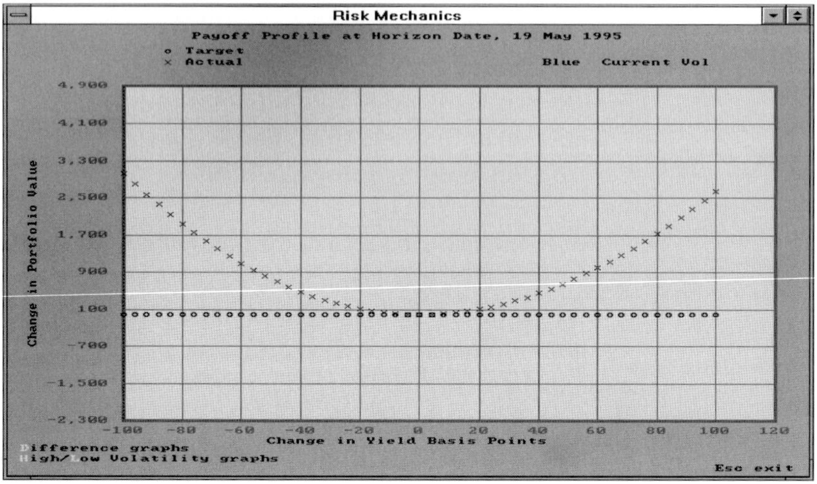

Window 3.1
Illustrating a long option delta hedged wih a FRA – producing positive gamma risk that profits from yield jumps in both direction

FRA contract rate and delta

When the underlying FRA is also used as an approximate hedge for the rho, or discounting risk, the face value of a FRA hedge depends on the FRA contract rate.

This fact is seen by observing *equations 1.4* and *1.4.1*, repeated below:

$$\Delta PV_{FRA.\Delta r} = d_{f\Delta} FV\left[\frac{1}{1+r_1 t} - \frac{1}{1+(r+\Delta r)t}\right] - d_f FV\left[\frac{1}{1+r_1 t} - \frac{1}{1+rt}\right]$$

Equation 1.4 FRA PV change, yield quote

$$\Delta PV_{FRA.\Delta r} = FVt[d_{f\Delta}(r - r_1 + \Delta r) - d_f(r - r_1)]$$

Equation 1.4.1 FRA PV change, discount quote

It is apparent that the change in present value of a FRA depends on its contract rate r_1. Therefore, the face value of a synchronous FRA used to hedge an option depends on the FRA contract rate if the FRA is being used to hedge the present value risk of its own unrealised profit. For example, if the FRA contract rate used to hedge the option in *exercise 3a* is changed from the market rate of 8.33 per cent to say 7.00 per cent, the FRA now has an unrealised loss of $16,869 and therefore its option hedge face value changes from $5.27 million to $5.34 million. The yield curve exposure of this future cashflow is compensated for by adjusting the FRA face value – assuming uniform yield curve shifts.

However, if a strip of FRAs, or a zero coupon bond, is used to hedge the rho risk, the face value of the synchronous FRA that hedges the option reflects the actual option delta (except for the $years delta adjustment). In this case the actual option delta adjusted for face value is $5.339 million and a FRA strip with face value $0.0124 million can be used to hedge the present value or rho risk. The face value of this FRA strip is rather small and therefore adjustment to the synchronous FRA may be the preferred method.

Delta hedging – yield, volatility and time risk

The option price is affected by yield and volatility shifts as well as time lapse. Therefore, the option delta is also affected by these three parameters. Or, in the lexicon of *Chapter 4 – Dimensionless Risk*, the delta is affected by spotik and voltime – that is, only two parameters in dimensionless terms.

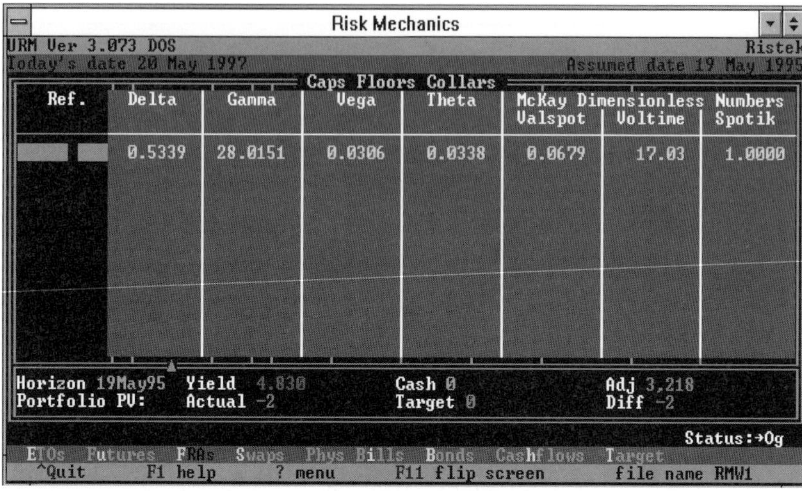

Window 3.2
Option FV Greek Letters and dimensionless numbers

The sensitivity results in *windows 3.3* and *3.4.* illustrate the tracking errors produced by variations in yield, volatility and time lapse for the option/FRA delta hedge portfolio studied in *exercise 3a.* These windows use 10bp yield and volatility shifts and 14 days time lapse. A perfect hedge would show zero in each cell.

Notice the FRA hedges the option quite well against small yield shifts with no time lapse. Notice also that the FRA does not hedge the option against pure volatility shifts (*window 3.3,* cells 4 and 6) or pure time lapse (*window 3.4,* cell 5). Also, as expected the positive gamma produces profits for both increases and decreases in yield (*window 3.3* cells 2 and 8).

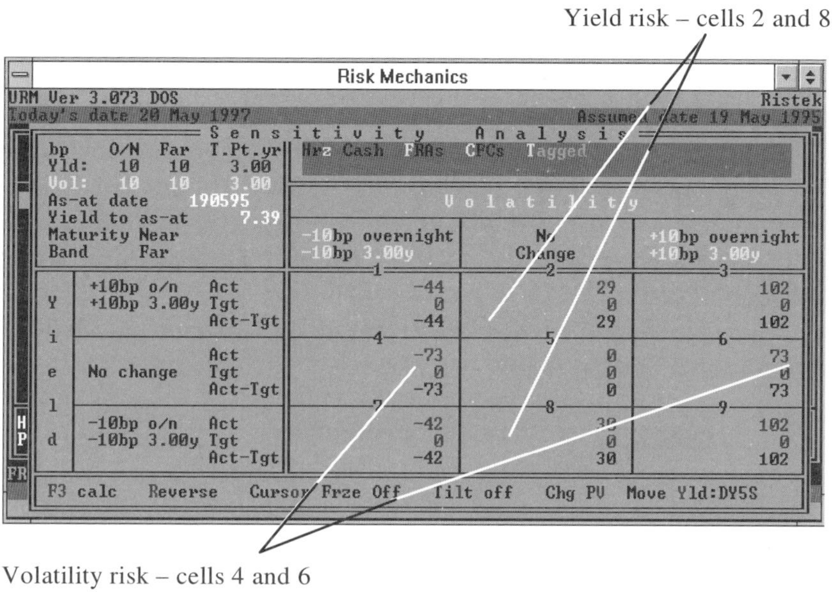

Window 3.3
Option/FRA delta hedge sensitivity – no time lapse

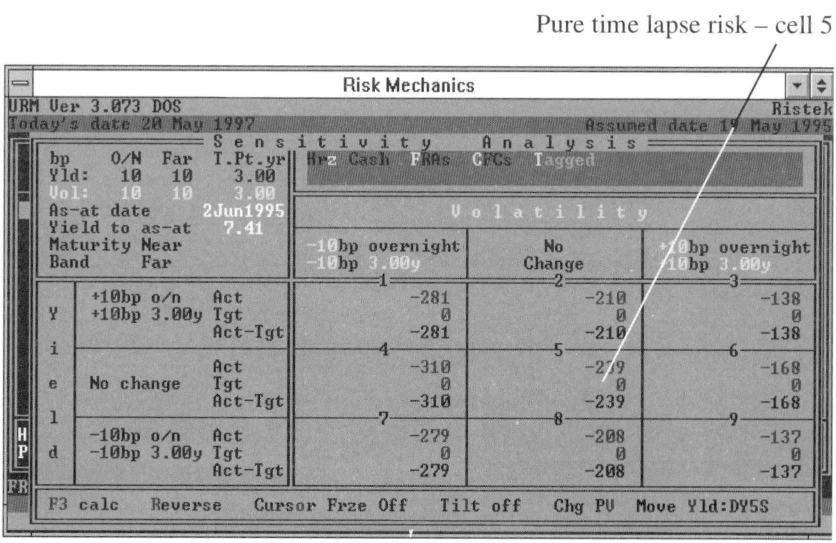

Window 3.4
Option/FRA delta hedge – 14 day time lapse

Option replication

We have seen that forwards can be used to hedge an option over small range yield shifts – the delta hedge technique. It follows, therefore, that forwards can also be used to replicate an option payoff over small range yield shifts.

The FRA position that *replicates* rather than hedges an option's price risk is exactly the same as the FRA that hedges the option but with reversed sign. The risk exposures are also the opposite to the option hedge. For example, a negative rather than positive tracking error results from a yield jump in either direction.

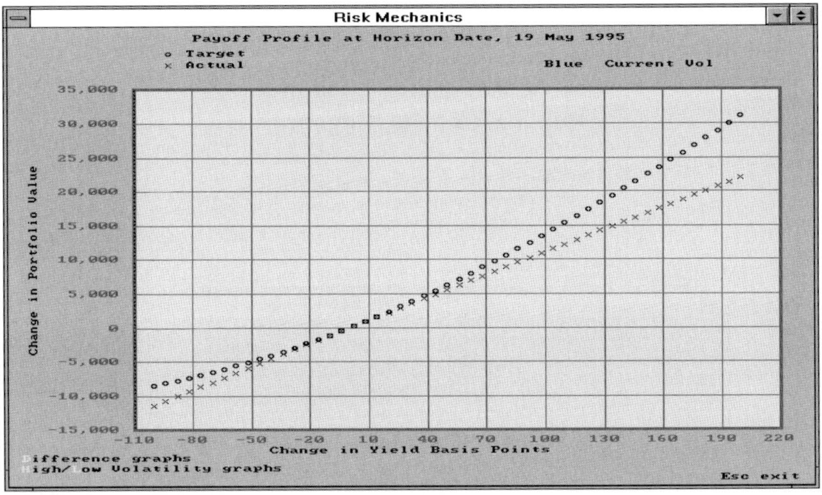

Window 3.5
Target option and replicating FRA payoff graphs

The replicating FRA and the target option payoff graphs are illustrated in *window 3.5*. Notice that the FRA payoff matches closely the target option payoff for small range yield shifts, after which the graphs diverge to produce a fishtail appearance.

Exercise 3b – Option delta replication – tracking error

Determine the expected tracking errors resulting from a sudden 50bp and 100bp instantaneous yield jump when a synchronous FRA is used to replicate the option studied in *exercise 3a.*

The FRA that replicates the option studied in *exercise 3a* is the reverse of the hedge position – that is, we start with a borrower's FRA with face value of $5.27 million.

Tracking errors are produced by determining the change in present value resulting from a defined yield shift for both the FRA and option separately and taking the difference.

The FRA valuation *equation 1.4* and option valuation *equation 1.9* are used. The sensitivity results are recorded in *windows 3.6* and *3.7.*

Notice that as the yield nudge increases the tracking error also increases and this is consistent with the fishtails illustrated in payoff graphs in *window 3.5.*

Dynamic delta matching

The previous exercise illustrates the risks associated with delta hedging – the near linear hedge instrument, in this case an FRA, only hedges or replicates accurately the option over small range market shifts. Obviously, this is because the face value of the FRA required to match the option's delta changes as yields, and to some extent time, change.

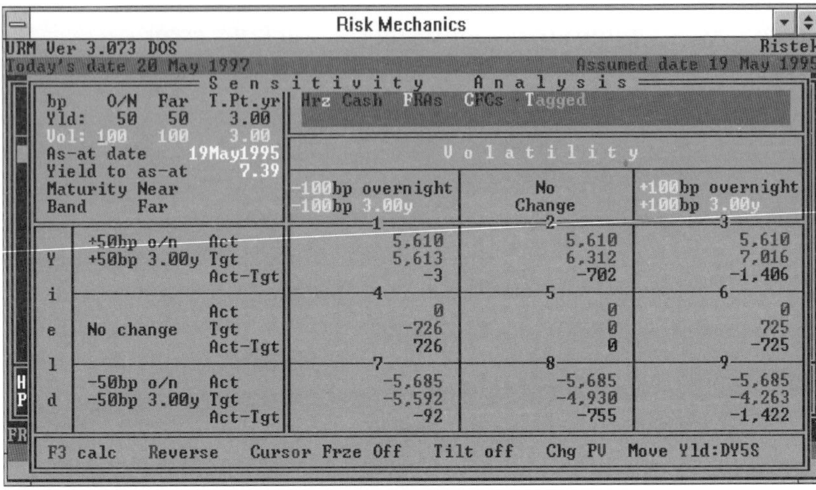

Window 3.6
Option replication using FRA delta hedge – illustrating tracking errors for 50 bp uniform yield jump

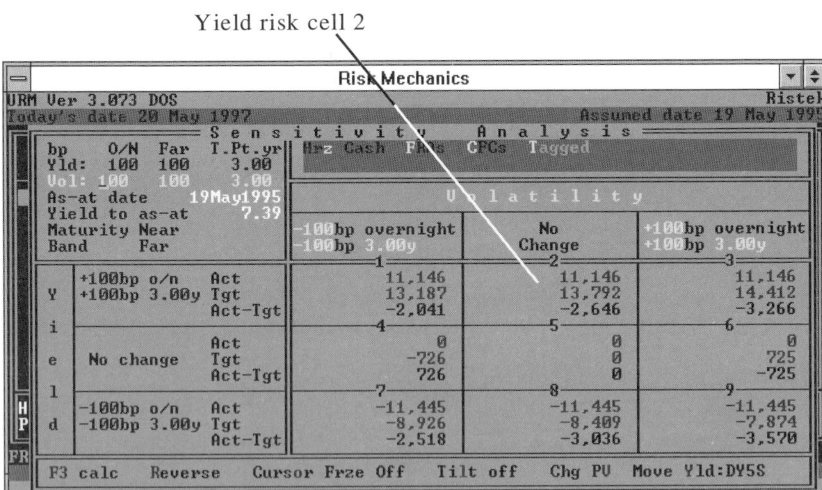

Window 3.7
Option replication using FRA delta hedge – illustrating tracking errors for 100 bp uniform yield and volatility jump

Can forwards be used to replicate options over larger range yield shifts? Yes, by adjusting or rebalancing the FRA portfolio from time to time. The expected replication accuracy tends to improve as the frequency of the rebalancing transactions increases. High gamma portfolios tend to be less stable and therefore are likely to require more frequent rebalancing. However, to minimise rebalancing costs it is usually sensible to avoid rebalancing until the rebalancing transaction exceeds a specified minimum size or trade hurdle.

Therefore, option hedge or replication tracking error can be reduced by adjusting, as required, the net delta of the delta matched portfolio so as to track the option delta through time. This is the process known as dynamic delta matching or replication. Importantly, the rebalancing adjustments must occur retrospectively, in response to market changes. Otherwise the process becomes dependent on speculative market forecasts.

A clear understanding of dynamic delta matching technique is central to all complex hedging and financial instrument manufacturing processes.

Exercise 3c – Option replication, tracking and rebalancing

Demonstrate that the tracking error of the target option studied in *exercise 3b* can be reduced by rebalancing the FRA portfolio before the yield shift reaches 100bp. Do this by simulating a delta rebalancing transaction after a 50bp yield shift. Assume no time lapse.

This is an elementary exercise in dynamic delta matching. We start with a perfect delta hedge – that is, the initial FRA position is a borrower's FRA with face value of $5.27 million. The semi-annual yield is increased by 50bp. Then the FRA and the target option are revalued. The option has a higher gamma than the FRA, so it increases in value faster than the

FRA. We know already from *window 3.6* that this difference or tracking loss is \$702. Immediately after the 50bp yield jump, the target option future value is 86.6bp or \$20,478 and its future value dimensionless unit delta is .6655. Also, from *equation 2.6* the option's delta in the alternative \$years dimension is .15687. The initial FRA position has an unrealised future value profit of \$6,231. And, from *equation 2.1* the FRA's future value \$years delta is .23618.

We need to perform a rebalancing transaction to bring the net FRA delta into line with the target option's new delta. First, ignoring the rho risk adjustment, the total FRA face value, $faceval_{FRA}$ required to replicate the option is equal to the option's face value, $faceval_{opt}$ multiplied by the ratio of the \$years option and FRA deltas. Thus, $faceval_{FRA}$:

$$faceval_{FRA} = 10{,}000{,}000\,(.15687/.23618)$$

$$= \$6.641 \text{ million}$$

Notice that $faceval_{FRA}$ is slightly less than the value obtained if the option's dimensionless delta is used. A small *risk hole* is avoided in this step.

Assuming that synchronous FRAs are used to hedge the rho, or present value risk associated with the option's value and the unrealised profit on the initial FRA position, a FRA adjustment, $rho_{adj.FRA}$ is needed to replicate the present value exposure of the difference between the option's future value and the initial FRA's future value. Thus $rho_{adj.FRA}$ is the FRA with equal exposure to uniform yield shifts as a cashflow with duration equal to the option's expiry and face value equal to \$20,478 - \$6,231 or \$14,247. This is a lender's FRA with face value of \$.06 million.

Therefore, the required rebalancing FRA, $rebal_{FRA}$ is:

$$rebal_{FRA} = 6.64 - 5.27 - .06$$

$$= \$1.31 \text{ million}$$

Thus we perform a rebalancing transaction by executing another borrower's FRA with face value of $1.31 million.

Now we determine the tracking error caused by the second 50bp. We perform a sensitivity analysis on the delta rebalanced FRA and option portfolio to determine the additional tracking error introduced by a further 50bp yield increase. These tracking errors are provided in *window 3.8.* A 50bp yield increase creates a further $585 tracking loss.

Therefore the total tracking error following a 100bp yield jump but with a midway delta rebalancing is:

$$\text{Total tracking loss} = 702 + 585$$

$$= \$1,287$$

Tracking error	=	$1,287	**Record 3.1**

Recall that the tracking loss without the delta adjustment at 50bp is $2,646, as recorded in cell 2 of *window 3.7.* Hence, the hedge adjustment saved the difference between $2,646 and $1,287 – that is $1,359.

Question 3a

What effect would the FRA rebalancing transaction have on the net tracking error if the yield immediately fell back to the starting rate, rather than continued to rise?

Answer

The rebalancing FRA would incur a loss. This form of "wipe-saw" loss is accounted for in the initial option premium estimate. That is, like the actual option premium, which has a volatility/time, or voltime, risk component – the option replication process based on FRA trading also has a voltime risk component.

However, if the volatility increases the "wipe-saw" FRA losses are likely to increase. Conversely, if volatility decreases, the synthetic FRA-based option is likely to cost less than the initial estimate. A volatility *risk hole* exists.

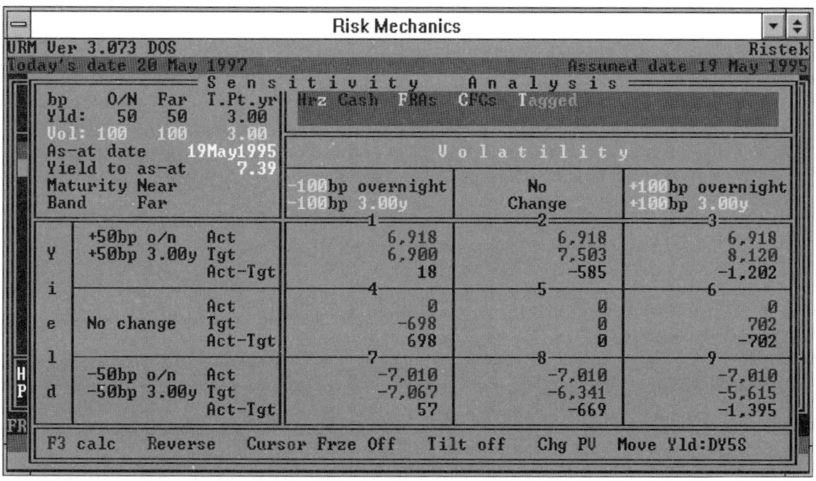

Window 3.8
Option replication tracking errors for second 50 bp yield shift with rebalanced delta hedge.

Question 3b

How does the tracking performance change if the trade hurdle is widened or narrowed and what effect does this have on the expected cost of replication?

Answer

This raises a complex issue. However, in a frictionless market – that is, with zero transaction costs – the expected cost is the same regardless of the trade hurdle. The wider the trade hurdle the larger the expected scatter around the expected result. However, in real markets with transaction costs, a trade hurdle that is too narrow is likely to result in excessive transaction costs.

Check using URM – Exercise 3a

Load file RMW1 – the same file used in *Chapter 1* – which contains both the FRA and option used in *exercise 3a*. Go to the FRA portfolio window <F> and enter the delta hedge estimate into the face value field <5.27 Enter>. Go to sensitivity analysis <F6> and check the as-at date is the same as the assumed date. Now test the impact of yield jumps of 10, 100 and 200bp.

With a perfect hedge, the portfolio shows no change in value for small yield shifts, both up and down. This hedge is not perfect, however the magnitude and sign of the hedge errors should be approximately the same for both the up and down yield shifts. In this case, the 10bp up and down errors are +$29 and +$30 respectively.

Now use *URM* to compute the FRA face value that delta hedges the option automatically. Return to the FRA portfolio window. Place the cursor on the face value field and press <Delete>, followed by <F3> to calculate. Notice the FRA delta hedge face value is computed automatically. The result should be $5.27 million, as predicted in *exercise 3a*.

Next check that the FRA face value is $5.27million. View the payoff graph <F8> <F8>. See *window 3.1*. Notice the "smile" effect – this option/FRA portfolio profits from both up and down yield shifts.

Check using URM – FRA contract rate and delta

Load RMW1. Unfix the FRA face value by moving the cursor to the face value field and pressing <Delete> and calculate <F3>. Notice the FRA face value is 5.27 million (or L5.27 meaning Lender's FRA). Now change the FRA contract rate to say, 7.00 <7 Enter>, watch the FRA face value field and again calculate <F3>. Notice the face value changes from L$5.27 million to L$5.34 million and that the FRA now has an unrealised future value loss of $16,869. The option Greek Letters appear in a Cap/Floor flip window <C> <F11> <F11>. Refer to *window 3.2.*

Now load file RMW1F. Calculate <F3>. This file contains exactly the same FRA and option as RMW1, except that it also includes a strip of FRAs spanning from our assumed date to the expiry of the FRA/option portfolio. Notice the FRA strip face value is $.01 million (it is actually closer to .0124 – however *URM* rounds to two decimal places) and the original synchronous FRA, expiring on 19 May 1996, now has a face value of $5.33 million – corresponding closely to the actual delta of the option.

Check using URM – Delta hedging – yield, volatility and time risk

Load file RMW1. Ensure that the FRA face value is set to the delta hedge value .527million. Go to sensitivity analysis <F6>, set both the volatility and yield nudges to 10bp and ensure that the as-at date is the same as the assumed date. The sensitivity result should be the same as *window 3.3*. Now place the cursor on the as-at date field and type <14 Enter>. The sensitivity result should be the same as *window 3.4*.

Check using URM – Option replication

Load file RMW1T. This file contains exactly the same two instruments as file RMW1 except that the option position appears in the target Cap/Floor window, <C> <T> instead of the actual portfolio window. This means that the hedge instrument, in this case the FRA, is formulated to replicate the option payoff, rather than hedge it.

Go to the FRA (actual) window. <T> <F>. Watch the FRA face value and calculate <F3>. Notice the calculated FRA face value is the same as for *exercise 3a*, but the sign is reversed -$5.27 million – a borrower's FRA. This position replicates the option payoff over small range movements. View the payoff graph <F8> <F8> and notice that the FRA graph matches closely the target option for small range yield shifts, after which the graphs diverge to produce a fishtail appearance. See *window 3.5.*

Check using URM – Exercise 3b

Use file RMW1T. Press <F3> to calculate the FRA face value required to replicate the option. Go to sensitivity analysis <F6>. Set the as-at date to zero. Set the yield shift to 50bp. Also set the volatility shift to 100bp. The tracking error is the third field in each cell of the sensitivity window and should be the same as *window 3.6.* The 50bp pure yield shift risk appears in cell 2. Next change the yield shift to 100bp. The tracking errors should be the same as *window 3.7.*

Check using URM – Exercise 3c

Load file RMW1TA. Go to the FRA window <F>. Notice the market yields have been increased by 50bp. Also, market rates for the option appearing in the target Cap/Floor window have also been increased by 50bp. (This involves a slight approximation as a 50bp move in the 90 day rate does not correspond exactly to a 50bp move in the semi-annual rate.)

View the sensitivity analysis <F6> and payoff graph <F8> <F8>. Notice the asymmetry in the tracking error. This is a sign of an unbalanced hedge – a *risk hole* exists! The option delta has changed substantially but the FRA delta is almost the same.

Now use *URM* to formulate the FRA delta rebalancing transaction. Go to the FRA window and press <Ctrl D>. This copies the current row, thereby creating a second FRA with the same market data but with blank contract rate and face value. Calculate <F3>. Notice the new FRA face value of $-1.31 million is computed automatically. The delta rebalancing transaction has the effect of lessening the tracking error over the next 50bp shift.

Notice the tracking error is displayed in the cash field labelled Adj. The amount showing should be $734. This tracking error is close to the error of $702 predicted using the sensitivity analysis as recorded in cell 2 in *window 3.6.* There is a slight difference because the sensitivity analysis moved the 90 day and semi-annual rates in a consistent manner, whereas the actual market nudge used here was 50bp for both rates.

Observe the sensitivity analysis and payoff windows again. Notice the tracking error is now more symmetric, indicating that the delta hedge is balanced again.

Next determine the tracking error caused by the second 50bp yield shift. Go to the sensitivity analysis and set the yield nudge to 50bp. Confirm your result with *window 3.8.* Cell 2 which shows a loss of $585. Thus the total tracking error is $1,287.

Summary

- ❑ The FRA delta hedge is effective over a small range of movements only.
- ❑ As the size of the yield shift increases the tracking error increases. The rate of change of this increase in error is a measure of gamma risk.
- ❑ Regular rebalancing of the delta hedge reduces tracking error.
- ❑ The FRA delta hedge also affects the portfolio's time lapse risk.
- ❑ The FRA delta hedge does not affect the portfolio's exposure to pure volatility shifts.
- ❑ A zero delta positive gamma portfolio profits from yield jumps in either direction and loses value with pure time lapse.

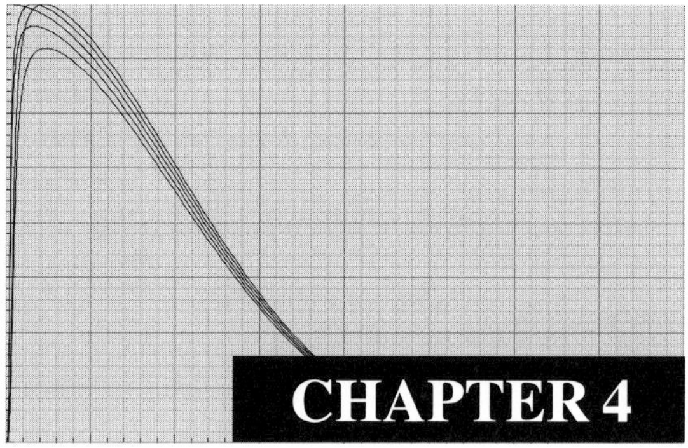

Dimensionless Risk™

This chapter introduces *McKay's dimensionless risk.* Using the European option pricing formula we demonstrate how to:

- produce universal pricing charts based on dimensionless numbers, and
- reduce the number of variables in a complex pricing formula.

Dimensionless numbers – spotik, voltime and valspot

Consider the currency option pricing formula repeated below:

$$C = e^{-r_f T} S N(x+\sigma\sqrt{T}) - e^{-r_d T} K N(x) \geq 0$$

$$P = e^{-r_f T} S[N(x+\sigma\sqrt{T})-1] - e^{-r_d T} K[N(x)-1] \geq 0$$

where:

$$x = \frac{\ln(S/K) + r_d T - r_f T - \sigma^2 T/2}{\sigma\sqrt{T}}$$

C = call price
P = put price
S = spot rate
K = strike
σ = annualised standard deviation of daily returns
T = years to maturity
r_d = base currency risk free continuous interest rate
r_f = dividend yield of underlying asset, or foreign currency risk free continuous interest rate
N = cumulative standard normal distribution function.

This Black-Scholes related pricing formula is complex. It also has a large number of variables. For this reason we tend to be very dependent upon computers and high quality programming skills to produce fair market option prices. Computers can fail. It is useful therefore, if not essential, to have a reliable checking mechanism. For the same reason it is important to develop a good "risk intuition" that reacts to suspicious prices or risk analyses.

One method is to produce a reference table of option prices representing all possible market variables. It would, however, be a very large table indeed. This may not practical. However, there is a technique of representing all option prices on one sheet of paper. The author calls this technique *Dimensionless Risk*.

Study the Black-Scholes related equation. It is apparent that the option price P depends on six variables:

$$P = fn(S, K, \sigma, r_d, r_f, T)$$

However, for interest rate options the future value is obtained by setting both r_d and r_f to zero. This reduces the number of variables by two. But we still have four variables left in the equation. Study the Black-Scholes equation again and notice that with both interest rate variables set to zero we can view S/K, $\sigma\sqrt{T}$, P/(SA) (A = face value) as the only variables in the equation. This reduces the number of variables to three. These three variables are dimensionless, as the dimensions cancel in each case. We will call these three dimensionless numbers *spotik*, *voltime* and *valspot* respectively.

Risk similitude

Since we only have three variables, all possible option prices can be represented on one graph. We could say a form of dimensionless risk similitude exists between any two options with two identical dimensionless numbers – meaning they must also have the same value for the third dimensionless number. For example, if two call options with different maturities have the same voltime and valspot they must also have the same value for spotik. This information may for example, be used to solve for the strike of the second option.

Chart 4.1 – McKay's dimensionless European call option represents all European call option prices[1]. This dimensionless chart can be used to obtain an approximate future value of any interest rate option. The value must be discounted to obtain the present value. Another dimensionless chart can be used to convert the future value into present value. Alternatively, a present valued form of valspot can be used to produce directly the present value option premium.

Chart reading accuracy depends on the size of the chart and the number of spotik plots[1].

Other dimensionless charts included are:

Chart 4.2 – McKay's dimensionless European call option delta chart, representing European call option deltas;
Chart 4.3 – McKay's dimensionless European put option chart, representing European put option prices;
Chart 4.4 – McKay's dimensionless European put option delta chart, representing European put option deltas, and
Charts 4.5, 4.6, 4.7 and 4.8 – McKay's dimensionless European option gamma charts, representing European call and put option gammas.

Put/call symmetry – put option risk from the call algorithm

In fact, separate charts for the put option are not essential because call option charts can be used for the put option by observing put/call symmetry as observed by Grabbe[2] and more recently in a more general sense by Kholodnyi and Price[3].

Expressed in a currency context, put/call symmetry means that a European or American call option on a unit of a foreign currency, with strike K priced in terms of the domestic currency, is the same as a put option on the domestic currency with face value K priced and strike 1/K in terms of the foreign currency.

That is:

$$\text{Call}(S, K, T, \sigma, r_d, r_f) \;=\; S \times K\ \text{Put}(1/S, 1/K, T, \sigma, r_f, r_d)$$

Therefore, we can use the call charts to produce put prices or risk measures by replacing spotik with 1/spotik and observing the SK adjustment.

Note put/call symmetry should not be confused with the more commonly understood put/call parity relationship which applies to European options only.

Put/call symmetry may be obvious intuitively because it is simply the recognition of the same asset viewed from the alternate currency. In fact, it is the same asset regardless of whatever third currency from which it is observed. However the symmetric strike is less obvious for some path dependent options, such as Asian options, where it is not simply 1/K.

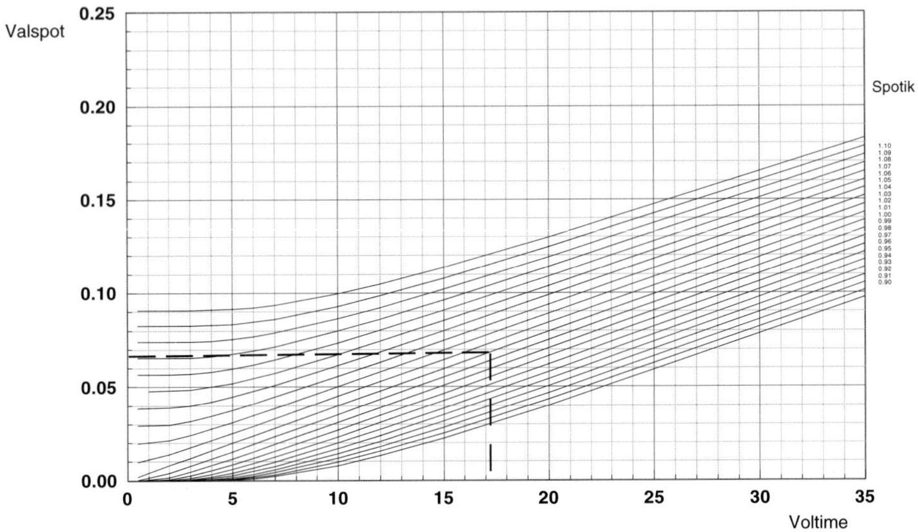

Chart 4.1
McKay's dimensionless European call option chart

where:

valspot	=	prem/spot
voltime	=	vol√time
spotik	=	spot/strike
time	=	years to maturity
vol	=	volatility expressed as a per cent.

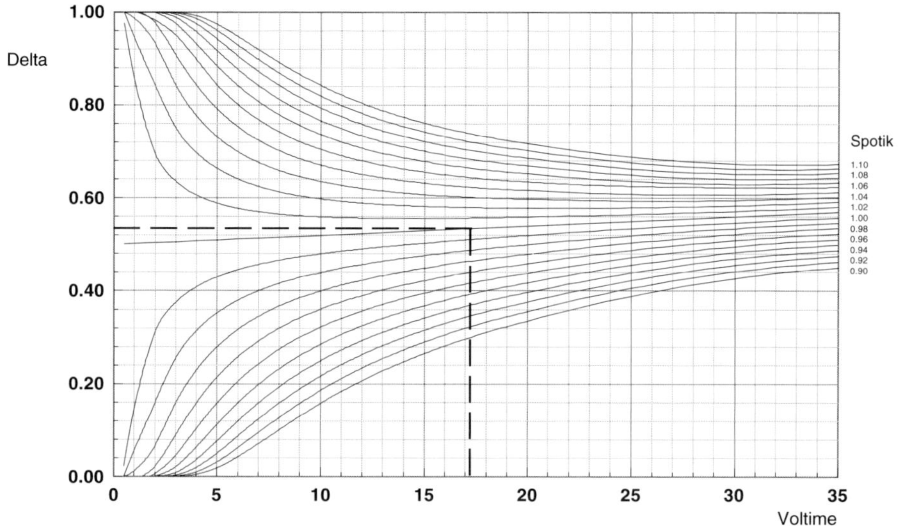

Chart 4.2
McKay's dimensionless European call option delta chart

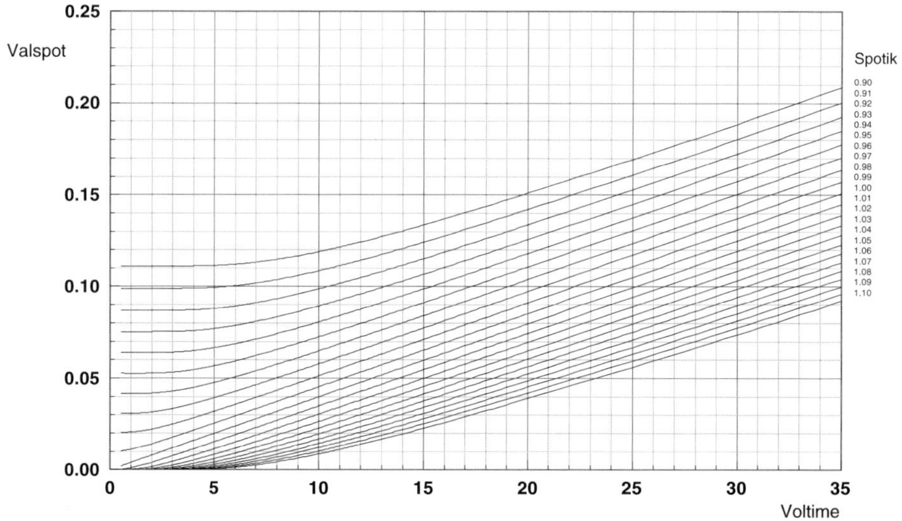

Chart 4.3
McKay's dimensionless European put option chart

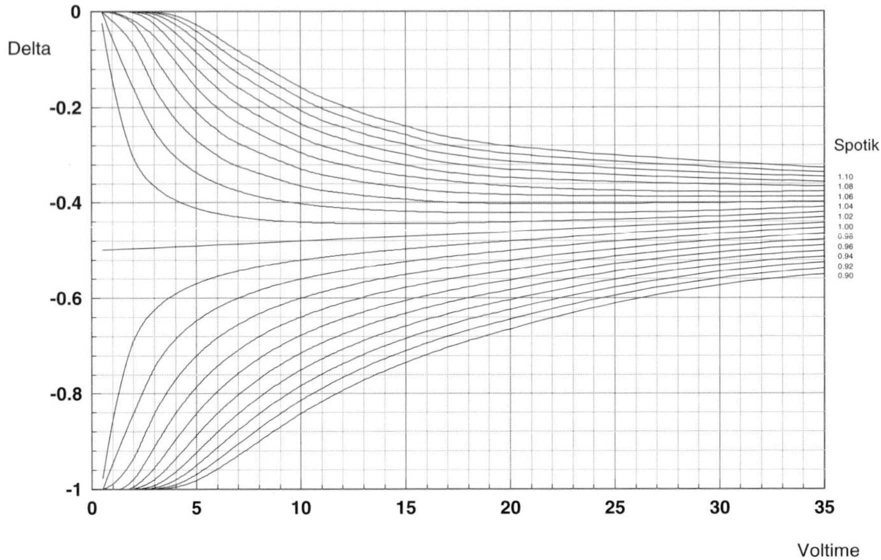

Chart 4.4
McKay's dimensionless European put option delta chart

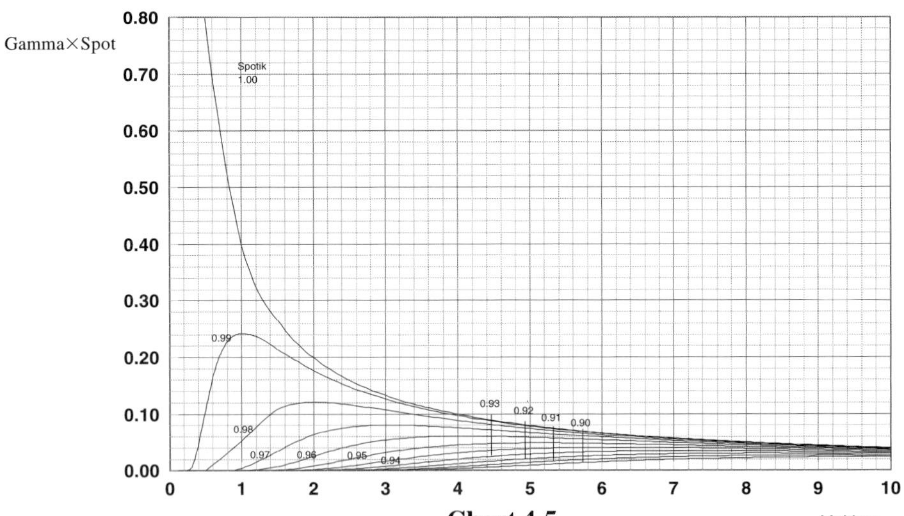

Chart 4.5
McKay's dimensionless European option gamma chart – voltime 0 - 10, spotik .90 – 1.00

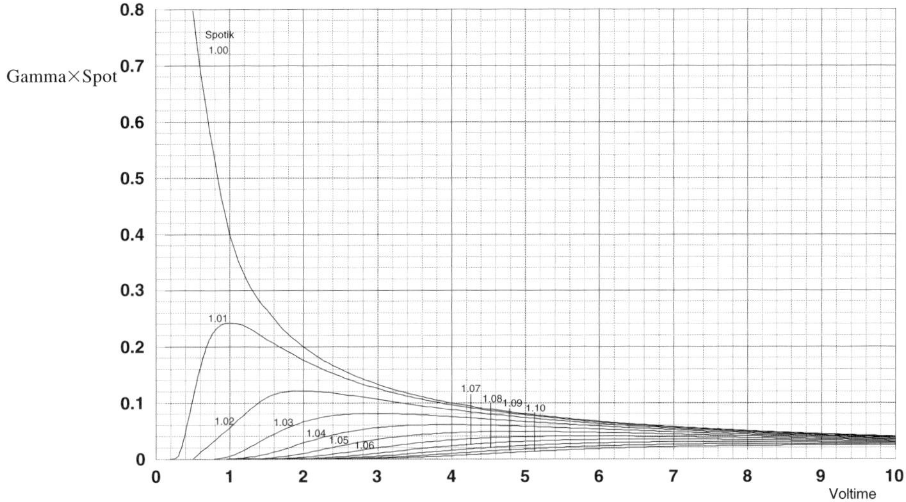

Chart 4.6
McKay's dimensionless European option gamma chart – voltime 0 - 10, spotik 1.00 – 1.10

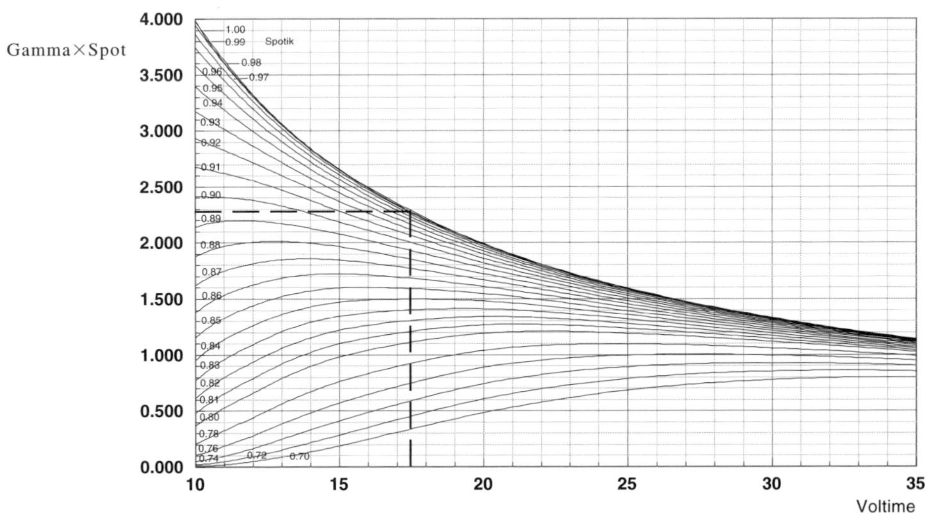

Chart 4.7
McKay's dimensionless European option gamma chart – voltime 10 - 35, spotik .70 – 1.00

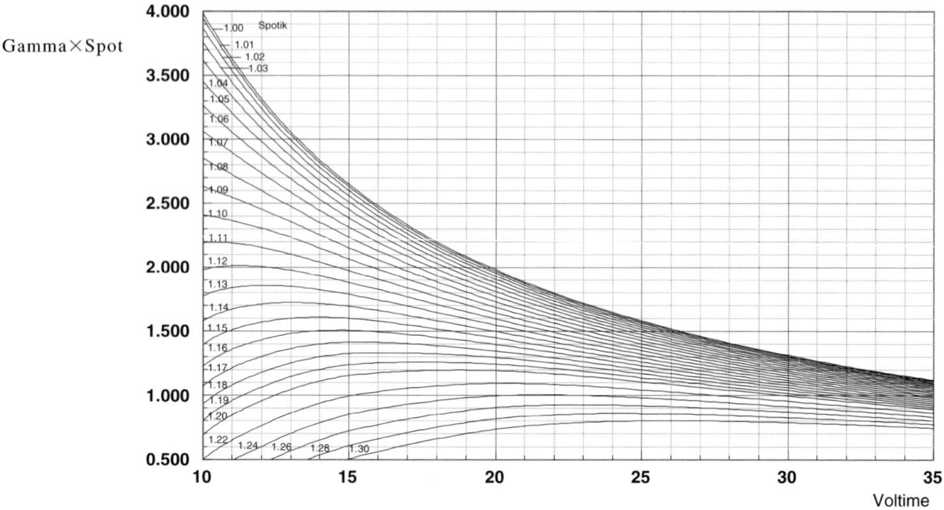

Chart 4.8
McKay's dimensionless European option gamma chart – voltime 10 - 35, spotik 1.00 – 1.30

Exercise 4a – Determining option prices and risk measures using dimensionless charts

Use the dimensionless call option *chart 4.1* to determine the fair market future value, FV_{opt} for a single at-the-money European call option on a $10 million 90 day FRA expiring in 12 months. Assume yield volatility of 17.01 per cent per annum and market forward rate of 8.33 per cent per annum. Note this is the same option studied in *exercise 2d*.

We will determine the option price based on yield rather than bill price.

The two known dimensionless numbers are:

$$\text{spotik} = \text{spot/strike}$$
$$= 8.33/8.33$$
$$= 1$$

and

$$\text{voltime} = \text{vol}\sqrt{T}$$
$$= 17.01\sqrt{366/365}$$
$$= 17.03$$

Next, use *chart 4.1* and locate the value 17.03 on the voltime (horizontal) axis and draw a vertical line up to find the intersection with the at-the-money spotik (1.00) line. Then draw a horizontal line from this voltime/spotik intersection to cross the valspot (vertical) axis. This gives valspot equal to .068.

$$\text{valspot} = \frac{FV_{opt.bp}}{\text{spot}}$$

Therefore:

$$FV_{opt.bp} = \text{valspot} \times \text{spot}$$
$$= .068 \times .0833$$
$$= .00566\text{ , or}$$

$$FV_{opt.bp} = 56.6\text{ basis points.}$$

Compare this option value of 56.6 bp with the value 56.537bp derived in *exercise 1d*. A small difference is expected since dimensionless charts tend to produce approximate values due to reading error.

This is converted to dollars using *equation 1.10*:

$$FV_{opt.\$} = faceval_{opt} \times bp \times t/(1 + rt)$$

$$= \frac{10{,}000{,}000 \times .00566 \times 90/365}{1 + .0833 \times 90/365}$$

Therefore:

$$FV_{opt.\$} \approx \$13{,}675 \text{ future value}$$

where *future value* means the option premium is paid at the option expiry rather than upfront.

This last step could also be achieved using another dimensionless chart.

Also from *chart 4.2* the option delta, $delta_{opt}$ is obtained directly:

$$delta_{opt} \approx 0.534$$

As recorded in *exercise 2d* the actual delta is 0.5339.

And the option gamma, $gamma_{opt}$ is determined using *chart 4.7:*

$$gamma_{opt} \times spot = 2.31$$

Therefore:

gamma $\approx$ 27.73

As recorded in *exercise 2d* the actual delta is 28.001.

Dimensionless charts are universal, not just because they represent all options in the same class but also because they can be used for any system of units. For example, the same charts, with adjusted scale, can be used to obtain the option price based on bill price rather than yield. Many financial relationships can be expressed as dimensionless charts. A selection of other dimensionless charts are illustrated in later chapters.

Summary

- The number of variables in a pricing formula is reduced by expressing its parameters as dimensionless numbers.
- Dimensionless charts are universal expressions of the pricing algorithm from which they are constructed.

Notes

1 For full-size dimensionless charts see R. McKay. *Dimensionless Risk.* Risk Technology. Sydney. 1997.

2 J. O. Grabbe. The Pricing of Call and Put Options on Foreign Exchange. *Journal of International Money and Finance*, 2:239-253, Dec. 1983.

3 V. A. Kholodnyi and J. F. Price. Foreign Exchange Option Symmetry based on Domestic-Foreign Payoff Invariance. Proc. IEEE/IAFE 1997. Conference on Computational Intelligence for Financial Engineers editors J. J. Marshall and R. J. Marks, pages 164-170. IEEE Service Centre, New Jersey.

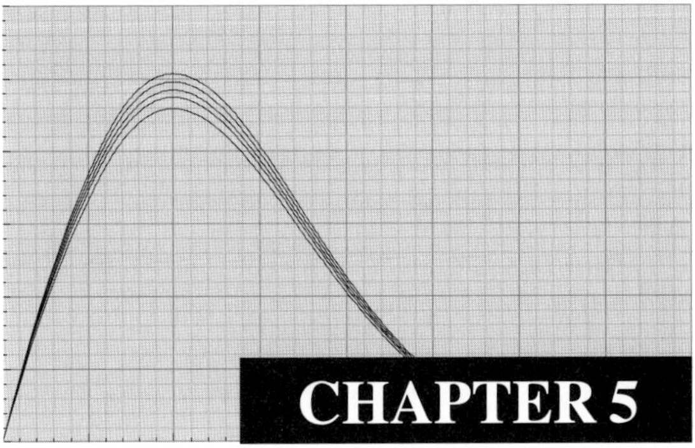

CHAPTER 5

Multirisk, Risklock and AAA Hedging Techniques

In this chapter we explore:

- the "bumps in the carpet" problem that often occurs with derivative portfolios;
- the *multirisk* and *risklock* risk control techniques and use them to minimise "bumps in the risk risk carpet" and market gap risk, and
- the principle underlying the *AAA hedge* technique – hedge Anything with Anything to achieve Anything.

Bumps in the risk carpet

In *Chapter 1 – PV Risk Components,* we learned that in general, the present value of a forward is sensitive to its forward rate, its discount factor, slightly sensitive to the rate of change of yields as well as being sensitive to time lapse – delta, gamma, rho and theta. Hence, if forwards are used with the intention of hedging a portfolio's yield or delta risk, the forward will also affect the portfolio's rho, theta and to some extent gamma.

On the other hand, option risk is sensitive to yield, the rate of change of yield, the discount factor, volatility and time lapse – delta, gamma, rho, vega and theta.

Therefore, if we use an option to delta hedge a portfolio, we will also affect the portfolio's gamma, rho, vega and theta.

This multi-risk nature of derivatives means that, when attempting to control the dominant risk component, we must be aware of the impact of our hedge on the other risk components. The hedge instruments may add a new risk component to the native position or inadvertently amplify other risk components.

Which means that the process of flattening one risk bump may cause other risk bumps to appear. This is the "bumps in the carpet" problem. In extreme cases, it may be that in the process of hedging one risk component, overall we make things worse.

Delta, gamma matching

In *Chapter 3.0 – Delta Hedging* we explored the process of replicating options using a dynamic delta hedge FRA position. That is, the FRA hedge is adjusted from time to time to track the option's delta. However, the accuracy of the replication suffers if market rates jump severely before the forward portfolio's delta can be rebalanced. This jump or gap risk is greatest when the option gamma is high, as is typically the case with short-dated, at-the-money options and some exotic options with highly asymmetric payoffs such as look-back, barrier and compound options (options on options).

Gap risk can be reduced or even eliminated by matching the gamma of the replicating portfolio with that of the target option.

This can be achieved by including options in the replicating portfolio. Frequently, the most liquid and competitively priced options are short-dated, exchange-traded options on futures (ETOs). ETOs are very useful instruments for improving the gamma match between the replicating and target portfolio. However, care should be taken not to introduce too much tilt risk due to the fact that short-dated ETOs are sensitive to the short end of the yield curve only.

When attempting to match both delta and gamma, it is necessary to determine the correct balance between the linear and non-linear instruments, in this case the FRA and ETO positions. The objective is to match, as closely as possible both the delta and the gamma simultaneously. FRAs are low gamma instruments. This means a FRA position can be adjusted to match a portfolio's delta without affecting significantly the portfolio's gamma. Therefore, a useful technique is to determine the number of ETOs required to match the target portfolio gamma first. This produces a linear *risk hole* in the replicating process that can then be "patched up" with a linear instrument such as a FRA.

Exercise 5a – Delta gamma matching

Use a short dated ETO position to reduce the gamma or yield jump risk evident in the option replication portfolio studied in *exercise 3c – Option Replication, Tracking and Rebalancing*. The tracking risk over a 50bp and 100bp yield jump, assuming no delta rebalancing, is illustrated in *windows 3.5, 3.6* and *3.7*. The 100bp tracking loss with no rebalancing is $2,646 and the tracking loss after a 100bp shift but with a delta rebalancing at 50bp is $1,287 – as provided in *record 3.1*.

The gamma risk exists because we tried to replicate an option, which has a high gamma, with a FRA which has a very low gamma. This gamma mismatch can be reduced by using ETOs and FRAs together in the replicating portfolio.

We will choose an ETO expiring on 1 December 1995 with strike 91.75. Based on our assumed date of 19 May 1995, this expiry represents a term of 196 days.

First, we determine the optimum number of ETOs to match the target option gamma. The short-dated ETO has a higher gamma than the target option. Therefore if we simply use 10 ETO contracts (and no FRAs) with a total face value of $10 million, the replicating portfolio gamma is too high. However, this replicating strategy has the advantage that the replicating portfolio outperforms the target in *both* directions under a sudden yield shift. However, the higher gamma of this replicating portfolio has the disadvantage of high pure time lapse risk. It also falls in value if volatility decreases – a theta and vega or voltime *risk hole* is created.

A balanced replicating portfolio has the same delta and gamma as the target. In this case, a smaller ETO position is required for gamma matching. The required number of ETOs can be determined from a simple sensitivity analysis. A yield sensitivity analysis, based on 100bp shift in both directions reveals that when seven ETOs are used, the tracking error is almost the same in both directions, but opposite in sign – producing a linear *risk hole* that can be closed with a linear instrument, such as a FRA. With seven ETOs and no FRAs in the replicating portfolio a sudden 100bp yield increase produces a tracking error of -$3,063 and a 100bp yield decrease produces an error of +$3,331. Also, for a 100bp yield increase a FRA with face value of $1 million increases in value by $2,115 and for a 100bp decrease it loses $2,173.

Thus, the FRA face value required to close the *risk hole* based on the up move is:

3,063/2,115 = $1.45 million

or based on the down move:

3,331/2,172 = $1.53 million

Taking the average:

(1.43 + 1.55)/2 = $1.49 million

Hence, a delta/gamma matched replicating portfolio can be formed using a synchronous borrower's FRA with face value $1.49 million and seven ETO puts (face value $7 million) with expiry 1 December 1995 and strike 91.75. Note that puts on the index (100 - interest rate) are equivalent to calls on the interest rate.

Window 5.1 illustrates the performance of the replicating (actual) and target portfolios along with the tracking errors for up/down shifts of 100bp in both the yield and volatility.

Notice that some smaller *risk holes* still exist. The replication process is quite exposed to volatility shifts.

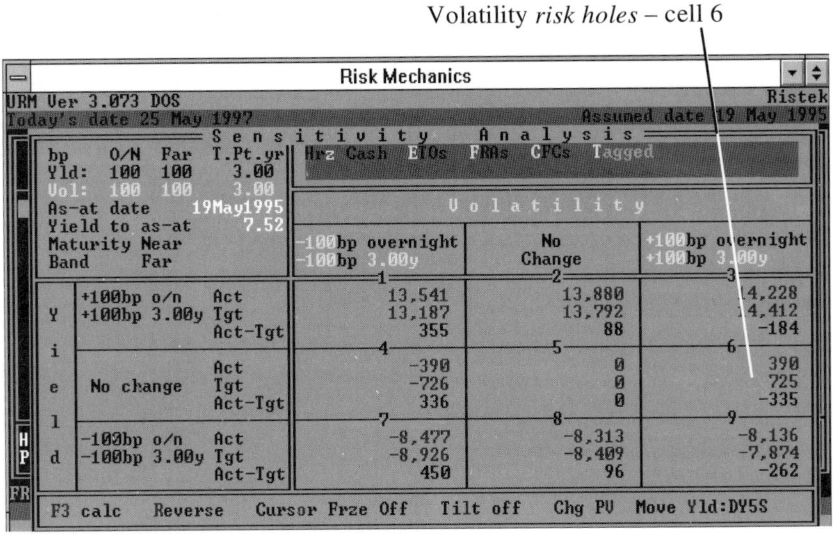

Window 5.1
Target option with delta and gamma matching – showing the change in PV of the actual and target portfolios and difference or tracking error

The next exercise demonstrates how the hedge can be improved further to include volatility matching.

Delta, gamma, vega matching

A more robust replicating portfolio, with smaller *risk holes* is formed by matching the volatility risk components as well as the delta and gamma. This can be achieved by including instruments in the replicating portfolio that are sensitive to volatility shifts.

In *Chapter 2 – Greek Letter Risk Components* we learned that options are also sensitive to volatility and therefore can be used to control volatility as well as gap risk. Compare the volatility risks appearing in cell 6 of *windows 3.7* and *5.1*. Notice that the ETOs used to control gamma, or gap risk also help to reduce volatility risk. However, cell 6 of *window 5.1* indicating significant volatility risk still remains and a tracking loss of $335 is incurred from a sudden 100bp increase in volatility.

Exercise 5b – Delta, gamma, vega matching

Following on from *exercise 5a,* attempt to eliminate the remaining tracking error related to a 100bp volatility shift, while continuing to control yield gap risk.

The sensitivity analysis recorded in *window 5.1* indicates that the portfolio is still exposed to a sudden increase in volatility. This means that when volatility increases, the replicating portfolio does not increase in value as fast as the target. Therefore the two right side cells 6 and 9 show a tracking loss. A long option position increases in value as volatility increases – or, more generally, as voltime increases. Therefore, taking extra ETOs should improve volatility tracking by reducing vega risk.

The first field in cell 6 indicates that the short-dated ETO which manages gap risk is not very sensitive to volatility. Cell 6 indicates that the replicating portfolio increases in value by $390, while the target increases by $725. Therefore, it is evident that the ETO position needs to be almost doubled to eliminate the volatility tracking loss. However, if we do this we will upset the balanced delta, gamma hedge – a "bumps in the carpet" problem.

However, a larger number of risk components can be managed simultaneously by increasing the number of hedge or replicating instruments.

Also, longer-term options tend to be more sensitive to volatility shifts. For example, we could use March 1996 ETOs with strike 91.50 along with December 1995 ETOs. In this case, the optimum solution is short 5 December 1995 ETO contracts and long 14 March 1996 ETO contracts and a borrower's FRA with face value $0.32million. The sensitivity analysis of this portfolio is illustrated in *window 5.2.*

Compare *window 5.2* with *window 5.1*. Notice, from cell 6, that the volatility risk is almost eliminated in *window 5.2.* However, the gamma risk is worse than in the simpler delta/gamma matched portfolio produced in *exercise 5a.* This can be seen by comparing cells 2 and 5 in *windows 5.1* and *5.2* – the "bumps in the carpet" again.

This imperfection in the tracking performance cannot be eliminated without adding more instruments to the replicating portfolio. However, we can "give up" some of the volatility-matching quality to improve the gamma risk.

That is, the potential for wealth to escape through the pure volatility *risk hole* represented in cell 6 can be increased as a trade off for decreasing the magnitude of the gamma *risk holes* in cells 2.

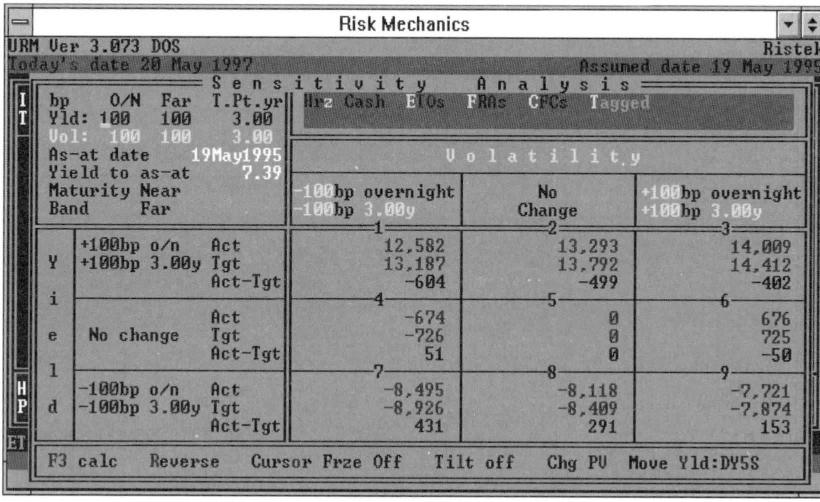

Window 5.2
Target option with delta, gamma and vega matching

The AAA hedge

In *exercises 5.1* and *5.2* we used interest rate forwards and exchange traded options together to replicate, or manufacture an over-the-counter option. The reverse sign portfolio of derivatives hedges an existing long option. Hedging and replicating are two sides of the same coin.

The replicating portfolio was constructed by matching its risk components with those of the option. As discovered, we can attempt to match one, several or all the risk components. The expected accuracy of the hedging process increases with the number of risk components matched. Matching the risk components means replicating the present value sensitivities of the risk components.

It is important to consider the stability of the matching process. For example, in the simple delta matched option replication studied in *exercises 3a, 3b* and *3c,* FRAs were used to replicate the option's sensitivity to small yield shifts. However, the quality of the replication diminishes quickly as yields shift. On the other hand, the ETO or ETO/FRA replicating portfolios produced in *exercises 5a* and *5b* are more stable and require less frequent adjustment.

In theory, any instrument that is exposed to any one or several of the same market risks as the target portfolio can be used in the hedge or replicating portfolio. Therefore, instruments such as bills, bonds, swaps, bill and bond futures, cashflows and options may be used in the construction of a replicating portfolio[1].

Hence, Anything can be hedged with Anything provided a reasonable match can be maintained in the risk components through time. Naturally, some tracking error is expected. The key point is that some instruments create more "bumps in the risk carpet" than others. For example, cashflows and bonds would not normally be used to hedge a single OTC option, since these instruments would add significant risks not matched by the option.

The third *A* in the *AAA* refers to "achieve Anything". Anything means any target risk. This means the target risk can be tailored to suit. The target can be any instrument or combination of instruments or an arbitrary payoff profile. The target payoff is manufactured by replicating its present valued risk components through time and thereby forming a risk-matched portfolio. The key to success with this process is the ability to identify the significant risk components and then replicate them, in a stable manner, through time. The replication process is more likely to be successful if the risk matching is stabilised by minimising gamma mismatch. This reduces the size and frequency of rebalancing transactions and therefore minimises market gap risk and transaction costs.

Check using URM – Exercise 5a

Reload file RMW1T. Go to the ETO portfolio window <E> and add a December 1995 ETO with strike 91.75 by typing <1295 Enter> in the expiry column and <91.75 Enter> in the strike column. Then press <Alt U> to update the market data fields. Set the entry rate fields the same as the market rate <.36 Enter>. Alternatively, load file RMW1B1.

Take a guess at the optimum number of ETO contracts to be included in the replicating portfolio – one contract has a face value of $1million. Begin by fixing the FRA face value to zero and attempt to replicate the option using only ETOs. No matter what number of ETOs we choose, the ETO tends to over-perform in one direction and under-perform in the other – unless 10 lots are used, in which case it outperforms the target option in both directions but is exposed to pure time lapse risk.

When you have chosen the ETO position, determine the appropriate FRA position to improve the quality of replication. Alternatively, you can let *URM* determine the FRA position by unfixing the FRA face value. To do this place the cursor on the FRA face value field and press <Delete>, then calculate <F3> and notice that the FRA position is computed automatically. The more ETOs, the smaller the FRA position. Use the sensitivity analysis and observe the tracking errors for a 100bp yield shift. Also study the payoff graph <F8> <F8>.

Notice that the sensitivity analysis <F6> can be used to confirm that a linear mismatch is produced using seven lots of the ETO. The appropriate FRA position to close this linear *risk hole* is determined quite easily using the delta matching technique.

Compare the tracking performance with the results recorded in *windows 3.6* and *3.7* with no rebalancing and also the tracking error with a midway rebalancing after a 50bp yield shift, as shown in *record 3.1*. Confirm that the hedge is effective and the inclusion of the ETOs reduces gap risk. This is a form of *risklock*. The payoff profile <F8> <F8> of the replicating portfolio tracks the target over a wide range of yield shifts. The two risk profiles are locked together.

Now use *URM* to formulate automatically the optimum quantity of ETOs so as to minimise gap risk over a 100bp range up and down in the yield curve.

Go to the ETO portfolio window <E>. Unfix the ETO quantity by pressing <Delete> with the cursor on the quantity field. Go to the risk control <F2> and set both the yield up and down fields to 100bp. This means that the hedge formulation process will try to minimise gamma risk over a 200bp yield range. Alternatively, load file RMW1C.

Press <F3> to formulate the hedge parcel quantities. Notice the calculated ETO quantity is seven lots and a borrower's FRA with face value $1.49 million. Also use the sensitivity analysis and payoff graphs to confirm that yield gap risk is reduced. Compare this result with your earlier estimate.

Go to sensitivity analysis <F6> and set both the yield and volatility shifts to 100bp and confirm the sensitivity tracking error records in the *window5.1*.

Check using URM – Exercise 5b

1. Manual

Using file RMW1T. Go to the ETO window and press <Ctrl Enter> to create a new row. Then type <0396 Enter> in the expiry column and <91.50> in the strike column. Press <Alt

U> to update the market data. Alternatively, load file RMW1D.

Experiment with a combination of December 1995 ETOs and March 1996 ETOs by either manually adjusting the quantities or letting *URM* calculate the quantities. Study the sensitivity analysis and notice the volatility tracking tends to improve.

2. *Automatic*

Now use *URM* to formulate automatically the optimum ETO/FRA quantities to achieve a balanced delta, gamma and vega hedge. Ensure that both ETOs and the FRA are unfixed. If necessary, use <Delete> to unfix any of the face values.

Go to risk control <F2> and activate volatility protection by pressing <V>. Notice the volatility matching range is already set to 100bp in both the up and down directions. Alternatively, load file RMW1E.

Press <F3> to formulate the hedge parcel quantities. Notice the ETO positions – short 5 December 1995 contracts and long 14 March 1996 contracts.

3. *Testing*

Study the sensitivity analysis <F6> and payoff graphs <F8> <F8>. In the payoff graph, the high and low volatility shifts are viewed with <H> and <L>. Notice the gamma and vega risks are now both controlled with high accuracy. The sensitivity tracking results appear in the *window 5.2*. Compare this with *window 5.1*. Notice, from cell 6, that the volatility risk is almost eliminated but the gamma risk is worse than in the simpler delta/gamma hedge recorded in *window 5.1* (cells 2 and 8) – the "bumps in the carpet" again.

This problem cannot be eliminated without adding more instruments to the hedge parcel. However, we can "give up" some of the volatility-matching quality to improve the gamma risk.

That is, the pure volatility *risk hole* represented in cells 4 and 6 can be increased as a trade-off for decreasing the size of the gamma *risk holes* in cells 2 and 8. This is done by shifting the weighting emphasis more towards the gamma matching in the *multirisk* optimisation process.

This effect can be observed by using *URM's* "risk levers" – the risk weightings in the risk control window <F2>.

4. Risk levers

Use *URM's* risk levers to reduce the gamma risk in cells 2 and 5 in *window 5.2.*

Leave the sensitivity window <Esc> and go to risk control <F2>. Move the cursor to the yield uniform shift weighting field and change the weighting to say 100 <100 Enter>. Calculate <F3>. Observe the number of ETO contracts and the sensitivity window <F6>. Repeat using a weighting of say 500.

Summary

- In theory, delta, gamma, vega and theta risks all can be controlled simultaneously.
- In general, the number of instruments required in the hedge parcel increases with the number of separate risks being controlled and the degree of precision required.
- Vega and gamma risk can be controlled using asymmetric instruments such as options.
- Tailored risk profiles can be manufactured through dynamic risk component matching.
- Linear *risk holes* are easier to seal than non-linear *risk holes.*
- Short dated ETOs are useful for controlling gamma risk but tend to introduce tilt risk.
- Longer term ETOs tend to be more sensitive to volatility shifts.
- Reducing gamma mis-match improves replication accuracy and reduces the size and frequency of rebalancing transactions.

Notes

1 In *URM*, any combination of these instruments can be included in the hedge parcel. The quantities of the chosen hedge instruments are optimised to form the closest match with the target risk.

CHAPTER 6

Forward/Futures Relationship

In this chapter we:

- explore the market risk relationship of forwards and futures;
- discover that in many cases forwards can be substituted for futures and vice versa provided we use an important adjustment, and
- learn that in general, forward/future hedges produce gamma risks.

The marked-to-market effect

Futures are marked-to-market, FRAs are not. Futures are settled daily, FRAs are settled at expiry or settlement date. This means that futures and FRAs are not equivalent. The value of a FRA, or any other forward, must be discounted to produce its present value. However, because futures are marked-to-market, futures values are automatically present values. Therefore forwards and futures that are otherwise identical in every way – such as expiry, face value, projection term and pricing formula – will in general have different present values and different risk exposures such as delta and gamma.

Exercise 6a – A mark-to-market effect

Consider a simple portfolio containing a long 90 day futures contract and a synchronous 90 day borrower's FRA. Both instruments expire on 12 June1997 – that is, in 755 days or 2.07 years from our assumed date of 19 May 1995. Assume the FRA and future are sensitive to the same interest rate or yield curve. Also assume that both the FRA and futures contract prices are based on the yield formula:

PV = FV/(1 + rt) using 365 day count basis. The entry or contract rate for both instruments is the current market rate at 8.69 per cent per annum – the equivalent futures index is

91.31. The yield to the expiry date is 8.295 per cent per annum using semi-annual compounding.

However, we will assume that the face value of the futures position is $10 million, or 10 contracts, and the face value of the FRA is $11 million.

Obviously the borrower's FRA produces a profit when yields rise and the long future position incurs a loss when yields rise. However, in this example, the FRA face value is $1 million greater than the futures contracts.

Will this FRA/futures portfolio incur a net profit or loss if yields rise? At first glance we might expect a profit. In fact this portfolio incurs a loss when yields rise. For example, if semi-annual yield rises 100bp this simple FRA/futures portfolio incurs a net loss of $2,038. Why? Futures are marked-to-market, FRAs are not. The futures loss is realised immediately. However, the FRA profit is not realised until expiry – in this case in 2.07 years. The FRA profit must be discounted to present value before it can be compared directly to the futures.

Oversights in the mixing of forwards and futures seem to be quite a common source of *risk holes.*

The risk component associated with the yield to maturity, referred to as the rho risk in *Chapter 2 – Greek Letter Risk Components,* does not exist with futures contracts.

FRA/future delta hedging

FRAs are sensitive to the settlement date discount factor. This means that the PVbp of a future will be larger in magnitude than the PVbp of a synchronous FRA with the same face value. Therefore, when FRAs are used to hedge or replicate futures or vice versa the face value of the hedge or replicating instrument must be adjusted to produce a PV delta match.

Exercise 6b – FRA/future delta hedging

Use the delta matching technique to determine the face value of the FRA that hedges the futures position studied in *exercise 6a*.

The change in the present value of both the FRA and futures contract is determined using *equation 1.4*, repeated below:

$$\Delta PV = d_{f\Delta}FV[1/(1 + r_1t) - 1/(1 + (r + \Delta r)t)] - d_fFV[1/(1 + r_1t) - 1/(1 + rt)]$$

In the case of a future, both d_f and $d_{f\Delta}$ are set to 1.

ΔPV	Future ΔPV	FRA ΔPV
+10bp	-2,312	1,950
-10bp	2,313	-1,959

Table 6.1

10bp PV change – synchronous 90 day forward/futures each with face value of $10 million

Table 6.1 summarises the changes in value of both the FRA and future based on a face value of $10 million and a semi-annual yield increase, as well as decrease of 10bp. Notice that as expected the FRA is less sensitive than the future to yield shifts. The FRA hedge adjustment factor, $adj.factor_{FRA}$ is equal to the futures change divided by FRA change. For a more accurate result we produce delta estimates based on both the up and down yield nudges and take the average. Hence the FRA adjustment factor is:

$$\text{adj.factor}_{FRA} = [(2{,}312/1{,}950) + (2{,}313/1{,}959)]/2$$

$$= (1.186 + 1.1807)/2$$

$$= 1.183$$

And, the FRA hedge face value face.val_{FRA} is equal to the FRA adjustment factor times the futures face value, face.val_{fut}, hence:

$$\text{face.val}_{FRA} = \text{adj.factor}_{FRA} \times \text{face.val}_{fut}$$

$$= 1.183 \times 10{,}000{,}000$$

$$= \$11.83 \text{ million}$$

Notice that as expected the FRA hedge face value is greater than the futures face value. This is a general feature of a correctly formulated FRA/future hedge with synchronous expiry dates and identical projection terms.

The FRA hedge face value of $11.83 million produced above using delta matching can also be produced using *equation 2.1*, repeated below:

$$\text{delta}_{FRA}\ \delta = \frac{\partial PV_{FRA}}{\partial r} = tFVK^{-nT}(1 + rt)^{-2}$$

Where for a future K =1.

Since adj.factor_{FRA} is equal to $\text{delta}_{fut}/\text{delta}_{FRA}$ then from *equation 2.1:*

$$\text{adj.factor}_{FRA} = K^{nT}$$

where:

$T = 755/365$

$n = 2$

$K = 1 + Y/n$

$= 1 + .08295/2$

Thus:

$$adj.factor_{FRA} = (1 + .08295/2)^{2(755/365)}$$

$$= 1.1831$$

This is a similar result determined above using delta matching based on a small yield shift – demonstrating that the gamma is low.

Notice that the FRA hedge adjustment factor is determined from the discount factor alone. In fact, it is the inverse of the discount factor or accumulation factor. The FRA/futures market rate has no effect on the adjustment factor.

Smiles and frowns – zero delta with gamma

The FRA/future hedge is not perfect. In fact, with the FRA/future portfolio the tracking error is negative for instantaneous rises as well as falls in yields – a *risk hole.* See *window 6.1.* This imperfect hedge is the best we can do with this FRA/future hedge, unless we can add more instruments to the hedge parcel. Notice, however, that the error curve is symmetric. This is a sign of a balanced hedge. Initially the net delta is zero but the net gamma is slightly negative – this produces a "frown" payoff.

The actual gamma values are produced using *equation 2.1.1* for $gamma_{FRA.r}$ and *2.1.4* for $gamma_{FRA.Y}$ – assuming yield quotes. Note that *equation 2.1.4* – which relates to the discounting interest rate Y – assumes that Y is discretely compounded. Therefore, a slight error occurs if these two components of the FRA gamma are combined directly without an appropriate adjustment. $Gamma_{FRA.r}$ for the futures contract is produced using *equation 2.1.1* with K set to 1. If discount quotes are used $gamma_{FRA.r}$ is zero and $gamma_{FRA.Y}$ is produced using *equation 2.2.3*. It follows that gamma is always zero for a discount quote type futures contract.

The FRA/futures hedge studied in *exercise 6b* uses a long futures position and a borrower's FRA and the tracking error is negative in both directions. Obviously, the tracking error is positive – producing a smiling graph – if the portfolio sign is reversed to a short futures position with a lender's FRA. See *window 6.2*.

These gamma related *risk holes* have a theta connection. In the case of the frowning payoff, the portfolio will tend to gain value with time lapse and in the case of the smiling payoff the portfolio will tend to lose value with time lapse. From an arbitrage theory point of view we cannot say one portfolio offers a better return than the other. The time decay component is expected to balance the gamma component so that the expected gain in wealth is the risk free rate in both cases.

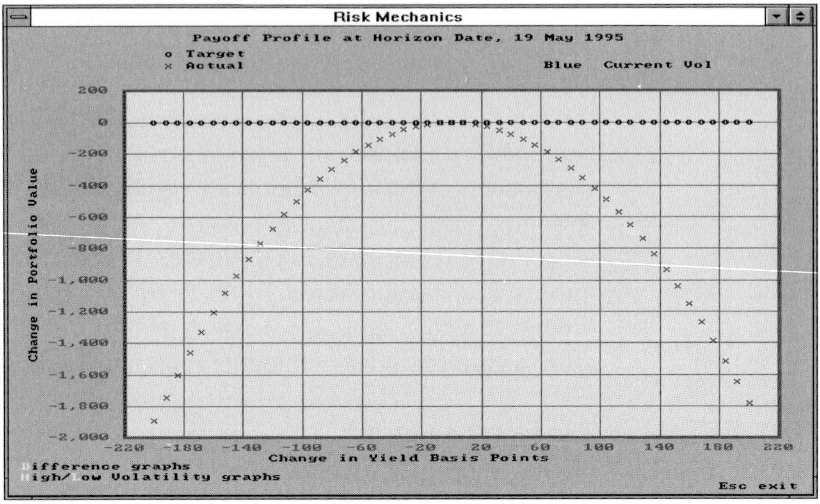

Window 6.1
Frown effect: long futures hedging a borrower's FRA

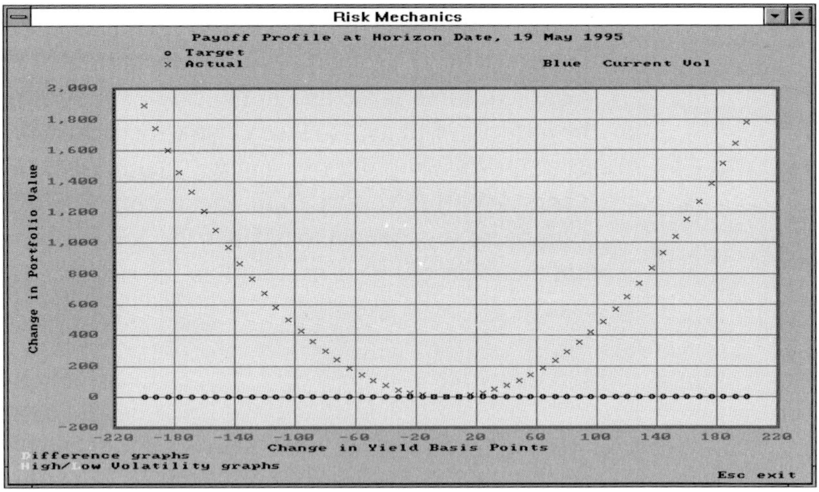

Window 6.2
Smile effect: short futures hedging a lender's FRA

It is apparent that gamma risk exists in a FRA/futures hedge – for both yield and discount quotes – and that this produces the smile and frown payoffs. However, the gamma exposure observed in FRAs and futures priced using yield quotes suggest that these instruments should be priced with a formula that contains a volatility component, as with options. Similarly, FRA and futures should not be priced using exactly the same yield curve[1]. Without an appropriate correction a pricing error exists and this error tends to increase as the time to expiry increases. This information may be important for astute traders involved in arbitrage activities and derivatives managers hedging large exposures involving FRAs, swaps, cashflows or bonds.

Another consequence of the gamma effect is that the FRA/ futures hedge ratio is not constant – it changes as the discounting interest rate changes or time lapses. For example, in *exercise 6b,* if yields increase by 100bp the FRA adjustment factor increases from 1.183 to 1.207 and if yields decease by 100bp the FRA adjustment factor decreases to 1.160. Obviously, as time to expiry diminishes the adjustment factor approaches one.

Check using URM – Exercise 6a

Load file RMW2. This file contains the forward/futures portfolio described in *exercise 6a.* Use the sensitivity analysis <F6> to confirm that when yields rise 100bp, this simple FRA/futures portfolio incurs a net loss of $2,038.

Also analyse the performance of this FRA/future hedge when the face values of the two instruments are the same. Go to the FRA window <F> and reset the FRA face value to be the same as the futures – that is, $10 million, by typing <10 Enter> in the face value field and study the sensitivity. As expected, it is not a good quality hedge.

Check using URM – Exercise 6b

Load file RMW2. Set the face value of both the FRA and future to $10 million. Go to sensitivity analysis <F6> and set the yield nudge to 10bp. Deactivate the FRA portfolio <F> and calculate <F3>.

Confirm the records in the first column of *table 6.1* – the PV changes for the futures position. Now reactivate the FRA <F> and deactivate the futures <U>. Calculate <F3> and confirm the records in the second column of *table 6.1.*

View the payoff graph <F8>, <F8>. Notice the asymmetric payoff, a sign of an unbalanced hedge – a *risk hole.*

Next use *URM* to formulate automatically the FRA hedge face value. Exit sensitivity analysis <Esc>. Go to the FRA window <F> and unfix the face value. Place the cursor on the face value field and press <Delete>. Calculate <F3> and notice that the FRA face value is $11.83 million as expected.

Now use the sensitivity analysis <F6> and the payoff graph <F8> <F8> to observe the performance of this FRA/future hedge portfolio. Notice that this portfolio incurs a loss for both rises and falls in the yield. Also notice that the error curve is symmetric – a sign of a balanced hedge.

Summary

- ❑ In a balanced FRA/futures hedge the futures face value is less than that of the FRA.
- ❑ The futures face value is determined by multiplying the FRA face value by the discount factor to the expiry date.
- ❑ In general, it is not possible to form a perfect FRA/futures hedge – some gamma risk remains.
- ❑ A symmetric smile or frown payoff graph is a sign of a balanced hedge.
- ❑ Forwards and futures should not be priced using exactly the same yield curves when using the conventional – volatility insensitive – pricing formulae.
- ❑ FRA/future hedges exhibit some gamma risk therefore requires occasional adjustment.

Notes

1 G. Burghardt and B. Hoskins. A Question of Bias. *Risk Magazine,* Vol 8 No 3 March 1995.

CHAPTER 7

Cashflow Risk and Hedging

In this chapter we:

- analyse cashflow risk in terms of duration measures, yield, gamma and time lapse risks;
- use forwards and futures to hedge cashflows, and
- develop several practical dimensionless cashflow risk sensitivity charts.

Representing instruments as cashflows

Many forms of financial exposure can be viewed as cashflows. For example, payables, receivables, bonds, fixed annuities, short term discount instruments, FRAs, swaps, assumed dividends, expenses and mortgages (without embedded options) can all be analysed as cashflows. However, it is important to note that options and most instruments with asymmetric payoffs cannot be represented accurately as simple cashflows.

Cashflow present value risk

The present value of a cashflow depends on its face value, maturity and yield to maturity. Thus, the present value risk of a given cashflow can be viewed in two components – the interest rate and time decay risk.

Recall the common interest rate types:

PV	=	FVe^{-rt}	Continuously compounded rate
PV	=	$FV/(1 + rt)$	Simple interest – yield quote
PV	=	$FV(1 - rt)$	Simple interest – discount quote
PV	=	$FV(1 + r/n)^{nt}$	Compound interest – yield quote
PV	=	$FV(1 - r/n)^{nt}$	Compound interest – discount quote

However, viewed in dimensionless terms, cashflow present value risk is exposed to only one parameter, rt.

Present value risk is important whenever there is a possibility of trading or liquidating the position at the market rate – the present value. Also, mark-to-market valuation must be based on present values or values discounted to a consistent date.

Hedging cashflows with futures

How can the present value of a cashflow be protected against yield shifts?

Clearly, an effective hedge can only be constructed using financial instruments or derivatives that are sensitive to the same yield curve segment as the cashflow. However, frequently it may not be possible to hedge a cashflow perfectly using a single derivative because there may not be any derivatives available which are sensitive to exactly the same interest rate as the cashflow.

For example, the present value of a cashflow is affected by the portion of the yield curve extending from today to the cashflow date – that is, the zero coupon discount rate. On the other hand, liquid hedging instruments such as 90 day interest rate futures are sensitive to yield curve forward rates.

Figure 7.1 illustrates a typical interest rate sensitivity mismatch between an interest rate future and a cashflow.

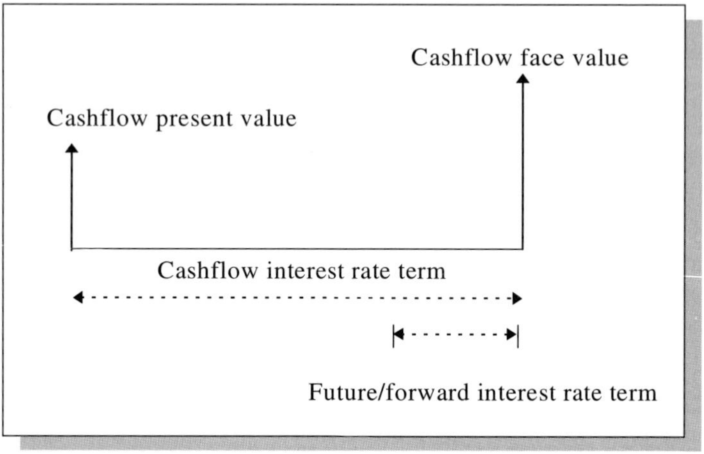

Figure 7.1
Illustrating different yield curve sensitivities of a cashflow and short-term forward interest rate instrument

Exercise 7a – Cashflow interest rate sensitivity

Analyse the interest rate sensitivity of a single, unhedged \$10 million positive cashflow occurring in three years. Assume the three year interest rate is 8.482 per cent per annum using semi-annual compounding.

The discount factor is:

$1/(1 + R/200)^{2T}$

where:

$R = 8.482$ and

$T = (366 + 365 + 365)/365$

$= 3.0027397$

Therefore, the cashflow present value is:

$$PV = 10{,}000{,}000/(1 + 8.482/200)^{2 \times 3.0027397}$$

$$= \$7{,}792{,}373$$

When the yield increases by 50bp, R changes to 8.982 and the present value becomes:

$$PV_1 = 10{,}000{,}000/(1 + 8.982/200)^{2 \times 3.0027397}$$

$$= \$7{,}681{,}077$$

Thus the change in present value is:

$$\Delta PV = -\$111{,}296$$

Table 7.1 records the cashflow PV changes for 50bp yield increments over a 200bp range up and down. The change in the change, representing gamma risk, is also presented. Notice that present values are more sensitive at lower interest rates.

ΔYld	ΔPV	Difference
200	-434,223	-105,850
150	-328,373	-107,631
100	-220,742	-109,446
50	-111,296	-111,296
0	0	0
-50	113,181	113,181
-100	228,285	115,181
-200	464,410	119,061

Table 7.1
Sensitivity results for $10 million three year cashflow with current semi-annual yield equal to 8.482 per cent per annum

Exercise 7b – Example of an ineffective hedge

Use the delta matching technique to hedge the three year \$10 million cashflow studied in *exercise 7a*. Use a single 90 day futures contract with maturity as close as possible to the cashflow maturity. Analyse the effectiveness of this hedge.

Based on our assumed date of 19 May 1995, the cashflow date is 19 May 1998. Therefore, the 90 day futures contract with maturity closest to the cashflow date is the March 1998 contract. Assume the three year semi-annual yield is 8.482 per cent per annum and the March 1998 futures index is 91.08 (interest rate equals 8.92 per cent per annum).

In the absence of reliable correlation parameters the delta hedge is formulated assuming the forward rates move uniformly and in parallel. We will base the delta matching on a 1bp shift in the semi-annual interest rate.

We will normalise the yield nudge using the approximation method demonstrated in *exercise 2a.*

First, the 90 day futures rate is converted to a semi-annual rate using *equation 1.7*:

$$R = n(1 + rt)^{1/nt} - n$$

$$= 2(1 + (.0892 \times 90/365))^{365/(2 \times 90)} - 2$$

$$= .090208408 \quad \text{(a)}$$

This semi-annual rate is nudged by 1bp to .090308408. This new rate is then converted back to a 90 day rate using *equation 1.7.1:*

$$r = [(1 + R/n)^{nt} - 1]/t$$

$$= [(1 + .090308408/2)^{2 \times 90/365} - 1]365/90$$

$$= .089297772 \quad (b)$$

Because futures are marked-to-market, *equation 1.3* provides the change in the futures contract value, except ΔFV is replaced with ΔPV:

$$\Delta PV_{fut} = FV[1/(1 + rt) - 1/(1 + (r + \Delta r)t)]$$

where:

$$r = (a), \text{ and}$$

$$r + \Delta r = (b)$$

In this case, a single futures contract has a face value of $1,000,000, therefore:

$$\Delta PV_{fut} = 1{,}000{,}000[1/(1 + .0892 \times 90/365) - 1/(1 + .089297772 \times 90/365)]$$

$$= \$23.08 \text{ for each short futures contract}$$

Next the change in PV of the cashflow arising from a 1bp yield shift is determined using:

$$PV = FV/(1 + R/n)^{nt}$$

Therefore:

$$\Delta PV_{cashflow} = FV[1/(1 + (R + \Delta R)/n)^{nt} - 1/(1 + R/n)^{nt}]$$

Thus:

$$\Delta PV_{cashflow} = 10{,}000{,}000[\ 1/(1 + .08492/2)^{2 \times 1096/365} - 1/(1 + .08482/2)^{2 \times 1096/365}$$

$$= -\$2{,}244$$

Hence, the number of 90 day futures required is:

$$\text{No. futures} = \frac{\Delta PV_{cashflow}}{\Delta PV_{fut}}$$

$$= -2244/23.08$$

$$= -97.23$$

A short position of 97 futures contracts hedges the cashflow against uniform shifts in the semi-annual yield.

This hedge is quite effective for uniform yield movements and produces a smile payoff. For example, a net gain of \$2,391 is incurred from a sudden increase of 100bp in the semi-annual rate. Also, a net gain of \$3,552 is incurred from a sudden yield decrease of 100bp. The smile effect occurs because the cashflow has a higher gamma than the futures position. Therefore the short futures contracts do not neutralise all the cashflow gamma. Note that if the futures are priced using discount quotes the futures gamma is zero and the smile effect is even stronger.

Of course, the major weakness of this hedge is the assumption of uniform yield shifts. Suppose, for example that the near-dated futures fall (rising interest rates) while the longer term futures remain unchanged. In this case, the cashflow discount factor increases and the cashflow present value decreases, while the futures hedge value remains unchanged: the hedge does not work.

For example, if we assume that the semi-annual rate tilts by jumping 100bp overnight, decreasing linearly to zero shift in three years, the future/cashflow portfolio incurs a loss of \$157,042. The hedge is not robust – a serious *risk hole*. See *window 7.1*.

Far yield shift set to zero

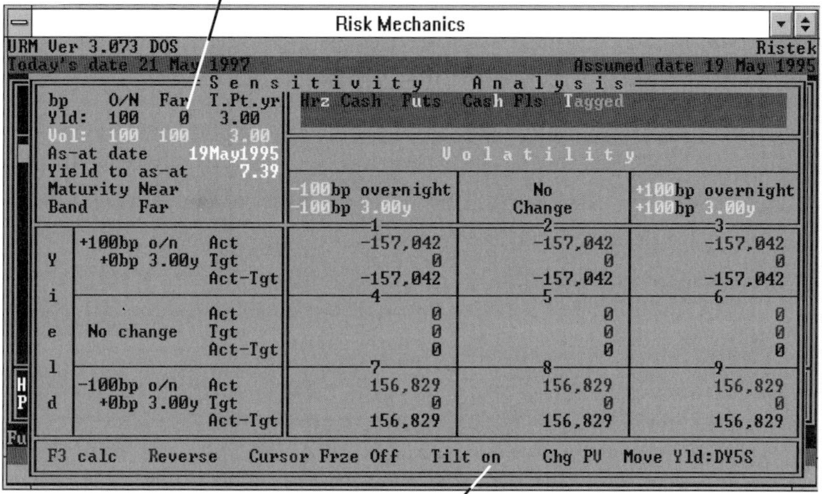

Tilt activated

Window 7.1
Cashflow hedged with a single futures contract illustrating exposure to yield curve tilt

Question 7a

Can the tilt *risk hole* observed in *exercise 7b* be eliminated using only futures?

Answer

Yes, the problem is that none of the 90 day futures are sensitive to exactly the same interest rate as the cashflow. However, a strip of futures can be used to replicate the cashflow's interest rate sensitivity although with some residual error.

Hedging cashflows with a futures strip

The present value of a cashflow, $PV_{cashflow}$ is sensitive to the interest rate from today to the cashflow maturity. We will represent this as a simple interest rate R over term T. However, the value of a future, PV_{fut} is sensitive to a short term forward interest rate. Call this simple interest rate r over term t.

That is:

$PV_{cashflow} = FV/(1 + RT)$ – yield quote

or

$PV_{cashflow} = FV(1 - RT)$ – discount quote

and PV_{fut} is sensitive to the price of a short term discount instrument, PV_{bill} priced off the forward curve.

$PV_{bill} = FV/(1 + rt)$ – yield quote

or

$PV_{bill} = FV(1 - rt)$ – discount quote

Obviously, the hedging problem arises because, in general:

$T \neq t$

We need to find a hedging instrument that is sensitive to R, the interest rate used to produce the present value of the cashflow. Although this cannot be achieved with a single 90 day future, the cashflow's interest rate sensitivity can be replicated using a strip of futures because the cashflow's discount factor, d_f is equal to the product of its component discount factors – that is:

$$d_f = 1/(1 + RT) = 1/[(1 + r_1t_1)\ldots(1 + r_it_i)\ldots(1 + r_nt_n)]$$
– using yield quotes

or

$$d_f = (1 - RT) = [(1 - r_1t_1)\ldots(1 - r_it_i)\ldots(1 - r_nt_n)]$$
– using discount quotes.

Where t_i represents the interest rate terms, in this case 90 days, and r_i is the futures rate, expressed as an interest rate, for the yield curve segment t_i. The curve segments t_i are assumed to be equal in duration and placed consecutively, as illustrated.

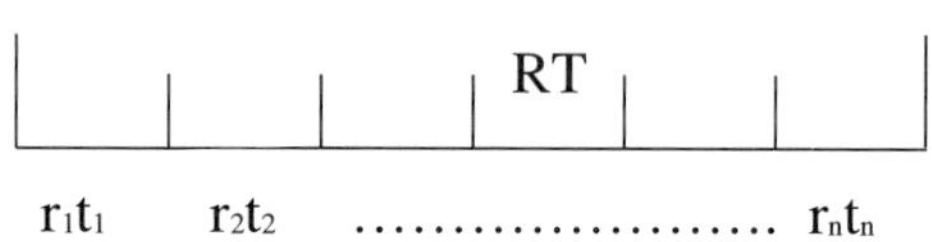

If r_i changes to $r_i + \Delta r_i$ then the new discount factor $d_{f\Delta}$ is:

$$d_{f\Delta} = 1/[(1 + r_1t_1)\ldots(1 + r_it_i + \Delta r_it_i)\ldots(1 + r_nt_n)]$$
– using yield quotes

or

$$d_{f\Delta} = (1 - r_1 t_1)\ldots(1 - r_i t_i - \Delta r_i t_i)\ldots(1 - r_n t_n)$$

– using discount quotes.

It is apparent that the effect on the cashflow's discount factor for a small defined change in r_i is basically the same regardless of which r_i changes. In fact, it is exactly the same when the yield curve is flat. There is a slight variation in the impact on the overall discount factor whenever the forward rate curve is not flat. In general, this effect is minor.

In fact, if forward rates are quoted as continuously compounded rates then the impact on the cashflow present value, or discount factor, is exactly the same for any forward rate nudge, even in the case of an arbitrarily shaped yield curve – providing the same nudge size and terms are used in each case. Therefore, it follows that the error in the simple interest rate nudge equivalence assumption is defined by the slight difference between a constant simple interest rate nudge and a simple interest rate nudge equivalent to a constant continuous interest rate nudge.

This observation means that the number of futures can be determined, quite accurately, simply by multiplying the number of futures required to hedge the cashflow against a uniform yield shift by the fraction t_i/T.

Hence, a strip of futures can be used to replicate or hedge cashflow exposure to yield shifts. This is valuable information because, as discussed, many forms of financial exposure can be viewed in terms of cashflows. It brings to light a mechanism for hedging cashflow related exposures with liquid, fungible instruments. A small gamma mismatch is expected.

Exercise 7c – Formulating a futures strip to hedge a cashflow

Formulate the 90 day futures strip that hedges the $10 million three year cashflow studied in *exercises 7a* and *7b* against uniform yield curve shifts, tilts and flexes.

In *exercise 7b* we determined that the total number of 90 day futures required to delta hedge the three year cashflow is 97 short. Therefore, a hedge strip must also contain a total of 97 short 90 day futures. We need to determine how to distribute this quantity across all the contract months.

We use the approximation discussed above – that is, the number of each futures contract as a fraction of the total is t_i/T. However, in this expression, t_i needs to be adjusted for any gaps not covered by the futures. For example, four 90 day futures do not completely span a 365 day year. Thus, with the exception of the first and last futures contracts, each contract needs to hedge, on average, 365/4 days or 366/4 days in the case of the leap year.

In this case, the first futures contract expires on 8 June 1995 and matures on 6 September 1995. The second contract expires on 14 September 1995. Therefore, we will assume that the June 1995 contract is used to hedge the portion of the yield curve from time zero to 10 September 1995. That is, 20 days from the assumed date of 19 May 1995, a further four days past the maturity of the June contract as well as the synchronous 90 day period. Thus the first futures is used to hedge the first (20 + 90 + 4) 114 days interest rate.

Hence, the number of June 1995 contracts required is:

No. first contract = -97 (114)/(365 + 365 + 366)

= -10.09, say short 10 contracts

Similarly, the last contract expiring 12 March 1998 overlaps with the cashflow term by only 68 days. Therefore, the number of March 1998 contracts required is:

No. last contract = -97 (68)/(365 + 365 + 366)

= - 6.02, say short 6 contracts

And, the number of each remaining or non-extreme contract in the hedge strip is:

No. n/e contracts = -97 (365/4)/(365 + 365 + 366)

= -8.08, say short 8 contracts.

Due to small rounding errors we have distributed 96 contracts rather than 97 as expected. The formulated futures hedge strip appears in *window 7.2*. The performance of this hedge strip under an instantaneous tilt produced by shifting the overnight rate 100bp with the shift decreasing linearly to zero at three years is illustrated in *window 7.3*. When yields increase, this linear tilt produces a net gain of $2,253 and when yields decrease the tilt produces a net loss of $2,409. This indicates that this futures hedge strip produces a robust hedge – particularly when compared with *window 7.1* – where the hedge error is approximately 70 times larger using the same tilt. In this case, the futures were very poorly distributed. The tilt *risk hole* has been almost eliminated. This futures strip provides very good protection against uniform shifts as well as tilts. *Window 7.4* illustrates the hedge payoff over a range of uniform yield shifts. Notice the smile effect caused by a residual positive gamma and the slight asymmetry about a vertical axis through zero yield. This indicates that the net delta is not quite zero.

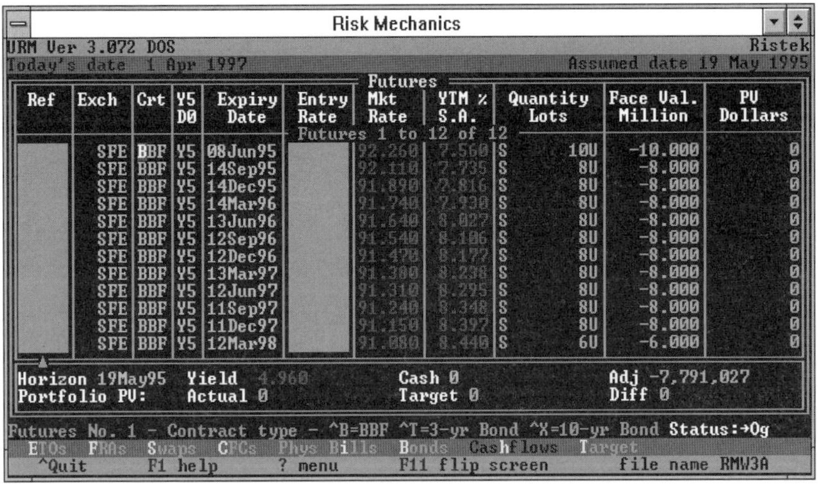

Window 7.2
Futures strip hedging three year $10 million cashflow

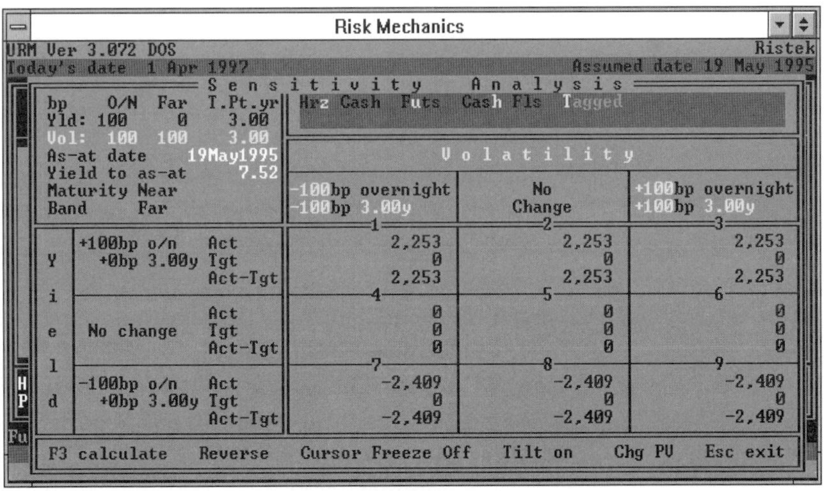

Window 7.3
Cashflow hedged with futures strip illustrating improved exposure to yield curve tilt

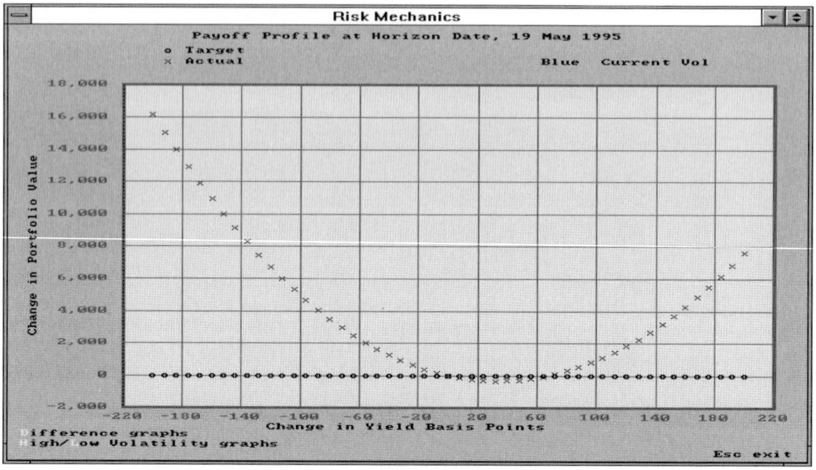

Window 7.4
Cashflow hedged with futures strip illustrating smile effect – near zero delta and positive gamma

Question 7b

Identify four sources of error that explain the small imperfections in the cashflow hedged with a 90 day futures strip?

Answer

The minimum futures contract size is $1 million dollars. Therefore, the contract quantities do not match the exposure perfectly. This is the reason why the net delta is not quite zero. A hedge gap exists at the near end since the first contract expires in 20 days and matures in 110 days. The last contract is sensitive to the 22 day forward rate beyond the cashflow maturity. This introduces tilt/flex risk. Also, a tiny error is introduced because four 90 day futures contracts do not quite span a full year. Small gaps exist since four consecutive contracts span (4 × 90) or 360 days, leaving small gaps totalling five or six days – a further source of tilt flex *risk holes*. A smile effect is caused by a small gamma mismatch.

Question 7c

What adjustment, if any, should be made if the cashflow is hedged with a strip of 90 day FRAs instead of futures?

Answer

From *Chapter 6 – Forward/Futures relationship* we know that the FRA equivalent risk position has a greater face value than the futures position because futures are marked-to-market and forwards are not. The FRA adjustment factor is the inverse of the discount factor to the futures expiry.

The forward/cashflow relationship

Interest rate forwards, such as FRAs and interest rate swaps, can be viewed as cashflows. This means that the market risk of a forward can be hedged perfectly with cashflows.

Exercise 7d – Hedging a FRA with cashflows

Consider a 90 day borrower's FRA, based on yield quotes expiring on 13 June 1996 – that is, in 391 days from our assumed date of 19 May 1995 – this date coincides with a futures expiry date. The face value is $10 million and the FRA contract rate is 8.36 per cent per annum. Specify the cashflows that hedge this FRA.

This instrument locks in the 90 day bill rate on 13 June 1996 for a borrower at 8.36 per cent per annum. It follows that cashflows with reversed signs would hedge the FRA.

A borrower would use this FRA to lock in a draw-down on 13 June 1996 of amount, PV:

$$PV = \$10{,}000{,}000/(1 + .0836 \times 90/365)$$

$$= \$9{,}798{,}026$$

As well, the borrower must repay the face value of

$10,000,000 on 11 September 1996.

Thus the FRA risk is equivalent to the two cashflows:

Receive $9,798,026 on 13 June 1996, and

Pay $10,000,000 on 11 September 1996.

Macaulay and modified duration

The Macaulay duration[1] dur_{mac}, is a present value weighted average of the terms of the payment stream. Therefore its dimension is time. Thus, the duration of a single cashflow is the same as its term to maturity.

$$dur_{mac} = \frac{\sum_{i=1}^{n} PV_i t_i}{\sum_{i=1}^{n} PV_i}$$

Equation 7.0 Macaulay Duration

What has this duration measure got to do with price risk? The dimension of time means that it is unlike the PV risk measures discussed in detail in *Chapter 1 – PV Risk Components*, which have the dimension of present value dollars. Duration is also quite a different measure to the Greek Letters discussed in *Chapter 2*.

Duration is significant because a portfolio can be delta hedged against *uniform* yield shifts, to a high degree of accuracy, using a single cashflow with maturity equal to the duration and face value equal to the portfolio present value accumulated at the internal rate of return to the duration. Frequently this face value is approximately equal to the net of all cashflows in the portfolio.

The derivation of the Macaulay based delta hedge of a portfolio of cashflows is quite straightforward and is now provided for those interested in the mathematics:

We will work with continuously compounded interest rates because this produces simpler mathematical expressions than discretely compounded rates. Recall that for a single cashflow:

$$PV = FV\ e^{-rt}$$

Therefore, the present value, PV_T of an arbitrary cashflow stream with internal rate of return r is:

$$PV_T = \sum_{i=1}^{n} FV_i e^{-rt_i}$$

We now make use of the mathematical relationship, given:

$$y = e^{ax} \text{ then}$$

$$\frac{dy}{dx} = ae^{ax}$$

Thus, taking the first derivative of PV_T with respect to r gives delta_{PV_T}:

$$\text{delta}_{PV_T} = \frac{\partial PV_T}{\partial r} = \sum_{i=1}^{n} -t_i FV_i\ e^{-rt_i}$$

Hence:

$$\frac{\partial PV_T}{\partial r} = \sum_{i=1}^{n} -t_i PV_i$$

Notice that the right side of this equation is the negative of the Macaulay duration multiplied by PV_T.

Therefore:

$$\text{delta}_{PV_T} = \frac{\partial PV_T}{\partial r} = -\text{dur}_{mac} \times PV_T$$

Equation 7.1 Cashflow portfolio delta – using continuous rates

Notice that if delta_{PV_T} is expressed as the rate of change of PV_T divided by PV_T then delta_{PV_T} is simply the negative of the duration.

Using the mathematical relationship:

$$\frac{\partial(\ln x)}{\partial x} = \frac{1}{x}$$

Equation 7.1 can be expressed as:

$$\frac{\partial \ln PV_T}{\partial r} = -\text{dur}_{mac}$$

Equation 7.1.1 Variation of equation 7.1

The Macaulay duration of a single cashflow is the same as its term to maturity. Therefore, it follows from *equation 7.1* that the sensitivity of a cashflow stream is similar to that of a single cashflow with duration equal to the Macaulay duration of the cashflow stream and face value equal to the present value accumulated to the Macaulay duration.

Remember, however, *equation 7.1* was derived using continuously compounded rates. How should the formula be adjusted if discretely compounded interest rates are used?

We start with a single cashflow based on yield quotes:

$$PV = FV/(1 + r/n)^{nt}$$

Taking the first derivative of PV with respect to r gives:

$$\frac{\partial PV}{\partial r} = -FVt/(1 + r/n)^{nt+1}$$

Therefore it follows that if r is the internal rate of return for a portfolio of cashflows:

$$delta_{PV_T} = \frac{\partial PV_T}{\partial r} = \frac{-dur_{mac} PV_T}{1+r/n}$$

Equation 7.2 Cashflow portfolio delta – using discrete compounding and yield rate

and if discount quotes are used:

$$PV = FV(1-r/n)^{nt}$$

Taking the first derivative of PV with respect to r gives:

$$\frac{\partial PV}{\partial r} = nt(-1/n)FV(1-r/n)^{nt-1}$$

$$= \frac{-tFV(1-r/n)^{nt}}{(1-r/n)}$$

Therefore for a portfolio of cashflows:

$$\frac{\partial PV_T}{\partial r} = \frac{-dur_{mac} PV_T}{1-r/n}$$

Equation 7.2.1 Cashflow portfolio delta – using discrete compounding and discount quote

Remember, n is the compounding frequency. Therefore n equals two for semi-annual rests. Notice that as n approaches infinity *equations 7.2* and *7.2.1* become *equation 7.1.*

The expression $dur_{mac}/(1 + r/n)$ is known as the *modified duration* for yield quotes. Note the equivalent expression for discount quotes is $dur_{mac}/(1 - r/n)$.

Note: *equations 7.1, 7.2* and *7.2.1* were derived using the internal rate of return. This means the formula involves a slight approximation since, in general, the combined effect of the first derivative of each cashflow with respect to its zero rate is not the same as the combined effect of the derivative of each cashflow with respect to the internal rate of return.

Equation 7.1 can be used to determine the approximate change in the present value of a cashflow or cashflow stream, resulting from a small instantaneous shift in the internal rate of return.

Using the approximation:

$$\frac{\Delta PV_T}{\Delta r} \approx \frac{\partial PV_T}{\partial r}$$

Therefore:

$$\frac{\Delta PV_T}{PV_T} \approx -dur_{mac} \times \Delta r$$

Equation 7.3 PV sensitivity/duration approximation – using continuous rates

This relationship is only approximate since the cashflow gamma is non-zero.

Also, for discrete rates, using *equation 7.2*:

$$\frac{\Delta PV_T}{PV_T} \approx -dur_{mod} \times \Delta r$$

Equation 7.4 PV sensitivity/duration approximation – using discrete compounding and yield quote

This approximation is less effective for larger yield shifts.

And for discount quotes, from *equation 7.2.1*:

$$\frac{\Delta PV_T}{PV_T} \approx \frac{-dur_{mac} \times \Delta r}{1 - r/n}$$

Equation 7.4.1 PV sensitivity/duration approximation – using discrete compounding and discount quotes

Exercise 7e – Calculating Macaulay duration

Determine the Macaulay duration for a simple portfolio with two positive cashflows. Assume the near cashflow has a duration of 365 days and face value of $1 million. Assume the far cashflow has a duration of 730 days and face value of $2 million. Also assume that the semi-annual zero rate is 10 per cent per annum for each cashflow.

First, we determine the discount factors used to form the present values of each cashflow.

The present value, PV is equal to the discount factor d_f multiplied by the future value, FV. Therefore, the discount factor is:

$$d_f = PV/FV$$

$$= 1/(1 + r/n)^{nt}$$

Note the dimension of both r and n is 1/time and, of course, the dimension of t is time. Hence the discount factor is a dimensionless number.

Thus, the discount factor for the near cashflow, $d_{f.near}$ is:

$$d_{f.near} = 1/(1 + .1/2)^2$$

$$= .9070$$

And the discount factor for the far cashflow, $d_{f.far}$ is:

$$d_{f.far} = 1/(1 + .1/2)^4$$

$$= .8227$$

Thus, using *equation 7.0*, the Macaulay duration is:

$$dur_{mac} = \frac{.9070 \times 1 \times 1 + .8227 \times 2 \times 2}{.9070 \times 1 + .8227 \times 2}$$

$$= 1.645 \text{ years, or } 600.43 \text{ days}$$

Refer to *figure 7.2.*

The Macaulay duration is 1.645 years. This means that for small *uniform* yield shifts this portfolio has the equivalent yield risk of a single cashflow with duration 1.645 years and face value close to $3 million.

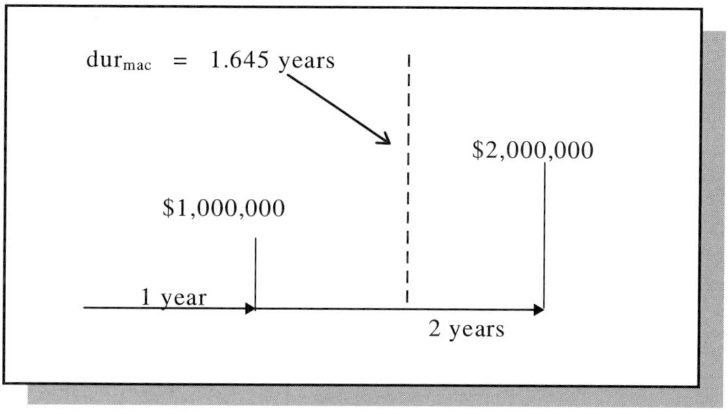

Figure 7.2
Macaulay duration of two positive cashflows

Exercise 7f – Duration hedging

Check the effectiveness of the Macaulay based hedge produced in *exercise 7e.* Assume uniform yield shifts only.

The net present value of the two cashflows is:

$$PV = 1{,}000{,}000[1/(1+.1/2)^{2\times 1} + 2/(1+.1/2)^{2\times 2}]$$

$$= 907{,}029 + 1{,}645{,}404$$

$$= \$2{,}552{,}433$$

After a 100bp rate increase the net present value is:

$$PV_{+100bp} = 1[1/(1+.11/2)^{2\times 1} + 2/(1+.11/2)^{2\times 2}]$$

$$= 898{,}452 + 1{,}614{,}433$$

$$= \$2{,}512{,}885$$

This is a decrease of $39,548.

The present value of the duration cashflow, assuming a duration of 600 days is:

$$PV_{dur} = 3{,}000{,}000/(1+.1/2)^{2\times 600/365}$$

$$= \$2{,}555{,}394$$

After a 100bp rate increase the present value is:

$$PV_{dur+100bp} = 3{,}000{,}000/(1+.11/2)^{2\times 600/365}$$

$$= \$2{,}515{,}793$$

This is a decrease of $39,601.

Thus, in this case the Macaulay based hedge produces an error of $53 or .002 per cent from a uniform instantaneous 100bp yield increase or .002 per cent.

Table 7.2 summariscs the change in present value both for the unhedged and Macaulay hedged portfolios over a ±200bp range in uniform semi-annual yield shifts.

As illustrated by the sensitivity results in *table 7.2* the Macaulay based hedge is quite effective. Note, we do not need to be actually considering initiating a Macaulay based hedge for this information to be valuable. The fact that the hedge is effective for *uniform* yield shifts means that we have a way of approximating the portfolio risk characteristics with those of a single cashflow. There are however, significant limitations of this risk approximation, as we will discover.

Δbp	**ΔPV**	
	Unhedged	**with Mac'Hdg**
200	-78,250	156
150	-39,548	53
0	0	0
-100	40,420	0
-200	81,730	56

Table 7.2
Illustrating PV change with Macaulay based hedge in place

Two features in *table 7.2* are worth noting. First, the portfolio incurs a profit for both increases and decreases in yields. This is a gamma effect – the non-linear payoff characteristic. The reverse position incurs a loss in both directions. Second, the payoff is asymmetric – it tends to profit more easily when yields rise. This indicates the hedge is not balanced perfectly and highlights the approximations referred to in the derivation of the Macaulay duration. *Table 7.3* illustrates the hedge performance when delta matching is used to determine the hedge cashflow's face value. Notice this produces a more accurate hedge.

Δbp	**ΔPV**	
	Unhedged	**with Mac' Hdg.**
200	155	103
150	53	26
0	0	0
-100	0	27
-200	56	111

Table 7.3
Comparing PV changes with Macaulay based hedge using face value equal to the sum of the portfolio face values and face value determined by delta matching

Exercise 7g – Testing PV sensitivity/duration approximation

Test the accuracy of *equation 7.4* over a range of yield shifts using the cashflow portfolio studied in *exercise 7e.*

We repeat *equation 7.4* and show the workings for a 100bp increase:

$$\Delta PV \approx -\,dur_{mod} \times (PV_T\,\Delta r)$$

$$dur_{mod} = 1.645/(1 + .1/2)$$

$$= 1.567 \text{ years}$$

$$PV_T = .9068 \times 1 + .8225 \times 2$$

$$= \$2.5518 \text{ million}$$

$$\Delta r = .01 \text{ per year}$$

Hence:

$$\Delta PV \approx \$39{,}986$$

Refer to *table 7.2* and notice the record of the actual loss, which is \$39,549. Therefore, the +100bp sensitivity result predicted by *equation 7.4* is \$437 lower than the actual, an error of 1.10 per cent. This is the gamma, or non-linear, effect. *table 7.4* compares the results predicted by *equation 7.4* with actual sensitivity results over a range of yield shifts.

Δbp	ΔPV		
	Actual	Eq. 7.4	$Error
400	-153,205	-159,944	-6,739
200	-78,251	-79,972	-1,721
100	-39,549	-39,986	-437
-100	40,418	39,986	-432
-200	81,730	79,972	-1,758
-400	167,136	159,944	-7,192

Table 7.4
Illustrating the PV sensitivity of the cashflow portfolio studied in *Exercise 7e* – actual and as predicted by *equation 7.4*

Note the error increases with the size of the yield shift. The error is 4.40 per cent for a 400bp yield increase. Notice the linear approximation produces a value that is less than the actual in *both* directions.

Duration problems

Macaulay developed his duration technique in 1938 – before computers were invented. Duration is a relatively simple measure to calculateand was a great advantage before computers. However, this duration measure provides a rather naive measure of yield curve exposure since it tells us nothing about yield tilt or flex risks. With the advent of computers more comprehensive risk measures can be used, perhaps together with duration.

Exercise 7h – Duration and tilt risk

Construct a portfolio with identical duration and net cashflow as the dual cashflow portfolio studied in *exercise 7e,* but with different yield tilt risk exposure.

By decreasing the duration of the shorter term cashflow and increasing the duration of the longer term cashflow, it is possible to keep the portfolio duration the same. In this case, the exposure to uniform shifts will change very little but the tilt exposure may change dramatically. For example, if the shorter term cashflow of $1million occurs in 27 days and the longer term cashflow occurs in 969 days, the portfolio duration is unchanged at 1.645 years.

Table 7.5 records the change in present values of the two portfolios after a linear tilt in the yield curve. The tilt is produced by moving the overnight rate up 100bp with the movement decreasing linearly to zero change for the three year yield. Notice the tilt risks are quite different for the two portfolios with identical duration.

Tilt \ Port	ΔPV	
	First	Second
100 - 0	-16,137	-5,163
-100 - 0	16,275	5,183
Duration	1.645	1.645

Table 7.5
Illustrating different yield curve tilt risks for two portfolios with identical duration

Exercise 7i – Identical duration different uniform exposure

Specify two portfolios with identical duration but quite different exposures to uniform yield shifts.

This is very easy to do. Consider a cashflow with a duration of say three years and face value $1million along with a second cashflow with exactly the same duration but different face value. Obviously, the two portfolios have different interest rate exposures even though they have identical duration.

Hence, the duration measure by itself is a meaningless measure of interest rate exposure.

Dimensionless cashflow sensitivity charts

Equation 7.4 ignores the non-linear effect. This is the source of the error observed in *exercise 7g*.

An accurate universal present value sensitivity chart can be formed by identifying all the parameters affecting the present value and then forming the dimensionless numbers. First we consider continuously compounded rates:

$$PV = FVe^{-rt}$$

$\Delta PV = FVe^{-rt}(e^{-\Delta rt} - 1)$

Hence:

$\Delta PV = fn(PV, \Delta r, t)$

$\Delta PV/PV = (e^{-\Delta rt} - 1)$

Therefore:

$\Delta PV/PV = fn(\Delta rt)$

where:

FV = face value

r = continuously compounded rate

Δr = change in r

t = duration in years

Both $\Delta PV/PV$ and Δrt are dimensionless numbers. *Chart 7.1* is produced using these two dimensionless numbers.

Subject to the limitations of scale and resolution, *chart 7.1* can be used to determine the change in present value of any cashflow given Δrt. Notice the value r is not required because the continuous rate is used in this case. However, because the continuously compounded rate is used, Δr must be converted from the commonly used discrete rate to the continuous rate. This can be avoided by including the compounding frequency in the pricing relationship.

Allowing for discrete rates with n as the compounding frequency:

$$\Delta PV = fn(PV, r, \Delta r, t, n)$$

Possibly the most obvious dimensionless parameters in this relationship are: $\Delta PV/PV$, rt, $r/\Delta r$ and r/n. With four variables this relationship is difficult to represent as a simple chart. We still have four variables even if we choose to hold either Δr or n constant, or even both constant.

Fortunately, however, an alternative set of dimensionless parameters can be formed: $\Delta PV/PV$, $\Delta r/n$, $r/\Delta r$ and Δrt.

This relationship has the practical advantage that we can hold $\Delta r/n$ constant, thereby reducing the number of variables to three. *Chart 7.2* was constructed with Δr fixed at 100bp and n fixed at 2 – that is, assuming semi-annual compounding. It provides an accurate representation of the cashflow present value change to a 1 per cent increase in the semi-annual yield. Other dimensionless charts could be formed using different size yield shifts.

Notice the graph is not highly sensitive to the value of R. Also, the present value sensitivity is slightly less than the duration but with reversed sign – the difference increases as the yield increases. This relationship can also be seen by observing *equation 7.4*.

Importantly, *charts 7.1* and *7.2* can also be used to determine the price sensitivity of cashflow streams, swaps, FRAs and bonds. In this case, the variable T is the Macaulay duration, R is the internal rate of return and PV is the portfolio present value. However, as discussed earlier in this chapter, the Macaulay cashflow is not a perfect representation.

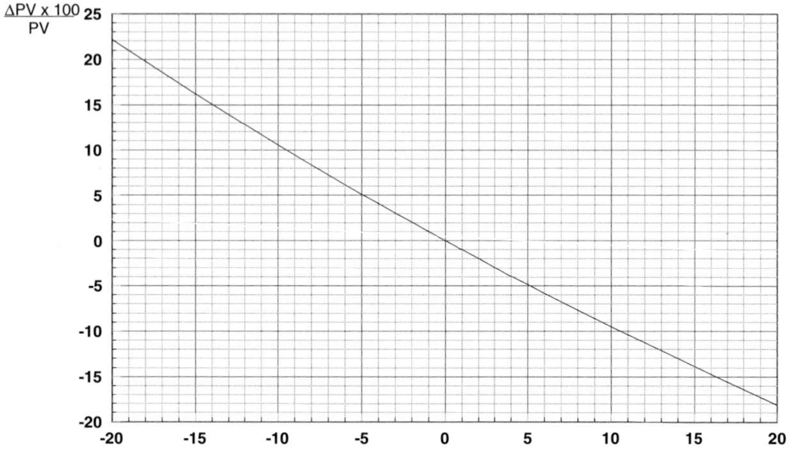

Chart 7.1

McKay's dimensionless cashflow sensitivity chart – using continuously compounded rate change ΔR per cent and T the duration in years

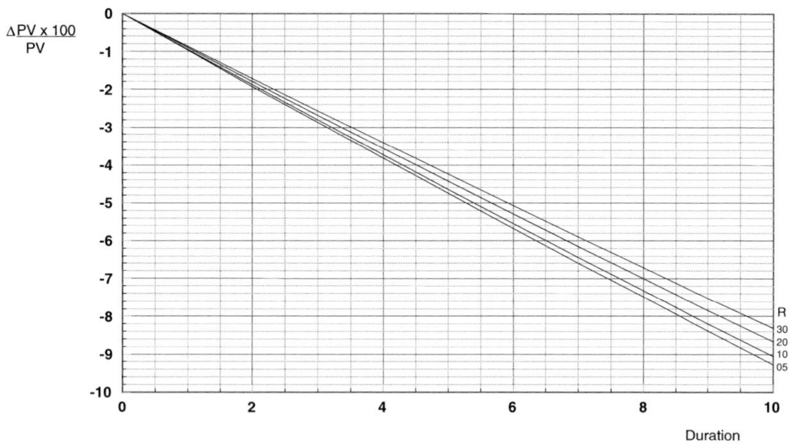

Chart 7.2

McKay's dimensionless cashflow sensitivity chart – using semi-annual compounding and Δr as +100bp

Gamma risk

The present value of a cashflow or portfolio of cashflows, has a non-linear relationship with yield. That is, the size of the change in the present value for a defined yield shift changes as the yield changes. This effect is illustrated in *table 7.4*. *Equation 7.4* assumes a linear relationship. The column labelled $Error shows the variation from this linear assumption. The mathematics describing this non-linear or gamma risk is quite straightforward.

Starting with:

$$PV = FV\ e^{-rt}$$

$$\frac{\partial PV}{\partial r} = -t\ FV\ e^{-rt}$$

Hence:

$$\frac{\partial^2 PV}{\partial r^2} = t^2 FVe^{-rt}$$

Equation 7.5 Cashflow gamma – using continuous rate

or

$$\frac{\partial^2 PV}{\partial r^2} = t^2 PV$$

Equation 7.6 Cashflow gamma – using continuous rate

and for discrete compounding using yield quotes:

Starting with *equation 7.2:*

$$\frac{\partial PV}{\partial r} = -t\,PV/(1 + r/n)$$

It can be shown that:

$$\frac{\partial^2 PV}{\partial r^2} = \frac{t(t+1/n)PV}{(1+r/n)^2}$$

Equation 7.7 Cashflow gamma – using discrete yield

And for discrete compounding using discount quotes:

From *equation 7.2.1:*

$$\frac{\partial PV}{\partial r} = -tFV(1-r/n)^{nt-1}$$

Taking the second derivative of PV with respect to r:

$$\frac{\partial^2 PV}{\partial r^2} = t(t-1/n)FV(1-r/n)^{nt-2}$$

$$= \frac{t(t-1/n)FV(1-r/n)^{nt}}{(1-r/n)^2}$$

Therefore:

$$\frac{\partial^2 PV}{\partial r^2} = \frac{(t^2-t/n)PV}{(1-r/n)^2}$$

Equation 7.7.1 Cashflow gamma – using discrete compounding and discount quote

and for a portfolio of cashflows, assuming r is the average rate:

$$\frac{\partial^2 PV_T}{\partial r^2} = \frac{\partial^2 (\Sigma PV_i)}{\partial r^2}$$

$$= \Sigma \frac{\partial^2 (PV_i)}{\partial r^2}$$

$$= \Sigma\left(\frac{\partial (-t_i PV_i)}{\partial r}\right)$$

$$= \Sigma -t_i \left(\frac{\partial PV_i}{\partial r}\right)$$

$$= \Sigma -t_i (-t_i PV_i)$$

Hence:

$$\frac{\partial^2 PV_T}{\partial r^2} = \sum t_i^{\ 2} PV_i$$

Equation 7.8 Cashflow portfolio gamma – continuous rate

and it can be shown that for discrete yield quotes:

$$\frac{\partial^2 PV_T}{\partial r^2} = \frac{\sum t_i^2 PV_i + 1/n \sum t_i PV_i}{(1+r/n)^2}$$

Equation 7.9 Cashflow portfolio gamma – discrete rate, yield quote

and for discount quotes, from *equation 7.7.1:*

$$\frac{\partial^2 PV_T}{\partial r^2} = \frac{\sum t_i^2 PV_i - 1/n \sum t_i PV_i}{(1-r/n)^2}$$

Equation 7.9.1 Cashflow portfolio gamma – discrete rate, discount quote

Strictly speaking, the gammas of two cashflow portfolios are not additive because infinitesimal average interest rates ∂r are not in general identical. However, frequently the summation error is minor.

Convexity

Convexity is defined as the rate of change of the duration.

$$\text{convexity} = \frac{\partial dur_{mod}}{\partial r}$$

Equation 7.9.2 Cashflow portfolio convexity

The convexity of a single cashflow is obviously zero, therefore convexity is not additive.

And it can be shown that the convexity of a cashflow portfolio is:

$$\text{convexity} = \frac{\partial dur_{mac}}{\partial r} = \frac{\left(\sum t_i PV_i\right)^2 - \left(\sum PV_i\right)\sum t_i^2 PV_i}{(1+r/n)\left(\sum PV_i\right)^2}$$

Equation 7.9.3 Cashflow portfolio convexity

Time lapse risk

The present value of a cashflow is exposed to time lapse as well as yield changes. We now derive the first and second derivatives of the present value with respect to time for continuously compounded as well as discrete rates.

Again, starting with the continuous expression:

$$PV = FV\ e^{-rt}$$

$$\frac{\partial PV}{\partial t} = -r\ FV\ e^{-rt}$$

Therefore:

$$\frac{\partial PV}{\partial t} = -rPV$$

Equation 7.10 Cashflow time lapse – using continuous rates

and:

$$\frac{\partial^2 PV}{\partial t^2} = r^2 PV$$

Equation 7.11 Cashflow rate of change of time lapse risk – using continuous rates

and for discrete compounding using yield quotes:

Since r is assumed to be constant we can substitute the conversion from continuous to discrete rates directly into *equations 7.10* and *7.11.*

First, we determine the discrete rate R in terms of the continuous rate r:

set $e^{-rt} = 1/(1 + R/n)^{nt}$

$-rt = \ln(1 + R/n)^{-nt}$

Therefore:

$$r = n\ln(1+R/n)$$

Equation 7.12 Continuous rate in terms of discrete rate

Remember ln is the natural log.

We now substitute *equation 7.12* in *equations 7.10* and *7.11* to form the first and second derivatives of the present value with respect to time. See *equations 7.13* and *7.14*.

$$\frac{\partial PV}{\partial t} = -n\ln(1+r/n)PV$$

Equation 7.13 Cashflow time lapse – using discrete compounding, yield quote

Now, we determine the discount rate R in terms of the continuous rate r:

set $e^{-rt} = (1-r/n)^{nt}$

$-rt = \ln(1-r/n)^{nt}$

$r = -n\ln(1-r/n)$

From *equation 7.10*:

$$\frac{\partial PV}{\partial t} = -r\ PV$$

Hence:

$$\frac{\partial PV}{\partial t} = -n\ln(1-r/n)PV$$

Equation 7.13.1 Cashflow time lapse – using discrete compounding, discount quote

From *equation 7.13*, taking the second derivative of the present value with respect to time t:

$$\frac{\partial^2 PV}{\partial t^2} = [n\ln(1+r/n)]^2\, PV$$

Equation 7.14 Cashflow rate of change of time lapse risk – using discrete compounding, yield quote

and

$$\frac{\partial^2 PV}{\partial t^2} = [n\ln(1-r/n)]^2\, PV$$

Equation 7.14.1 Cashflow rate of change of time lapse risk – using discrete compounding, discount quote

Note that in *equations 7.13* and *7.14* we reverted to using r, rather than R, for the discrete rate. Recall that *equations 7.3* and *7.4* express the present value change for a small yield shift in terms of the present value, duration and the yield nudge. A similar set of equations can be formed for a time nudge using *equations 7.10* and *7.13.*

Equation 7.10 gives:

$$\frac{\Delta PV}{PV} \approx -\, r\Delta t$$

Equation 7.15 Cashflow PV sensitivity to time lapse approximation – using continuous rates

Equation 7.13 gives:

$$\frac{\Delta PV}{PV} \approx -n\ln(1+r/n)\Delta t$$

Equation 7.16 Cashflow PV sensitivity to time lapse approximation – using discrete compounding, yield quote

and *equation 7.13.1* gives:

$$\frac{\Delta PV}{PV} \approx -n\ln(1-r/n)\Delta t$$

Equation 7.16.1 Cashflow PV sensitivity to time lapse approximation using discrete compounding, discount quote

Exercise 7j – Time lapse risk

Use *equation 7.16* to determine the present value change for the simple cash portfolio, studied in *exercise 7e,* for a time lapse of 1, 7, 14 and 28 days.

We repeat *equation 7.16*:

$$\Delta PV \approx -n\ln(1 + r/n)\ \Delta t\ PV$$

$$n\ln(1 + r/n) = 2\ln(1 + .1/2)$$

$$= .09758032$$

Δt = -1/365
and -7/365
and -14/365
and -28/365

$$PV = \text{discount factor} \times FV$$

We determined the discount factors for the two cashflows in *exercise 7e*.

Therefore:

$$PV = .9070 \times 1 + .8227 \times 2$$

$$= \$2.5524 \text{ million}$$

Thus, when Δt is equal to -1/365:

$$\Delta PV = \$682$$

The results based on *equation 7.16* for the various time lapses are recorded in *table 7.6*. The exact result is also recorded for comparison.

Notice that *equation 7.16* is quite accurate even for longer-term time lapses.

Time Lapse days	ΔPV	
	Eq. 7.16	**Actual**
1	682	683
7	4,775	4,782
14	9,550	9,572
28	19,101	19,179

Table 7.6
Illustrating PV change with time lapse as predicted by *equation 7.16* and the actual

Check using URM – Exercise 7a

Load file RMW3. This file contains a single $10 million positive cashflow maturing in three years. Inspect the cashflow window <H>. Calculate <F3>. Observe the present value.

Go to sensitivity analysis <F6> and observe the cashflow PV exposure to uniform yield shifts. Confirm the results recorded in *table 7.1*.

Can we hedge this cashflow's yield risk using 90 day bank bill futures? Which contract maturities should we use? *Exercise 7b* introduces these issues with an example of a poorly constructed hedge.

Check using URM – Exercise 7b

Load file RMW3A. The three year cashflow appears in the cashflow window <H>. The March 1998 futures contract appears in the futures window <U>. Calculate <F3>. As expected, the futures delta hedge position is short 97 contracts. Each contract has a face value of $1 million.

Go to sensitivity analysis <F6> and analyse the effectiveness of this hedge. Notice the hedge is quite effective for uniform yield movements. A net gain of $2,391 is incurred from a sudden increase of 100bp in the semi-annual rate. Also, a net gain of $3,552 is incurred from a sudden yield decrease of 100bp. Observe the payoff graph <F8> <F8>.

Notice the smile effect. Return to sensitivity analysis. Now activate the sensitivity tilt by pressing <L> and leave the yield tilt point on the default setting of 3.0 years and use 100bp for the yield near point and 0 bp for the far point. The hedge performance is recorded in *window 7.1*. Notice the hedge is not robust.

Check using URM – Exercise 7c

Load file RMW3A. Go to the futures window and delete the first row <Ctrl E>. Access the add menu <A>. The contract type defaults to BBF (90 bank bill futures). Move the cursor to the last field labelled *Number of futures* and type <12 Enter>. Press <Crtl A> to create the futures strip in the futures portfolio window. Press <Alt U> to update the market data. Press <F3> to calculate.

The hedge parcel contract lots are calculated automatically. Twelve separate futures contract months are used. Each futures contract has a face value of $1 million.

As expected, the futures strip consists of short 10 lot of the nearest month, short 8 lots for each of the next 10 contract months and short 6 lots of the last contract. See *window 7.2*

Observe the sensitivity analysis <F6>. The 100bp uniform yield up-move shows a net gain of $919 and the 100bp uniform down-move also shows a net gain of $5,032. Now observe the 100 - 0 tilt hedge. Notice this hedge is robust, the yield up tilt case shows a net gain of $2,253 and the yield down tilt shows a net loss of $2,409. See *window 7.3* and compare with *window 7.1*. Also observe the payoff graph <F8> <F8> to see the smile effect. See *window 7.4*.

Check using URM – Exercise 7d

Load file RMW3B. The FRA appears in the FRA window <F>. The two cashflows appear in the cashflow window <H>.

Go to sensitivity analysis <F6>. Notice that the FRA is hedged perfectly by the two cashflows. The hedge is perfect for both uniform yield shifts and tilts. The sensitivity of the cashflow and FRA portfolios can be viewed separately by deactivating the FRA or cashflow alternately. Now use *URM* to formulate the cashflow and FRA face values. Escape sensitivity analysis <Esc> and go to the cashflow portfolio <H>. *URM* can be used to solve for either cashflow or both cashflows together. Place the cursor on the face value field of either cashflow and press <Delete>, followed by <F3> to calculate. Notice that the face values of the cashflows that hedge the FRA are formulated automatically.

Also, the FRA that hedges these two cashflows can be computed. Fix the cashflow face values (if they have just been unfixed) by placing the cursor on the face value fields and pressing <X>. Go to the FRA portfolio <F> and unfix the face value using <Delete>. Calculate <F3>. Notice the calculated FRA face value is $10 million, as expected. This is an elementary example of the *AAA Hedge* technique process – hedge *Anything with Anything to achieve Anything*. In this case we achieve a zero risk position.

Check using URM – Exercise 7e and 7f

Use *URM's* sensitivity analysis to test the results illustrated in *figure 7.2.*

Load file RMW3C. The two cashflows appear in the cashflow portfolio <H.>. Calculate <F3>. Notice the duration measure displayed is 1.645 years, as expected.

Go to sensitivity analysis <F6>. Notice this portfolio incurs a loss of $39,549 when yields rise 100bp and a profit of $40,418 when yields fall 100bp. The slight difference in the magnitude of the profit and loss illustrates the gamma risk.

Now return to the cashflow window <Esc> and add the Macaulay based hedge. Press <Ctrl Enter> to create a new row. Move the cursor across to the date column and type

<1.645y Enter> in the maturity column, <10 Enter> in the YTM column and <-3m Enter> in the face value column. Press <F3> to calculate.

Go to sensitivity analysis and observe the portfolio profit and loss with the Macaulay based hedge in place. The 100bp and 200bp yield shift results are summarised in *table 7.2.*

We can also use *URM* to formulate the precise face value of the single cashflow hedge.

Return to the cashflow window, place the cursor on the face value field of the second (Macaulay hedge) row and press <Delete> to unfix the face value. Press <F3> to calculate. Notice the new face value is $2,997,994. Use the sensitivity analysis to confirm the results recorded in *table 7.3.*

The payoff, as illustrated in *table 7.3,* is now quite symmetric. This is a sign of a balanced hedge. Therefore, *URM* produced a more accurate hedge using the delta hedge matching technique.

Check using URM – Exercise 7h

Load file RMW3C. Go to sensitivity analysis <F6> and activate the tilt function <L>.

Move the cursor to the second, or far, yield field and type <0>. Leave the overnight yield shift set to 100bp. This specifies a move in the semi-annual zero curve of 100bp at the near end decreasing linearly to zero at three years. Confirm the results recorded in the first column of *table 7.5.*

Now press <Esc> and load file RMW3D. Go to the cashflow window and press <F3> to calculate. Notice the duration of the first cashflow is much less and the duration of the second cashflow is much greater than for the first portfolio. But both cashflows have the same face values as the first portfolio. Also notice the duration of this new portfolio is 1.645 years, as with the first portfolio in RMW3C.

Go to sensitivity analysis <F6> and repeat the tilt sensitivity exercise. Confirm the results recorded in the second column of *table 7.5*

Check using URM – Exercise 7g

The actual changes in value can be checked using *URM*. Load file RMW3C. Go to sensitivity analysis <F6>. Move the cursor to the as-at field and type <1 Enter>. Also change the yield as-at field to <10 Enter>.

The present value change from a one day time lapse appears in the middle cell, numbered 5. Repeat for seven, 14 and 28 days.

Summary

- The present value of a cashflow is sensitive to yield change and time lapse.

- The Macaulay duration is a present value weighted average of the terms of the payment stream.

- Interest rate forwards can be hedged/replicated using two cashflows straddling the span of the forward's projection term.

- For small uniform yield shifts, the change in present value of a cashflow stream is equal to the negative of the portfolio's modified duration, multiplied by the present value, times the yield shift.

- Forward and futures strips can be used to hedge cashflows against yield curve shifts, tilts and flexes but some gamma risk usually remains.

- Duration measures do not model tilt risk.

Notes

1 Frederick R. Macaulay. Some Theoretical Problems Suggested by the Movement of Interest Rates, Bond Yields and Stock Prices in the United States since 1856. *New York National Bureau of Economic Research.* 1938.

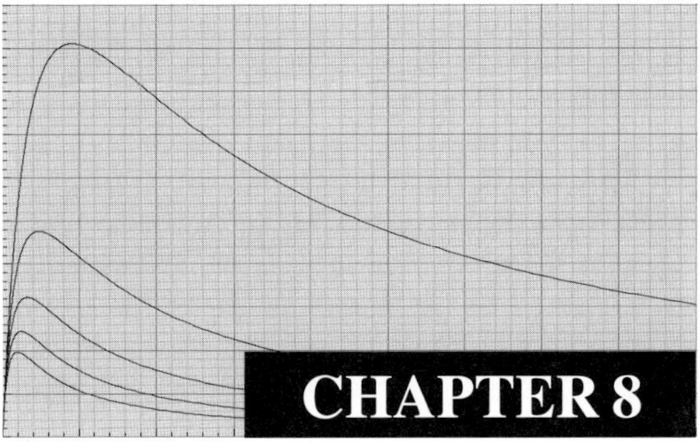

CHAPTER 8

The Bin Technique and Term Structure Hedging

In this chapter we discuss:

- interest rate term structure risks and hedging, and
- use a sophisticated delta hedging process known as the bin technique for measuring and reshaping term structure tilt/ flex risks.

Term structure risks

Frequently, the number of risk components increases with the complexity of the portfolio. For example, short and long term interest rates do not always move in parallel. Short term rates may rise or fall faster than longer term rates, or even move in opposite directions. Portfolios with exposures to many different durations are exposed to numerous possible yield curve tilts and flexes.

The effect of this yield curve dynamics can be modelled by breaking down the interest rate exposure of each financial instrument into separate risks for each point on the yield curve – say, monthly intervals. This produces many different yield risk components. This procedure is referred to as the bin technique. The process of calculating accurate risk measures for each bin can be quite complex, particularly when different instrument types are mixed in the same portfolio.

The commonly used duration based measures do not model exposure to term structure tilts and flexes. On the other hand, the bin technique can be used to produce realistic representations of yield curve risk. These bin risks can be used to form intelligent hedges that manage yield curve tilt and flex risks.

The bin technique can also be used to manage volatility risk which also exhibits term structure characteristics.

The bin technique

The bin technique is a practical method of dealing with the yield curve tilt/flex problem. It is really a sophisticated form of delta hedging technique. The techniques' great advantage is that it does not rely on detailed knowledge of the term structure dynamics such as correlations between different points along the yield curve.

The yield curve is divided into separate "bins" or "buckets". The sensitivity of the portfolio's present value to isolated movements in the forward rate for each bin is determined and treated as comprising separate risk components. Term structure risk is then hedged using a separate delta matching process for each bin by assuming that forward movements within each bin are uniform. Intuitively, the assumption of uniform local movements is sound, provided the bin width is not too wide. With complex portfolios it is more important to keep the bin width narrow at the shorter end of the curve – say less than two years.

The objective is to delta hedge independently those instruments sensitive to segments of the forward curve prone to change which may be less correlated with the trend.

Placing the bin walls

In theory, a single cashflow only needs one bin since the cashflow's present value can be expressed in terms of only one yield curve segment – that is the yield to its maturity (YTM).

However, as discussed in *Chapter 7 – Cashflow Risk and Hedging,* usually it is impossible to obtain a single hedging instrument that is sensitive to exactly the same yield curve segment as the cashflow. In this case, a combination of hedge instruments, that is a hedge parcel such as a futures or forward strip, may be used to replicate or hedge the underlying exposure. The appropriate number of bins and location of the bin walls depend on the nature of the hedge parcel instruments. Frequently, the most effective hedge is produced by creating a separate bin for each instrument in the hedge parcel.

The bin sensitivity exercise is more complex when several instruments in the hedge parcel or native portfolio are sensitive to the same segment of the forward curve. Also, it is not unusual to encounter instruments that extend across two or more bins.

Further, it is important to ensure that, for each bin, that its forward rate affects at least one of the hedge parcel instruments. Also, there should not be any hedge gaps. That is, at least a portion of the native portfolio must overlap, at least partially, with each bin. The danger of *risk holes* arising from this type of oversight is illustrated in *exercise 8b.*

Cashflow bin hedging using forwards

Consider a positive cashflow with face value, or future value FV. The first step in formulating a bin hedge is to choose the preferred hedging instruments. Commonly, the most effective and flexible hedging method uses a strip of forwards or futures. We will assume that the forward or futures are sensitive to exactly the same yield curve as the cashflow.

The bin walls are placed so as to straddle each forward/future to which the cashflow is sensitive – that is, forward/futures that expire after the cashflow maturity are ignored.

Each bin must be delta hedged separately using the forward/ future in the same bin. The delta hedge technique uses the forward/future and cashflow pricing formulae and a small yield shift or nudge in the forward/future rate of each bin. The key to an effective hedge is to determine accurately the change in present value of a unit of each forward/future and the cashflow corresponding to each bin nudge. The appropriate forward/futures position to achieve a risk neutral position is the forward/futures face value that produces equal but opposite present value exposure to the cashflow.

The discount factor of the cashflow, $d_{f.cf}$ can be specified in terms of the discount factor of the forward spanning the full width of the bin, $d_{f.bin}$ and a discount factor representing the remainder of the curve to which the cashflow is sensitive, $d_{f.nbin}$.

This simple relationship is expressed as:

$$d_{f.cf} = d_{f.bin} \times d_{f.nbin}$$

When the bin forward rate is nudged, its discount factor changes to say, $df_{bin+\Delta}$, the new cashflow discount factor $df_{cf+\Delta}$ is:

$$d_{f.cf+\Delta} = d_{f.bin+\Delta} \times d_{f.nbin}$$

Thus the change in present value of the cashflow, ΔPV_{cf} is:

$$\Delta PV_{cf} = FV(d_{f.cf+\Delta} - d_{f.cf})$$

$$= FV(d_{f.bin+\Delta} \times d_{f.nbin} - d_{f.cf})$$

$$= FV(d_{f.bin+\Delta} \times d_{f.cf} / d_{f.bin} - d_{f.cf})$$

$$= FVd_{f.cf}(d_{f.bin+\Delta} / d_{f.bin} - 1)$$

Thus:

$$\Delta PV_{cf} = FVd_{f.cf}\left[\frac{d_{f.bin+\Delta}}{d_{f.bin}} - 1\right]$$

Equation 8.1 Change in cashflow present value produced by an isolated forward yield nudge

Equation 8.1 provides the change in present value of the cashflow in terms of the cashflow discount factor before the nudge and the bin discount factor both before and after the nudge.

Exercise 8a – Cashflow bin hedging using futures

Demonstrate how the bin technique can be used to formulate accurately a 90 day futures strip to hedge the cashflow studied in *exercises 7a, 7b* and *7c* – a \$10 million positive cashflow with three year duration. The three year semi-annual interest rate is 8.482 per year per annum.

In *exercise 7b* we determined the number of futures required to hedge the cashflow against uniform yield shifts – that is 97 contracts. Then, in *exercise 7c* the 97 contracts were distributed across all futures with expires preceeding the cashflow duration. This creates a hedge strip that protects the cashflow present value against uniform yield curve shifts, as well as tilts and flexes.

The manner of distributing the futures used in *exercise 7c* is a form of bin technique where, in effect, separate bin walls are placed at zero time and the maturity of each futures contract. However, *exercise 7c* used a simplifying assumption. The impact on the cashflow discount factor, from a defined isolated change in the futures rate, was assumed to be the same for each futures contract. This assumption can result in slight errors, or *risk holes*, when the yield curve is not flat. Of course, yield curves are rarely flat. A more accurate form of bin technique determines directly the impact of an isolated movement in the forward or futures rate in each bin.

Consider the futures contract with the shortest expiry. At the time of the assumed date of 19 May 1995, the nearest 90 day futures contract expires on 8 June 1995 – that is, in 20 days.

Therefore, in this case futures cannot be used to produce a perfect hedge. Another instrument, such as a near dated FRA, may be used in combination with the futures strip to compensate for this gap. However, we will accept some correlation risk in the accuracy of the hedge and use the nearest futures (June 1995) contract to hedge the first 20 days, as well as the 90 day interest rate out of 20 days. Therefore, the first bin must span at least the first 110 days. In fact, we will place the first bin wall at 111 days to allow for the slight gap between the maturity of the June contract and the expiry of the adjacent September contract.

The market rate of the nearest (June 1995) contract expressed as an index is 92.26, or 7.74 as a simple yield rate. The 111 day interest rate is 7.729 per cent per annum using semi-annual compounding. We will nudge the semi-annual rate in each bin by 1bp.

Equation 8.1, repeated below, is used to produce the change in present value of the cashflow:

$$\Delta PV_{cf} = FVd_{f.cf}(d_{f.bin+\Delta}/d_{f.bin} - 1)$$

where in this case:

$$FV = \$10{,}000{,}000$$

$$d_{f.cf} = 1/(1 + .08492/2)^{2 \times 1096/365}$$

$$= .779012894$$

$$d_{f.bin} = 1/(1 + .07729/2)^{2 \times 114/365}$$

$$= .976593164$$

$$d_{f.bin+\Delta} = 1/(1 + .07739/2)^{2 \times 114/365}$$

$$= .976563798$$

Therefore using *equation 8.1*:

$$\Delta PV_{cf} = -\$234.32$$

Next, we determine the change in value of a single June 1995 futures contract when the semi-annual rate increases by 1bp.

First, the futures rate of 92.26, or 7.74 per cent per annum as a simple yield quote, is expressed as a semi-annual rate using *equation 1.7*. This gives 7.8159 per cent per annum. This semi-annual rate is then increased, or nudged 1bp to 7.8259 and then converted back to a simple rate using *equation 1.8*. This gives 7.74981 per cent per annum.

Then we determine the change in value of the futures contract when its (simple interest) rate increases from 7.74 to 7.74981 per cent per annum. This produces a change of $23.28 for each contract with face value of $1,000,000.

Thus, the number of futures contracts required to hedge the first bin is -234.32/23.28 or -10.07. This is rounded up to short 10 contracts. Notice this result is very close to the result of -10.09 determined in *exercise 7c*. The delta hedge quantities of the other futures in the strip can be determined in a similar manner using bins placed to straddle each of the futures contacts.

The full futures strip is illustrated in *window 8.1*.

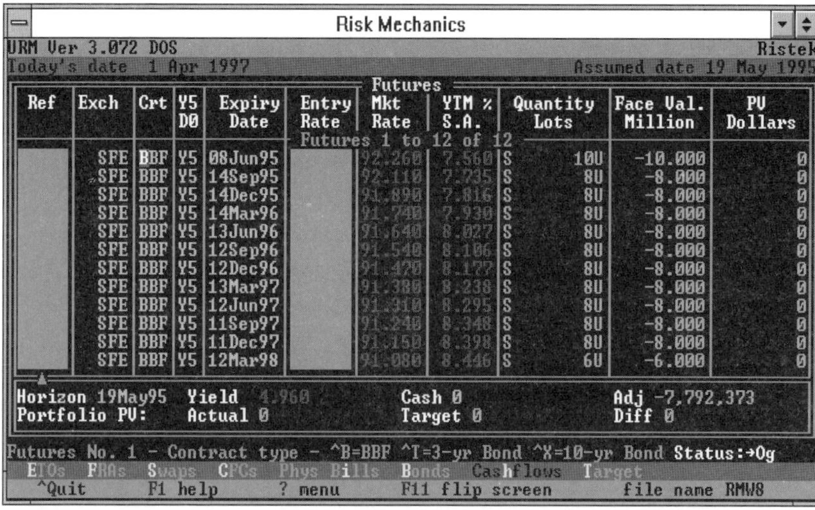

Window 8.1
Futures strip hedging a cashflow formulated using the bin technique

Eight futures contracts are used for all but the first and last contract. Only six of the last futures contract (March 1998) are used – this is because the last futures contract only partially overlaps with the cashflow. Therefore its amount is proportionally reduced. Notice this is the same futures hedge strip formulated in *exercise 7c*.

Window 8.2 displays the location of the bin walls and width of each bin, expressed in months, along with the results of an up and down 1bp semi-annual rate sensitivity analysis for each bin. Separate sensitivity analyses are provided for the hedge parcel (left side columns), the actual portfolio (middle columns) and the combined effect (right side columns). In this case, the actual portfolio is the single cashflow and the hedge parcel is the futures strip. The actual portfolio columns show the portfolio's present value exposure to isolated movements in the forward rates in each bin.

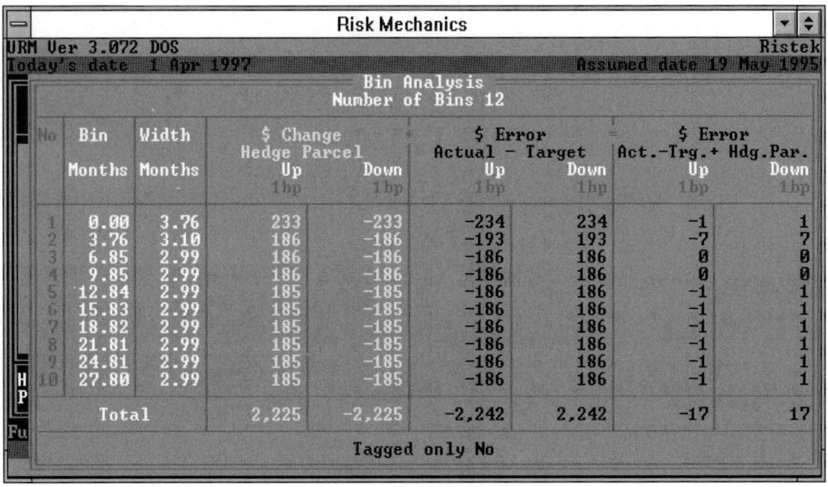

No	Bin Months	Width Months	$ Change Hedge Parcel Up 1bp	Down 1bp	$ Error Actual – Target Up 1bp	Down 1bp	$ Error Act.-Trg.+ Hdg.Par. Up 1bp	Down 1bp
1	0.00	3.76	233	-233	-234	234	-1	1
2	3.76	3.10	186	-186	-193	193	-7	7
3	6.85	2.99	186	-186	-186	186	0	0
4	9.85	2.99	186	-186	-186	186	0	0
5	12.84	2.99	185	-185	-186	186	-1	1
6	15.83	2.99	185	-185	-186	186	-1	1
7	18.82	2.99	185	-185	-186	186	-1	1
8	21.81	2.99	185	-185	-186	186	-1	1
9	24.81	2.99	185	-185	-186	186	-1	1
10	27.80	2.99	185	-185	-186	186	-1	1
	Total		2,225	-2,225	-2,242	2,242	-17	17

Window 8.2
Illustrating bin wall location and widths along with the sensitivities for the futures hedge strip and cashflow

Twelve bins have been created because the hedge parcel contains 12 futures. Generally a separate bin is formed for each instrument in the hedge parcel.

Notice, the two right-side columns illustrate that when the futures strip bin risks are added to the cashflow bin risks the risk in each bin is reduced to almost zero. This means the cashflow is hedged in a balanced manner regardless of how the yield curve may tilt or flex. The effectiveness of the tilt risk hedge can be tested using the sensitivity analysis window <F6>.

In *window 8.2* the bin walls have been placed between the maturity and expiry of adjacent futures contracts so that a separate bin is formed for each futures contract and each contract fits neatly within a bin – except for the first and last bins. *Window 8.3* displays the cashflow/futures portfolio payoff assuming uniform yield shifts. Notice the smile effect. The graph is not quite symmetric because the delta is not quite zero due to the limitation of the $1,000,000 minimum futures contract face value – a near zero delta, positive gamma portfolio.

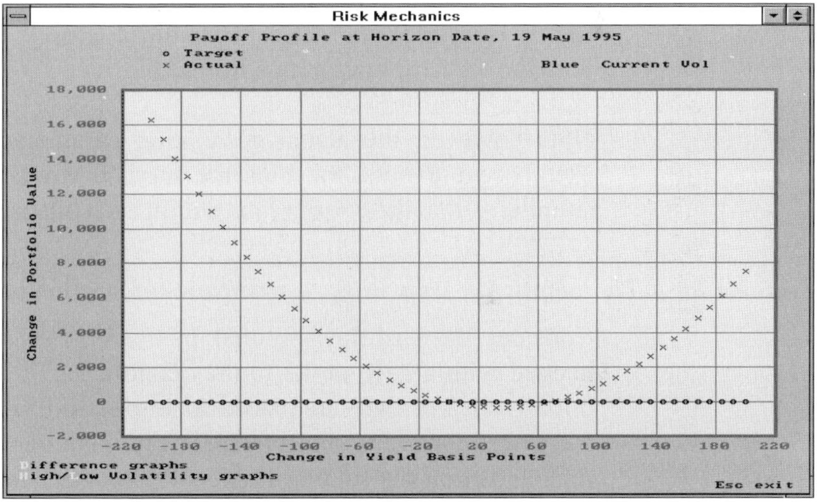

Window 8.3
Cashflow hedged with futures strip – near zero delta, positive gamma

The empty bin trap

It is important to ensure that there is at least one instrument in the chosen hedge parcel which is sensitive to an isolated movement in the forward rate in each bin. In general, there should be as many instruments in the hedge parcel as there are bins. If the value of the hedge parcel is insensitive to change in the forward rate of a particular bin it will be impossible to reshape the risk in that bin. In such cases, it is necessary to either include another instrument in the hedge parcel which is sensitive to the particular bin forward rate or merge the exposed bin with an adjacent bin.

Adding more instruments will produce a more robust hedge. However, frequently this is not practical and smaller bins must be merged into fewer larger bins.

This bin-merging step relies on the assumption that the forward rate in each of the exposed bins is closely correlated with the forward rate of an adjacent bin.

Note however, the actual correlation parameters are not used, because once the bins are merged we assume, for simplicity, that the correlations within each bin are perfect.

Exercise 8b – The empty bin trap using a cashflow/futures hedge

Consider the cashflow studied in *exercise 8a,* which is hedged with a strip of 12 futures contracts. Suppose that initially the bin walls are placed so as to straddle each of the 12 futures contracts – but say the last four contracts are then removed from the futures hedge strip because they are too illiquid – without adjusting the bin walls. Explain why a *risk hole* exists and express its size in terms of futures contracts.

A *risk hole* exists because, in a straightforward bin sensitivity analysis none of the remaining eight 90 day futures contracts is sensitive to isolated movements in the last four bins. By "straightforward" we mean that we ignore any possible correlations between the forward rates of each bin when performing the bin-by-bin sensitivity analysis. In this case, the last four bins will remain totally unhedged. In terms of futures contracts, this *risk hole* is equivalent to a long position of 8+8+8+6, or 30 futures contracts. This futures strip provides a poor hedge of the cashflow when the yield curve tilts because the last four bins are exposed. The hedge is not even effective as a hedge against uniform shifts because the total number of futures is 30 less than it should be – a serious *risk hole!*

One solution to this problem is to collapse the last five bins into one large bin containing 38 futures contracts – leaving a total of eight bins .

This illustrates an essential point in the placement of bin walls – that is, it is important to consider the nature of both the native exposure, as well as the chosen hedge parcel.

Exercise 8c – Cashflow bin hedging using FRAs

Assume the three year $10 million cashflow studied in *exercise 8a* is hedged with FRAs instead of futures. Illustrate the adjustment required for a FRA hedge by determining the face value of the FRA that delta hedges the first bin. Assume the FRA rate set dates and maturities are identical to the futures contract expires and maturities. Also assume that the FRA rates are priced off the same forward curve as the futures rates. The 20 day interest rate is 7.560 per cent per annum using semi-annual compounding.

This calculation is the same as in *exercise 8a* except that the change in the value of a FRA with face value of $1,000,000 for a 1bp nudge in the semi-annual yield must be discounted to present value. The future value price change of $23.28, recorded in *exercise 8a,* is a cashflow that occurs in 20 days' time. We will assume that the 20 day interest rate of 7.560 also increases by 1bp to 7.570 per cent per annum.

Therefore, the $PVbp_{FRA}$ is:

$$PVbp_{FRA} = -23.28(1/(1 + .07570/2))^{2 \times 20/365}$$

$$= -23.28 \times .99593690$$

$$= -23.19$$

Thus the FRA face value required to hedge the first bin is 234.32/23.19 – that is, a borrower's FRA with face value of $10.10 million. In this case, the FRA face value is only slightly different to the equivalent futures position of $10.07 million. However, the FRA/futures difference is more pronounced as the FRA/future duration increases. Also, in practice, the FRA rate set dates and maturities are likely to be adjusted to eliminate the small hedge gaps experienced with futures.

The full FRA strip, formulated using the bin technique, appears in *window 8.4*. Notice that the FRA face values tend to increase with the duration of the FRA. Compare this with the futures hedge strip recorded in the *window 8.1*. The payoff graph appears in *window 8.5.* Notice the payoff graph is symmetric and frowning – a zero delta, negative gamma portfolio. Compare the FRA/cashflow portfolio payoff with that of the slightly asymmetric, smiling payoff of the futures/ cashflow portfolio illustrated in *window 8.3*.

Question 8a

Why do the face values in the FRA strip tend to increase with the duration of the FRA, while the futures face values tend to be the same for each expiry?

Answer

As discussed in *Chapter 6 – Forward/Futures Relationship*, FRA face values must be adjusted by the accumulation factor – that is 1/discount factor. The accumulation factor increases with duration – it also increases with the interest rate.

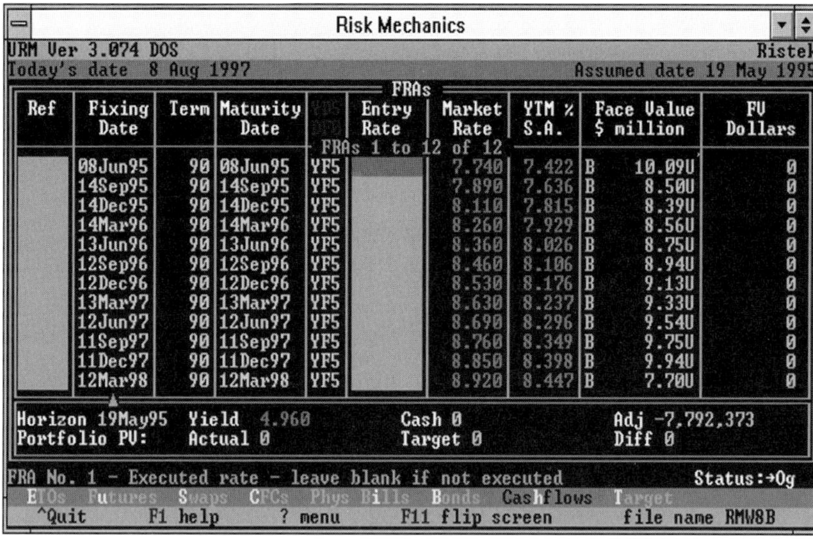

Window 8.4
FRA strip hedging three year cashflow

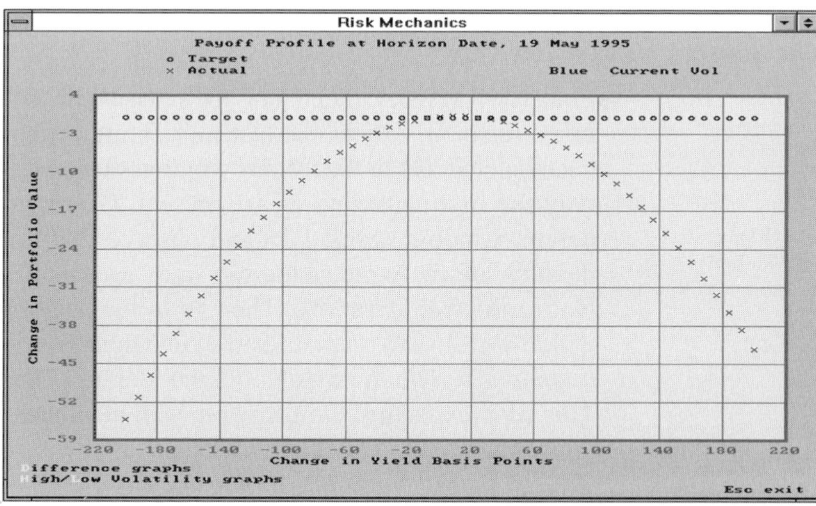

Window 8.5
Cashflow hedged with FRA strip – zero delta, negative gamma

Check using URM – Exercise 8a

Load file RMW8. The cashflow appears in the cashflow window <H> and the futures strip appears in the futures window <U>. Calculate <F3>. The bin-adjusted futures quantities appear in green. Notice, as determined in *exercise 8a*, the number of June 1995 contracts used is 10. (Before rounding, the actual value produced by *URM* Version 3.072 is 10.05 slightly different from 10.07 as calculated. This is cause by the use of a slight approximation that produces a value of -233.41 for ΔPV_{cf} instead of -234.32.) See *window 8.1*.

View the bin analysis <F7>. See *window 8.2*. Generally a separate bin is formed for each instrument in the hedge parcel – the futures strip in this case. This process has been automated in *URM*.

The effectiveness of the tilt risk hedge can be tested using the sensitivity analysis window <F6>. Observe the payoff graph <F8><F8>. See *window 8.3*.

Check using URM – Exercise 8b

Load file RMW8A. This file is the same as file RMW8 used in *exercise 8a,* except the last four futures contracts have been deleted. Go to the futures window <U> and notice that only the first eight futures are present. Go to the bin wall default window <Shift F7> and observe that the bin wall defaults are the same as the bin walls used in *exercise 8a.* Notice the wall durations. Then go to the hedge parameter window <F2> and press <A> to switch the bin analysis from *automatic* to *default walls.* Notice the "defaults" flag appears. This suppresses the automated bin wall placement and uses the default walls. Calculate <F3>.

Go to the futures window <U>. Notice that, as with *exercise 8a,* the first bin has 10 futures contracts and the following seven bins have the same eight contracts yet the remaining four bins are empty. Therefore, the total number of futures is only 66 rather than 96, as with *exercise 8a*. Observe the bin analysis <F7>. Notice that the last four bins in the hedge parcel are empty. Observe the sensitivity analysis <F6>. As expected, this is a very poor hedge.

Now reset the bin wall setting to automatic <F2> <A> and calculate <F3>. Observe the futures window <U> and bin analysis <F7>. Notice that this time only eight bins were formed. The last five bins have been collapsed into one large bin containing 38 contracts. Both the sensitivity analysis and bin analysis indicate that this hedge is quite effective.

Check using URM – Exercise 8c

Load file RMW8B. A FRA strip, similar to the futures strip used in *exercise 8a* appears in the FRA window <F>. Calculate <F3>. Notice the face value of the first FRA is $10.09 million. See *window 8.4*. (As with the futures, this is slightly less than the value of $10.10 million determined earlier in this exercise due to an approximation method used in the calculation of ΔPV_{cf}).

Compare this with the futures hedge strip recorded in the *window 8.1*. Observe the payoff graph <F8> <F8>. See *window 8.5*.

Summary

- The bin technique is a practical method of modelling market price risk related to yield curve dynamics.
- Delta matching the native exposure and the hedge parcel on a bin-by-bin basis can produce a balanced hedge which is sensitive to arbitrary yield curve tilts and flexes.
- Risk measures and hedge accuracy improve as the bin width is narrowed.
- At least one instrument in the hedge parcel must be sensitive to an isolated change in the forward rate in each bin.
- All interest rates to which the native portfolio is sensitive must be captured by the bins.

Notes

1 URM optimises the placement of the bin walls to ensure the most effective use of each instrument in the hedge parcel.

CHAPTER 9

Bond Sensitivity, Duration and Hedging

In this chapter we:

- analyse fixed interest rate instruments beginning with basic bond pricing and sensitivity;
- analyse the significance and some limitations of duration measures;
- use futures to hedge a three year bond, and
- develop a dimensionless bond volatility chart.

Bond pricing

A fixed interest rate bond is a stream of cashflows – coupons and principal. The following unit bond pricing formula is derived by assuming the bond's price is the sum of the present values of the payment stream using discrete compounding for the average yield R.

$$\text{Bond Price} = \frac{C}{F}\left[\frac{Y^{N(1/F-T_1)} - Y^{-NT}}{Y^{N/F} - 1}\right] + Y^{-NT}$$

Equation 9.1 Unit bond price using average yield and semi-annual compounding

where:

R	=	average bond yield
Y	=	1+R/N
C	=	coupon rate
F	=	coupon frequency
N	=	yield conversion frequency
T	=	duration of principal payment in years
T_1	=	duration of first coupon in years

NB. There are four different day count types in common usage for T. See note 1 *Derivaties Maths.*

If the yield R is expressed as a continuously compounded interest rate, *equation 9.1* becomes:

$$\text{Bond Price} = \frac{C}{F}\left[\frac{e^{R(1/F-T_1)} - e^{-RT}}{e^{R/F} - 1}\right] + e^{-RT}$$

Equation 9.2 Unit bond price using average yield and continuous compounding

Given the bond's price, the average yield R or internal rate of return can be solved iteratively using *equation 9.1* and Newton's approximation. Newton's approximation says that if x = a is an approximate solution to f(x) = 0, then a closer approximation to the solution is x = a - f(a)/f'(a) – providing the function is reasonably well behaved. Where f'(a) is the derivative of the function f(x) at x = a.

Bond delta

A bond's delta is the rate of change of its price with respect to its average yield. *Equation 7.2,* repeated below, is used to produce a bond's delta where PV_T is the bond's price.

$$\text{delta}_{PV_T} = \frac{\partial PV_T}{\partial r} = \frac{-\text{dur}_{mac} PV_T}{1+r/n}$$

Equation 7.2 Cashflow portfolio delta – using discrete compounding and yield rate

Bond gamma

A bond's gamma is the rate of change of its delta with respect to its average yield. *Equation 7.9,* repeat below, is used to produce a bond's gamma.

$$\frac{\partial^2 PV_T}{\partial r^2} = \frac{\sum t_i^{\,2} PV_i + 1/n \sum t_i PV_i}{(1+r/n)^2}$$

Equation 7.9 Cashflow portfolio gamma – discrete rate, yield quote

Bond convexity

A bond's convexity is the rate of change of its duration with respect to its average yield. *Equation 7.9.3*, repeated below, is used to produce a bond's convexity:

$$\text{convexity} = \frac{\partial dur_{mac}}{\partial r} = \frac{\left(\sum t_i PV_i\right)^2 - \left(\sum PV_i\right)\sum t_i^{\,2} PV_i}{(1+r/n)\left(\sum PV_i\right)^2}$$

Equation 7.9.3 Cashflow portfolio convexity

Exercise 9a – Determining a bond's price, duration, delta, gamma and convexity

Determine the price of a three year bond with face value \$10 million and 12 per cent semi-annual coupon. Assume an average yield of 8.4441 per cent per annum using semi-annual compounding. Using *equation 9.1*:

R = .084441
Y = 1.0422205
C = .12
F = 2
N = 2
T = 1096/365
T_1 = 1096/365 - 2.5

This gives a bond unit price of \$1.0922850. Thus, for a face value of \$10 million the bond price is \$10,922,850.

From *equation 7.0* the Macaulay duration is 2.628 years. Also, the modified duration is 2.522 years.

From *equation 7.2* the bond's delta is 27,547,427.7 \$years, after adjusting for the face value.

From *equation 7.9* the bond's gamma is 80,067,489 \$(years)^2, after adjusting for the face value.

And from *equation 7.9.3* the bond's Macaulay convexity is -.535 (years)^2.

Table 9.1 summaries these results – with the bond's face value expressed as 100 units.

Maturity	3 years
Coupon	12 per cent
Coupon frequency	semi-annual
Yield	8.4441 per cent
Face value	\$100
Price	\$109.2285
Macaulay duration	2.628 years
Modified duration	2.522 years
Delta	275.47 \$years
Gamma	800.67 \$year^2
Convexity$_{mac}$	-.535 years^2

Table 9.1
Bond specification with price and risk measures

See *window 9.1.*

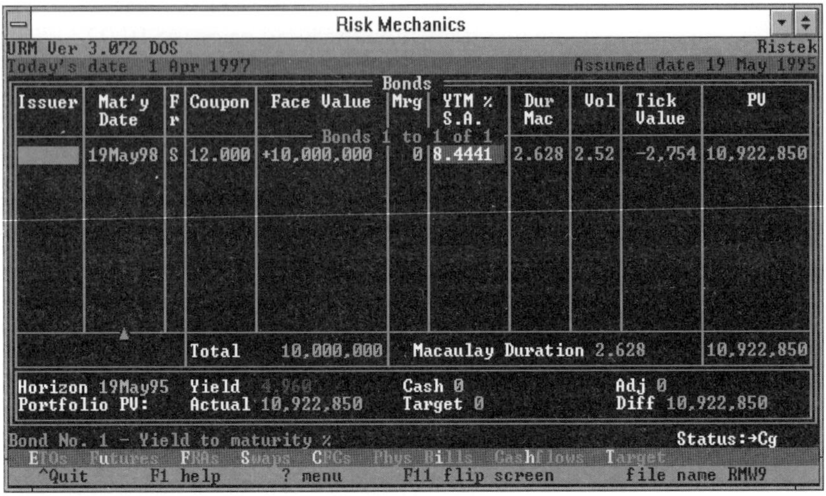

Window 9. 1
Three year 12 per cent semi-annual coupon bond with yield, various risk measures and price

Bond yield sensitivity

The sensitivity of a bond's price is determined by producing its change in price – that is, the change in the net present value of its coupon and principal payment stream from a defined change in the yield curve. However, we need to decide which type of interest rate is moved. For example, in earlier chapters we usually moved the semi-annual zero coupon rate. In this case, we need to determine the impact of this zero curve move on each bond coupon and the principal payment separately.

When a single bond is analysed we may instead choose to nudge the average yield – a much simpler process. However, in the case of a portfolio of bonds, small inconsistencies may arise when average yields are nudged. This is because a defined movement in the zero curve does not, in general, produce exactly the same shift in the average yield in all bonds.

The change in the average yield for bonds with different coupon rates, coupon frequencies and principal payment dates may be different for the same zero curve movement. A more accurate sensitivity analysis is produced by nudging the zero rates.

Also bonds showing similar sensitivities to uniform yield shifts may show quite different exposures to tilts and flexes in the zero curve.

Determining the price after a tilt is a little more complex. The most accurate method requires knowing the zero rate for each coupon, applying the linear tilt, then determining the net present value of the payment stream from the adjusted zero rates (or using the new implied average yield – after the tilt – in the bond-pricing formula). Alternatively, a simpler but approximate method involves using the average yield as the zero rate for each coupon, tilting this average rate for each coupon, then repricing the bond using the new implied average rate.

Exercise 9b – Bond sensitivity

Analyse the price sensitivity of the bond priced in *exercise 9a* to both a 10bp and 100bp shift in its average yield. Also analyse a tilt in the zero curve of 100bp overnight decreasing linearly to zero at three years and beyond. The change in the bond's price under a 10bp and 100bp shift in the average yield is determined directly by adjusting the average yield and using the bond pricing formula *equation 9.1*.

The 10bp and 100bp sensitivity results appear in *windows 9.2, 9.3*. The tilt analysis appears in *window 9.4*. We used the approximation method, referred to above, for the tilt risk. When the tilt is applied to the actual zero rate for each coupon separately the positive tilt produces a loss of $14,865 instead of approximate result of $14,788.

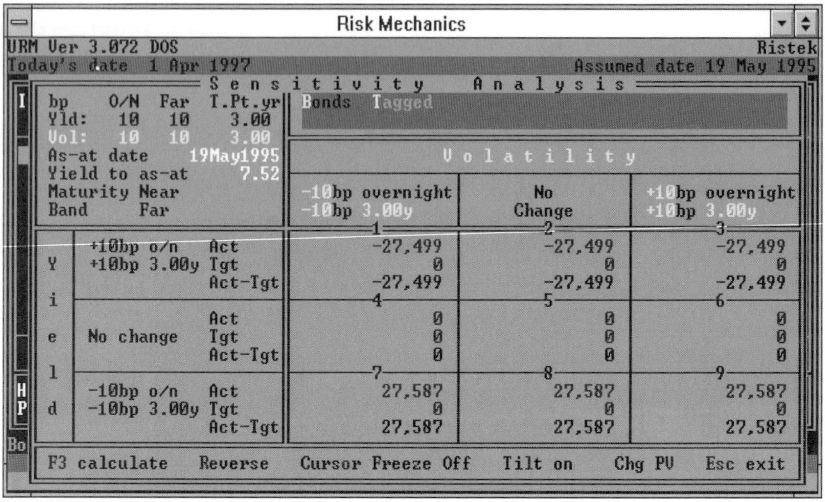

Window 9.2
Bond sensitivity 10bp yield shift

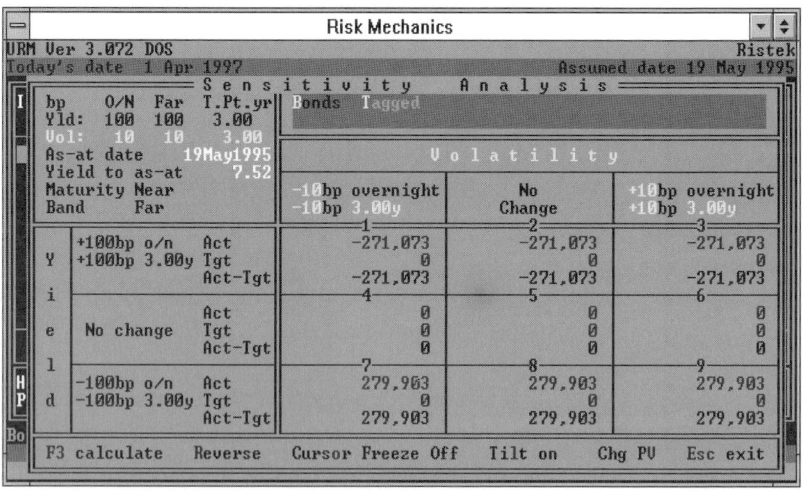

Window 9.3
Bond sensitivity 100bp yield shift

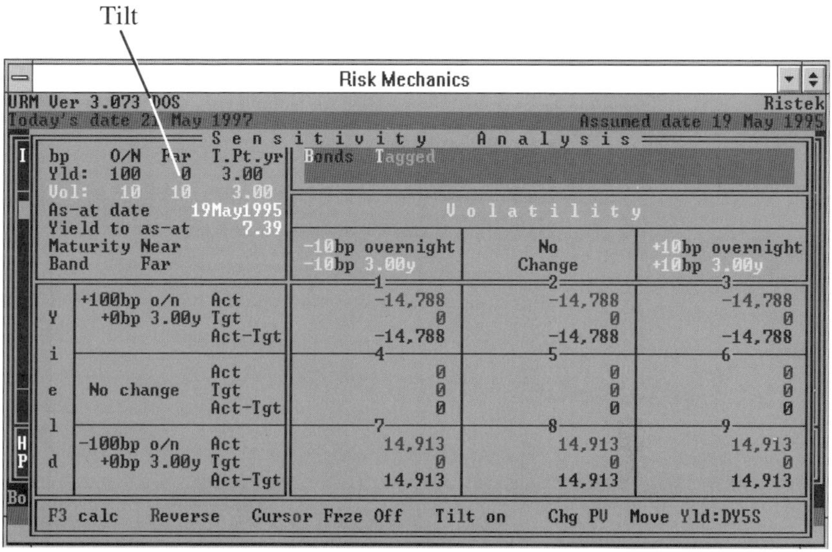

Window 9.4

Bond sensitivity 100bp ⟶ 0bp yield tilt

Duration delta hedging

Bonds are often analysed in terms of their duration. The significance of the duration is that the bond's exposure to uniform zero curve zero yield shifts is similar to a cashflow with face value equal to the sum of the payment stream and duration equal to the bond's duration.

Exercise 9c – Bonds and duration hedging

Test the effectiveness of a single Macaulay based cashflow as a hedge of the three year bond studied in *exercise 9a.*

As determined in *exercise 9a* the Macaulay duration of the bond is 2.628 years and the sum of the cashflow stream is $13,600,000.

Assume the cashflow interest rate is 8.410 per cent per annum using semi-annual compounding. See *window 9.5.*

The change in the present value of the cashflow is determined using the present value formula with semi-annual compounding:

$$PV = 1/(1 + r/2)^{2t}$$

Where r is .08410 and t is 2.628. This gives a present value of $805,337 per $million face value.

We then nudge r 10bp to .08510. This gives a new present value of $803,309 per $million face value. Therefore, the change in the present value of the cashflow after a 10bp increase in the semi-annual yield per $million face value is:

$$\Delta PV_{mac.cashflow} = -\$2,027.94$$

We have already determined that the bond's change in price, ΔPV_{bond} in response to a 10bp yield increase is -$27,499. See *window 9.2*.

Therefore, the delta matched cashflow face value, $faceval_{rep.cashflow}$ is:

$$faceval_{rep.cashflow} = \frac{\Delta PV_{bond}}{\Delta PV_{mac.cashflow}}$$

$$= -27{,}499/-2{,}027$$

$$= \$13{,}560{,}058.$$

Notice this is very close to the sum of the cashflows, $13,600,000.

Window 9.6 demonstrates the bond/Macaulay hedge portfolio sensitivity to a ± 100bp uniform yield shift. In this case the hedging (Macaulay) cashflow has a face value of $13,000,000. *Window 9.7* illustrates the same sensitivity analysis when the hedging cashflow face value is $13,560,058 as determined by delta matching. Notice that with the delta matched cashflow the 100bp yield shift hedge error is reduced from $999 to $168 or .00999 per cent to .00168 per cent.

Hedging bonds with futures and forwards

In *exercise 9b* we saw that a single cashflow can hedge or replicate a bond reasonably well, providing the yield curve moves uniformly. However in reality, yield curves frequently tilt and flex quite dramatically. Therefore the single cashflow hedge has limited practical value. A more robust bond hedge needs to replicate the bond's present value sensitivity to yield curve tilts and flexes. This can be achieved using a strip of futures or forwards formulated using the bin technique, as discussed in *Chapter 8 – The Bin Technique and Term Structure Hedging.*

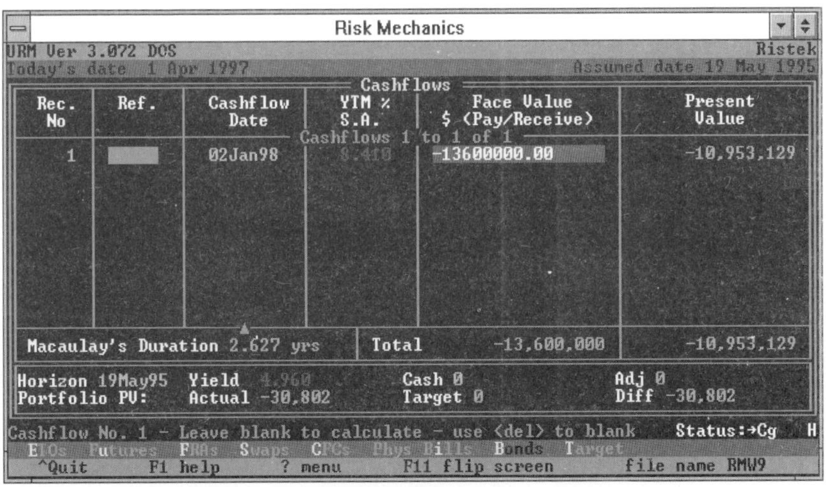

Window 9.5
Macaulay based cashflow hedging three year bond

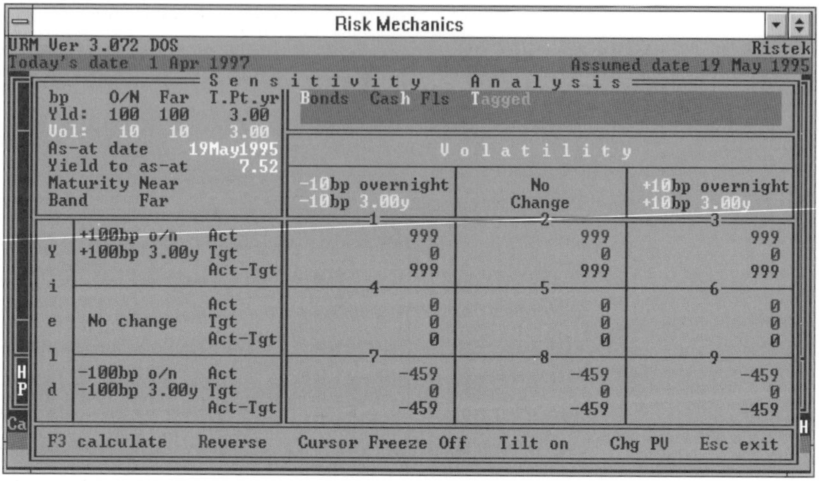

Window 9.6
Bond with Macaulay based hedge illustrating sensitivity to a 100bp yield shift

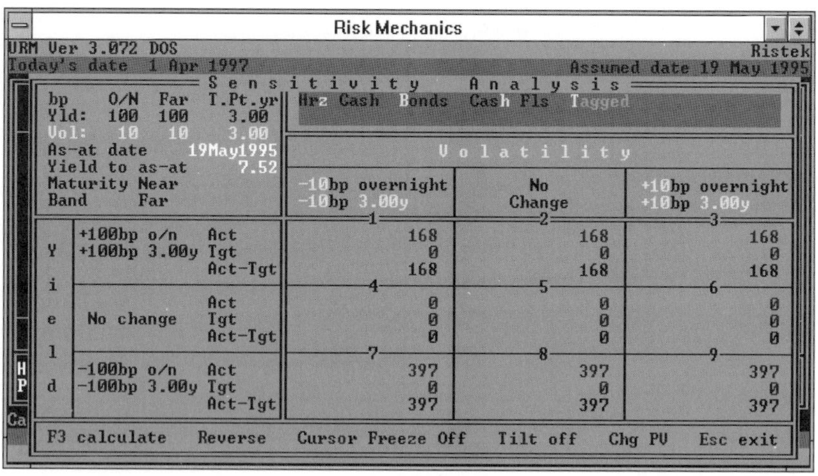

Window 9.7
Bond with delta matched cashflow hedge illustrating sensitivity to a 100bp yield shift

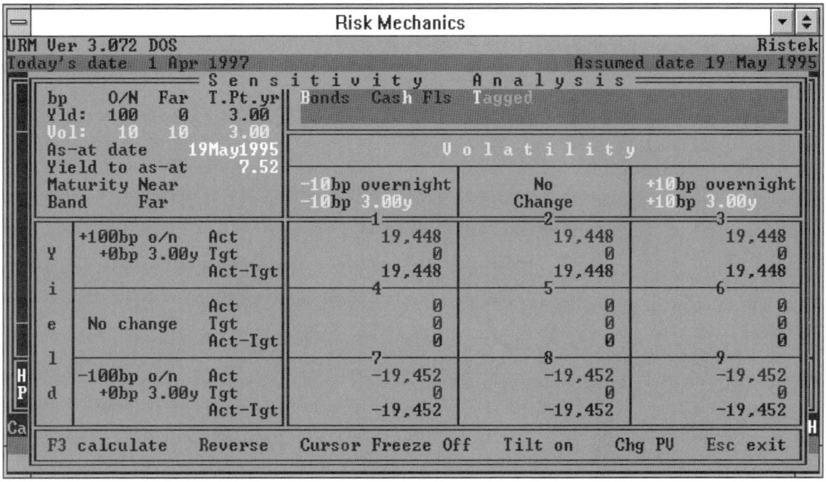

Window 9.8

Bond with Macaulay based hedge illustrating sensitivity to a 100bp → 0bp three year yield tilt

Exercise 9d– Hedging bonds with futures strips

Use the bin technique discussed in *Chapter 8 – The Bin Technique and Term Structure Hedging* to formulate a 90 day futures strip to hedge the three year 12 per cent coupon bond studied in *exercises 9a, 9b* and *9c*.

First we represent the bond as an annuity and principal payment – see *window 9.9.* Which also provides the zero rate for each cashflow. The bin walls are placed so as to straddle each futures contract with expiry less than three years. The first bin wall is placed at zero time and the remaining bin walls are placed midway between the maturity of each futures contract and the expiry of the next contract. Then, for each bin, the precise futures face value to hedge the exposure in that bin is determined for each cashflow. The face values are then combined and rounded to the nearest contract multiple. Note the rounding of the face values is done after the net position is formed. The futures hedge strip is illustrated in *window 9.10.*

The bin analysis is illustrated in *window 9.11*. This window displays the location of the bin walls, along with a ±10bp sensitivity analysis for each bin. Separate sensitivity analyses are provided for the futures strip hedge parcel (left columns), the bond in the actual portfolio (middle columns) and the combined effect (right columns).

The two right side columns show that when the futures strip is combined with the bond the delta risk is reduced greatly in each bin. This sensitivity analysis also confirms that this futures strip provides a balanced hedge against arbitrary yield shifts tilts, as well as uniform shifts.

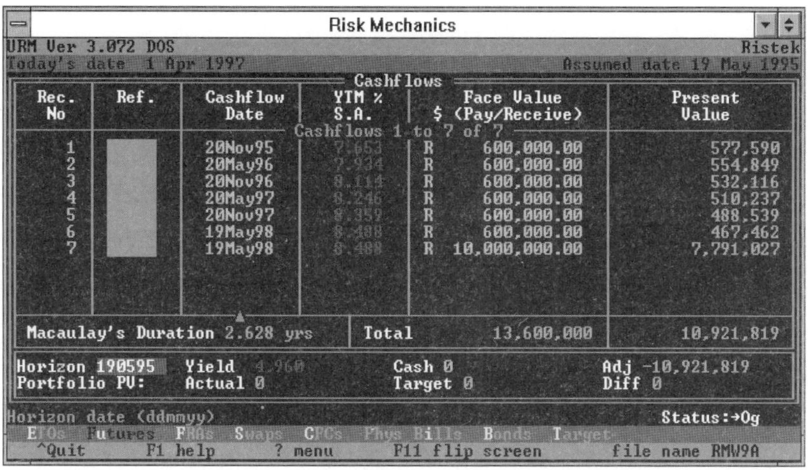

Window 9.9
Cashflows representing a three year 12 per cent semi-annual coupon bond, face value $10 million

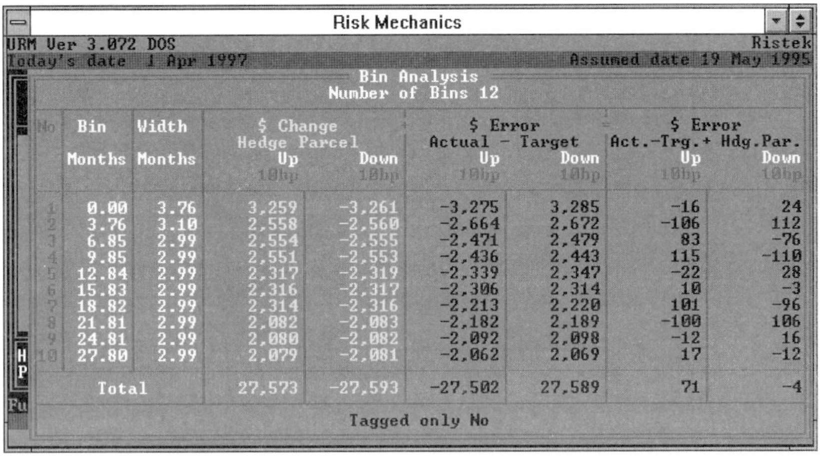

Risk Mechanics

URM Ver 3.072 DOS Ristek

Today's date 1 Apr 1997 Assumed date 19 May 1995

Bin Analysis
Number of Bins 12

No	Bin Months	Width Months	$ Change Hedge Parcel Up 10bp	Down 10bp	$ Error Actual − Target Up 10bp	Down 10bp	$ Error Act.-Trg.+ Hdg.Par. Up 10bp	Down 10bp
1	0.00	3.76	3,259	-3,261	-3,275	3,285	-16	24
2	3.76	3.10	2,558	-2,560	-2,664	2,672	-106	112
3	6.85	2.99	2,554	-2,555	-2,471	2,479	83	-76
4	9.85	2.99	2,551	-2,553	-2,436	2,443	115	-110
5	12.84	2.99	2,317	-2,319	-2,339	2,347	-22	28
6	15.83	2.99	2,316	-2,317	-2,306	2,314	10	-3
7	18.82	2.99	2,314	-2,316	-2,213	2,220	101	-96
8	21.81	2.99	2,082	-2,083	-2,182	2,189	-100	106
9	24.81	2.99	2,080	-2,082	-2,092	2,098	-12	16
10	27.80	2.99	2,079	-2,081	-2,062	2,069	17	-12
	Total		27,573	-27,593	-27,502	27,589	71	-4

Tagged only No

Window 9.10
90 day futures strip hedging a three year 12 per cent coupon semi-annual bond, face value $10,000,000

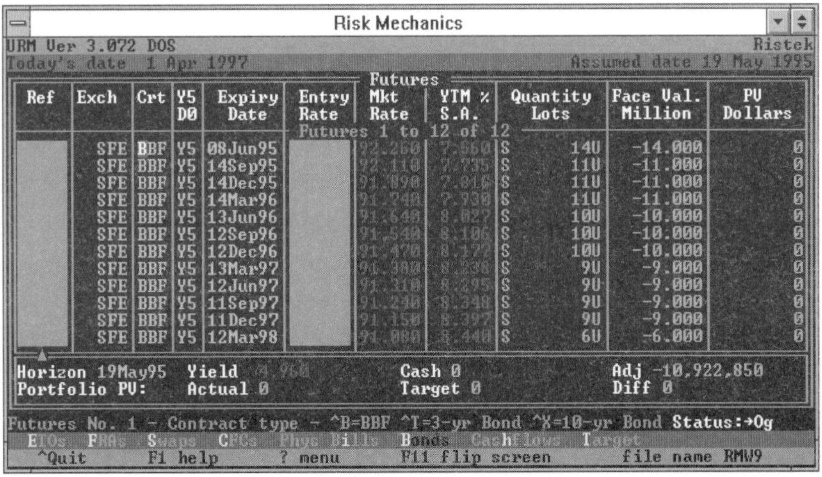

Risk Mechanics

URM Ver 3.072 DOS Ristek

Today's date 1 Apr 1997 Assumed date 19 May 1995

Futures

Futures 1 to 12 of 12

Ref	Exch	Crt	Y5 D0	Expiry Date	Entry Rate	Mkt Rate	YTM % S.A.		Quantity Lots	Face Val. Million	PV Dollars
	SFE	BBF	Y5	08Jun95		92.260	7.560	S	14U	-14.000	0
	SFE	BBF	Y5	14Sep95		92.110	7.735	S	11U	-11.000	0
	SFE	BBF	Y5	14Dec95		91.890	7.816	S	11U	-11.000	0
	SFE	BBF	Y5	14Mar96		91.740	7.930	S	11U	-11.000	0
	SFE	BBF	Y5	13Jun96		91.640	8.027	S	10U	-10.000	0
	SFE	BBF	Y5	12Sep96		91.540	8.106	S	10U	-10.000	0
	SFE	BBF	Y5	12Dec96		91.470	8.172	S	10U	-10.000	0
	SFE	BBF	Y5	13Mar97		91.380	8.238	S	9U	-9.000	0
	SFE	BBF	Y5	12Jun97		91.310	8.295	S	9U	-9.000	0
	SFE	BBF	Y5	11Sep97		91.240	8.348	S	9U	-9.000	0
	SFE	BBF	Y5	11Dec97		91.150	8.397	S	9U	-9.000	0
	SFE	BBF	Y5	12Mar98		91.080	8.440	S	6U	-6.000	0

Horizon 19May95 Yield [illegible] Cash 0 Adj -10,922,850
Portfolio PV: Actual 0 Target 0 Diff 0

Futures No. 1 - Contract type - ^B=BBF ^T=3-yr Bond ^X=10-yr Bond Status:→Og

EIOs FRAs Swaps CFCs Phys Bills Bonds Cashflows Target

^Quit F1 help ? menu F11 flip screen file name RMW9

Window 9.11
Bin analysis – futures strip hedging a three year 12 per cent semi-annual coupon bond, face value $10,000,000

Question 9a

Which bin has the highest exposure to yield shifts. Take a guess before studying the bin analysis – see *window 9.11*.

Answer

Results from the *First Risk Olympics - Heat 2*[2] indicate that approximately 50 per cent of people guess that a bond is more exposed to one of the more distant bins. Either that or they believe that the answer is unlikely to be known without a detailed sensitivity analysis. In fact, the bond is always more exposed to isolated forward shifts in the first bin. This can be seen from the bin analysis. The first bin is the widest bin – but this is not the real explanation since it still has the highest exposure even if it is as wide as the other bins. Notice the first bin produces a $3,285 profit from a 10bp yield increase and that the bin profits decreases steadily for each bin to $2,069 in the last bin.

The first bin has the highest exposure because all cashflows are sensitive to changes in the forward rate in this bin, whereas only the principal cashflow and last coupon are sensitive to the forward rate in the last bin.

It follows that bonds are more exposed to movements in near term forward rates than movements in longer term forward rates.

Window 9.12 illustrates the bin analysis for the first coupon only. Notice the bin exposure is zero in all bins except the first two bins. *Window 9.13* illustrates the bin exposure for the principal payment only. Notice that all bins are exposed to this most distant cashflow.

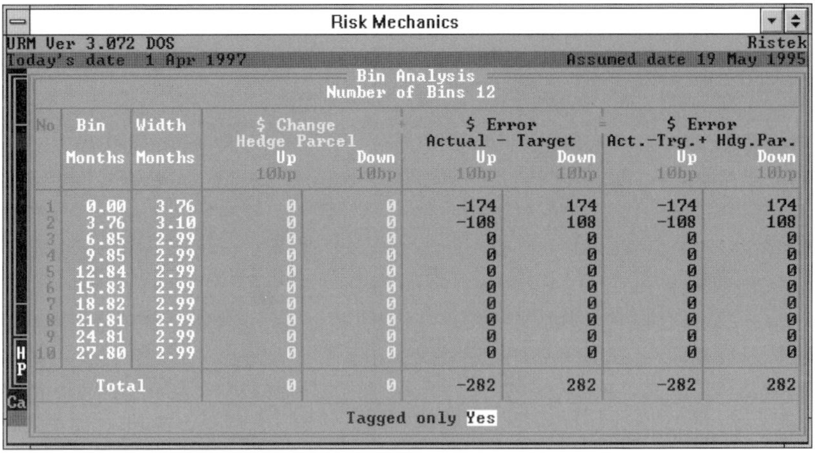

Risk Mechanics

URM Ver 3.072 DOS Ristek

Today's date 1 Apr 1997 Assumed date 19 May 1995

Bin Analysis

Number of Bins 12

No	Bin Months	Width Months	$ Change Hedge Parcel Up 10bp	$ Change Hedge Parcel Down 10bp	$ Error Actual - Target Up 10bp	$ Error Actual - Target Down 10bp	$ Error Act.-Trg.+ Hdg.Par. Up 10bp	$ Error Act.-Trg.+ Hdg.Par. Down 10bp
1	0.00	3.76	0	0	-174	174	-174	174
2	3.76	3.10	0	0	-108	108	-108	108
3	6.85	2.99	0	0	0	0	0	0
4	9.85	2.99	0	0	0	0	0	0
5	12.84	2.99	0	0	0	0	0	0
6	15.83	2.99	0	0	0	0	0	0
7	18.82	2.99	0	0	0	0	0	0
8	21.81	2.99	0	0	0	0	0	0
9	24.81	2.99	0	0	0	0	0	0
10	27.80	2.99	0	0	0	0	0	0
	Total		0	0	-282	282	-282	282

Tagged only Yes

Window 9.12
Bin analysis of a cashflow representing the first coupon in a $10 million three year 12 per cent semi-annual coupon bond

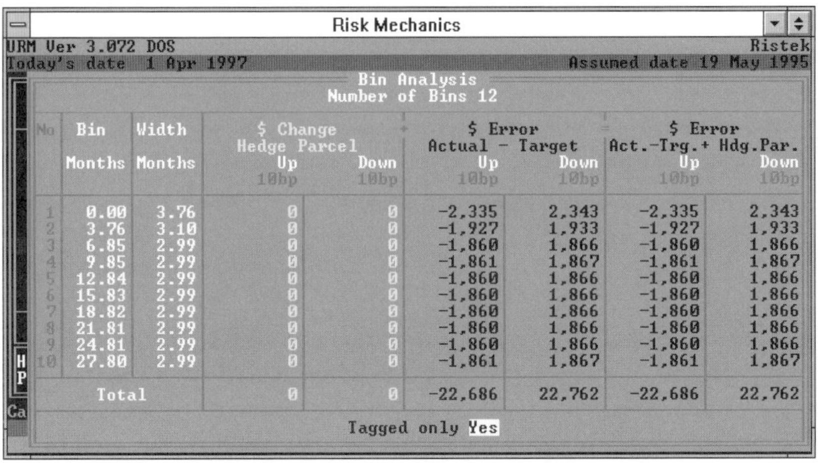

Risk Mechanics

URM Ver 3.072 DOS Ristek

Today's date 1 Apr 1997 Assumed date 19 May 1995

Bin Analysis

Number of Bins 12

No	Bin Months	Width Months	$ Change Hedge Parcel Up 10bp	$ Change Hedge Parcel Down 10bp	$ Error Actual - Target Up 10bp	$ Error Actual - Target Down 10bp	$ Error Act.-Trg.+ Hdg.Par. Up 10bp	$ Error Act.-Trg.+ Hdg.Par. Down 10bp
1	0.00	3.76	0	0	-2,335	2,343	-2,335	2,343
2	3.76	3.10	0	0	-1,927	1,933	-1,927	1,933
3	6.85	2.99	0	0	-1,860	1,866	-1,860	1,866
4	9.85	2.99	0	0	-1,861	1,867	-1,861	1,867
5	12.84	2.99	0	0	-1,860	1,866	-1,860	1,866
6	15.83	2.99	0	0	-1,860	1,866	-1,860	1,866
7	18.82	2.99	0	0	-1,860	1,866	-1,860	1,866
8	21.81	2.99	0	0	-1,860	1,866	-1,860	1,866
9	24.81	2.99	0	0	-1,860	1,866	-1,860	1,866
10	27.80	2.99	0	0	-1,861	1,867	-1,861	1,867
	Total		0	0	-22,686	22,762	-22,686	22,762

Tagged only Yes

Window 9.13
Bin analysis of a cashflow representing the principal payment in a $10 million three year 12 per cent semi-annual coupon bond

Exercise 9e – Hedging bonds with bond futures

Estimate the number of June 1995 three year bond futures contracts with face value $100,000 and 12 per cent semi-annual coupon required to hedge the three year bond with 12 per cent semi-annual coupon, studied in *exercises 9a*, *9b, 9c* and *9d*.

The three year bond future price is based on a semi-annual coupon of 12 per cent and is close to its expiry. Obviously, the number of bond future contracts is very close to 10,000,000/ 100,000 – that is, 100. In general, the face value of the bond futures contract that delta hedges the physical bond will not have the same face value as the physical bond. This is because the futures contract is not sensitive to exactly the same portion of the yield curve as the physical bond – except on the day of expiry. Of course, the futures face value is also influenced by the bond's maturity, coupon rate and frequency.

The duration/volatility relationship

Bond volatility is defined as the change in a bond's price for a defined yield shift divided by the current bond price, vol_{bond}:

$$vol_{bond} = (PV_h - PV_l)/PV$$

where P_h is the price of the bond after an instantaneous fall of in the internal yield of $\Delta R/2$, and P_l is the price of the bond after an instantaneous rise in the internal yield of $\Delta R/2$. Notice vol_{bond} is a dimensionless number.

Note that this definition of volatility has nothing to do with the volatility used in the option pricing Black-Scholes equation, which is a measure of dispersion about the mean.

If we use continuous rates, vol_{bond} depends on the current yield

R, the yield nudge ΔR, the bond maturity T, the coupon C, and coupon frequency F, expressed as:

$$vol_{bond} = fn(R, \Delta R, T, C, F)$$

However, a bond can be approximated as a single cashflow with duration equal to the bond's Macaulay duration, dur_{mac}. And, the volatility of a single cashflow, $vol_{cashflow}$ with duration T, can be expressed as:

$$vol_{cashflow} = fn(R, \Delta R, T)$$

Or, in dimensionless form:

$$vol_{cashflow} = fn(R \times T, R/\Delta R)$$

Therefore:

$$vol_{bond} \approx fn(R \times dur_{mac}, R/\Delta R)$$

This last expression is accurate to the extent that a duration-based cashflow approximates the bond's price behaviour. It can be used to represent the relationship between a bond's volatility, continuous yield and Macaulay duration on a single dimensionless chart – effective for all values of ΔR.

However, bonds are usually quoted as semi-annual yields, rather than continuous yields. In this case vol_{bond} is also a function of the yield conversion frequency N. Thus:

$$vol_{bond} \approx fn(R, \Delta R, dur_{mac}, N)$$

and in dimensionless form:

$$vol_{bond} \approx fn(R/\Delta R, dur_{mac} \times \Delta R, N/\Delta R)$$

We now have four dimensionless numbers, one too many for convenience. However, the dimensionless number $N/\Delta R$ can be treated as a constant by setting $N = 2$ and $\Delta R = 1$. This reduces the number of variables to three. And, since $\Delta R = 1$, $R/\Delta R = R$ and $dur_{mac} \times \Delta R = dur_{mac}$.

Therefore:

$$vol_{bond} \approx fn(R, dur_{mac})$$

Refer to *chart 9.1 – McKay's dimensionless volatility/duration/yield chart.* This chart can be used to determine the approximate volatility of any bond regardless of its maturity, coupon or yield. Notice that, allowing for the sign change, *chart 9.1* is almost the same as the cashflow volatility *chart 7.2*. Also, the nudge is centred in *chart 9.1*.

Exercise 9f – Determining bond volatility using dimensionless charts

Use the dimensionless bond volatility/duration/yield, *chart 9.1*, to determine the volatility of the three-year 12 per cent coupon bond studied in *exercise 9a*.

From *window 9.1* we see that the average yield for the bond is 8.4441 per cent per annum using semi-annual compounding and the Macaulay duration is 2.628 years.

To check this result using *chart 9.1*, we locate the value on the X axis equal to the duration 2.628. Then we draw a vertical line to find the intersection with a line representing R=8.444 per cent per annum. (Slightly above the R=10 line on the chart). Move horizontally to find the intersection with the Y axis. We get a value close to 2.62, as expected. Note that the accuracy of this technique improves greatly when a larger chart is used.

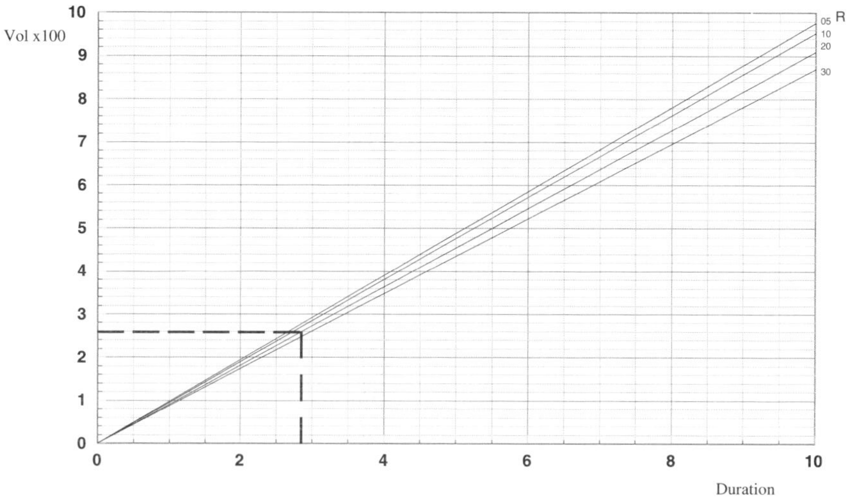

Chart 9.1
McKay's dimensionless bond volatility/duration/yield chart based on Macaulay duration, semi-annual compounding and 100bp centred yield shift

where:

vol = $\dfrac{PV_{-50} - PV_{+50}}{PV}$

R = Internal rate of return using semi-annual compounding

Duration = Macaulay duration

Check using URM – Exercise 9a

Load file RMW9. The bond studied in *exercise 9a* appears in the bond portfolio window <B>. See *window 9.1*. Calculate <F3>. The duration, volatility and price appear.

Check using URM – Exercise 9b

Load file RMW9. View the bond portfolio window <B>. The bond specified in *exercise 9a* appears in the bond portfolio window <B>.

Press <F3> to calculate. The bond duration, volatility and price appear in green. Confirm the sensitivity results displayed in *windows 9.2, 9.3* and *9.4* using the sensitivity analysis <F6>.

Notice the bond is exposed to yield shifts and tilts but not volatility shifts. (We have assumed a conventional bond pricing formula that ignores the volatility component)

Check using URM – Exercise 9c

Load file RMW9. View the cashflow window <H> and type <2.628y Enter> in the maturity column and <-13.6m> in the face value column. Press <Alt U> to update the market data fields. The duration based hedge is now created. See *window 9.5*.

Study the sensitivity analysis <F6> and test the effectiveness of this duration based cashflow hedge.

Notice that it is quite an effective hedge against uniform yield shifts. See *window 9.6*. However, it is not effective as a tilt hedge. Confirm the 100 - 0 tilt result recorded in *window 9.8*. Compare this result with *window 9.4* - tilt without the cashflow hedge.

Now use *URM* to formulate automatically the face value of the duration-based cashflow hedge. Also try changing the maturity of the new (hedge) cashflow and let *URM* formulate the face value.

Return to the cashflow portfolio window and unfix the face value of the cashflow by placing the cursor on its face value field and pressing <Delete>. Press <F3> to calculate. Notice that the optimised face value produced of -$13,558,457 is close to the Macaulay value of -$13,600,000 and even closer to the value of $13,560,058 (*URM* produces the *hedge* cashflow rather than the *replicating* cashflow, hence the sign is reversed) determined above using a +10bp delta matching. Note: the *URM* value is more accurate because it delta matches over a range of movements, both up and down, and produces the best overall match.

Use the sensitivity analysis <F6> to confirm that this calculated face value – based on the delta hedge technique – produces a more accurate hedge against uniform yield shifts than the Macaulay hedge. See *window 9.7.*

Return to the cashflow window and change the maturity of the new (hedge) cashflow by placing the cursor on its maturity field and pressing <+> or <-> several times. (These keys change the date one day at a time). Then press <F3> to calculate. A new (calculated) face value now appears. Return to sensitivity analysis <F6>. You will discover that the bond can be hedged against *uniform* yield shifts with a cashflow with any duration, not just the Macaulay duration but the face value of the cashflow changes. Note, however, the tilt risk exposure changes when the hedge maturity is adjusted. For example, a very short-dated cashflow provides very poor tilt protection.

Check using URM – Exercise 9d

Load file RMW9. Go to the futures portfolio window <U> and press <A> to access the add menu and use the default futures type (BBF) and select 12 futures <12 Enter> in the last field labelled *number of futures*. The futures strip appears. Press <Alt U> to update the market data, then <F3> to calculate. The bin optimised futures strip appears. See *window 9.9.* Note that each futures contract has a face value of $1,000,000.

Now view the bin analysis <F>. This window displays the location of the bin walls, along with a ±10bp sensitivity analysis for each bin. Separate sensitivity analyses are provided for the futures strip hedge parcel (left columns), the bond in the actual portfolio (middle columns) and the combined effect (right columns).

The two right side columns show that when the futures strip is combined with the bond the delta risk is reduced greatly in each bin. This sensitivity analysis also confirms that this futures strip provides a balanced hedge against arbitrary yield shifts tilts, as well as uniform shifts.

The same futures strip can be produced by representing the bond as its component cashflows in the cashflow portfolio window. Load file RMW9A. Go to the cashflow portfolio window <H> and notice the cashflows representing the bond coupons and principal appear. See *window 9.9.* Also notice the futures strip appear in the futures window <U>. Calculate <F3>. Notice the futures strip and bin analysis produced are the same as *windows 9.10* and *9.11* produced using the actual bond.

Check using URM – Exercise 9e

Load file RMW9. Access the add menu <A> and select TYB as the contract type. Then, in the last field labelled

Number of Contracts specify one (the nearest) contract only, by typing <1 Enter>. Press <Crtl A>. The June bond contract appears in the futures portfolio window. Update the market date fields <Alt U> then calculate <F3>.

Notice that as expected, the number of bond futures formulated is 100.

Check using URM – Question 9a

Load file RMW9A. Go to the cashflow portfolio window <H>. Ensure the cursor is on the first row, representing the nearest coupon, and press <Alt T> to tag this row only. Press <Alt I> to highlight the tag. Go to bin analysis <F7> and press <T> to isolate the tagged row. See *window 9.12*. Notice that only the first two bins are sensitive to yield shifts. This is because the first coupon is sensitive to changes in the first two 90 day futures only. Return to the cashflow window <H> and switch off the tag on the first cashflow representing the first coupon <Alt T> and move the cursor to the last row representing the principal cashflow and press <Alt T> to tag it. Go back to the bin analysis <F7> and press <T> to activate tagged only. Notice that the principal payment is sensitive to movements in all the futures in the strip.

See *window 9.13*.

Summary

- The unit price of a bond is a function of its coupon rate, coupon payment frequency, term to maturity, internal rate of return and compounding frequency.
- A bond's internal rate of return can be determined iteratively from its price.
- A bond's price behaviour can be approximated by the price behaviour of a single cashflow with duration equal to its Macaulay duration and face value equal to the sum of the coupon and principal payment stream.
- A bond's yield exposure can be hedged using a swap, FRA or futures strip – although significant gamma risk may remain when futures are used.
- A defined movement in the zero curve does not, in general, produce the same shift in the average yield for bonds with different maturities, coupon rates and frequencies.
- Bonds showing similar sensitivity to uniform shifts may show quite different exposure to tilts.
- Bonds are more exposed to isolated movements in their near term bins.

Notes

1 John Martin. *Derivatives Maths,* IFR Publishing, London, 1996. page 29.

2 *First Risk Olympics* is a series of questions designed to test risk intuition. Heats 1 and 2 were run in mid 1996. The results appear on the Ristek Web site http://www.ristek.com/~ristek/olympics.htlm.

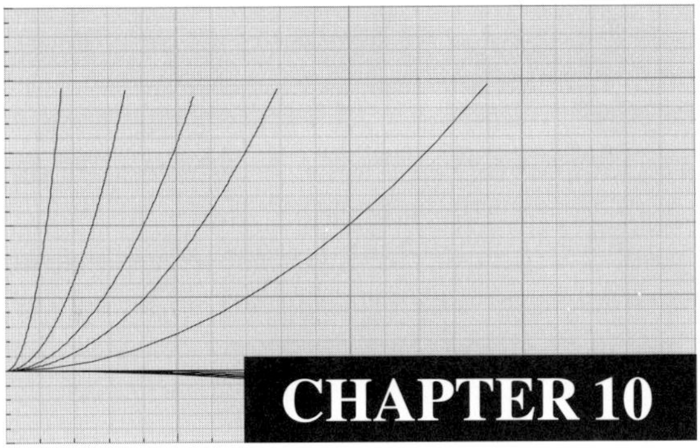

Replicating, Hedging and Modifying Swaps Caps and Floors

In this chapter we explore:

- techniques for replicating, hedging and modifying interest rate swaps, caps and floors, and
- useful techniques for mixing different instrument types to achieve a specified risk profile with exposure to various points along the yield curve.

Manufacturing risk and flexibility

The ability to manufacture derivatives is of fundamental importance to market makers. It is also useful for end users to know how to manufacture tailored payoffs using liquid fungible instruments such as futures. The same skills can be used to modify synthetically swaps to produce asymmetric payoffs similar to caps and floors, synthetically adjust option strike rates and reduce asymmetry in option based instruments.

Manufacturing interest rate swaps from futures

The market value of any instrument can be manufactured using a different instrument type, or combination of instruments, provided the market value of the instrument is replicated through time. This is achieved by maintaining a replicating portfolio with the same present value and market risk sensitivities as the target instruments. Often, in practice, a perfect replication is not possible. In such cases, *risk holes* must be minimised to an acceptable level. However, even though the present value of the target may be tracked through time, the actual cashflows may differ from that of the target instrument depending on the replicating instruments used and movements in market rates. For example, short term futures may be used to replicate the market value of an interest rate swap. The target swap cashflows occur at known specified intervals in time, while the futures trading cashflows occur daily and are path-dependent because futures are marked-to-market.

Exercise 10a – Manufacturing a fixed-to-floating swap using futures

Formulate a 90 day futures strip that replicates, as near as possible, the payoff of a $100 million two year fixed-to-floating swap which receives the fixed rate. For simplicity, we assume the swap's first rate set date coincides with the nearest futures expiry – 8 June 1995 in this case. The target swap appears, in exploded form, in *window 10.1*

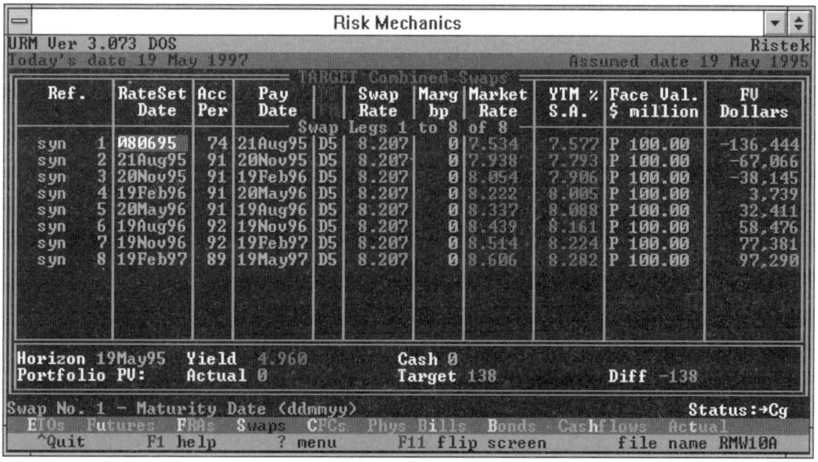

Window 10.1
Two year fixed-to-floating target swap in exploded form

The swap increases in value when interest rates rise. Therefore, obviously we need to take a short position in futures. But should we simply short 100 of the first eight futures contracts? Beware of the *risk hole*! With swaps the face value is likely to indicate the discounted amount before interest whereas with futures the face value is likely to be the full face value which includes interest. This will tend to increase the number of futures required. See *figure 10.1*.

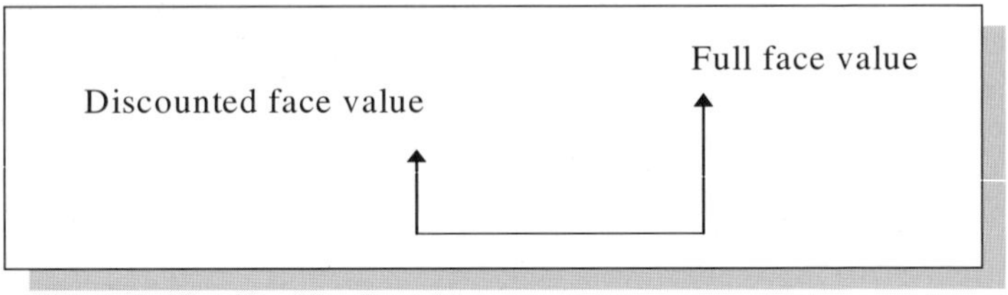

Figure 10.1
The face value of the same instrument may be quoted in two different ways. Either the discounted amount or the full amount with interest may be called the face value.

We should check the interest rate conventions used – is the yield quote PV = FV/(1+rt) or the discount quote PV = FV(1 - rt) being used? Is it the same for both swaps and futures? In this case we will assume the yield quote is used for both.

Also, four 90 day futures span a total of 360 days, not quite a full year – this also tends to increase the number of futures. However, on balance, the number of futures required to construct a balanced hedge is less than the face value of the swap. This is because futures are marked-to-market and therefore are more sensitive to interest rate movements than forwards. This effect is more pronounced with longer duration instruments. Refer to *Chapter 6 – Forward/Futures Relationship*. The futures face value needs to be adjusted by the appropriate discount factor. This reduces the number of futures required to match the present value sensitivity of the swap.

The futures strip that replicates the swap is formulated using a bin-by-bin delta matching. See *Chapter 8 – The Bin Technique and Term Structure Hedging.*

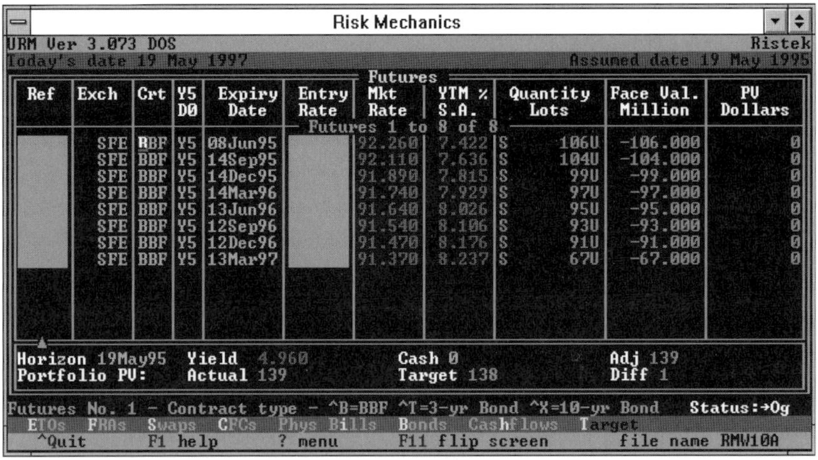

Window 10.2
Futures strip replicating the swap presented in window 10.1

Used correctly, the bin technique automatically produces the appropriate futures face values. In this case, the futures strip is illustrated in *window 10.2*. *Window 10.3* illustrates the tracking error for a range of instantaneous parallel yield shifts. Notice the tracking error is positive for both rises and falls in the yield – a smile effect.

Window 10.4 illustrates that the futures strip in *window 10.2* produces a good quality bin-by-bin match and therefore is expected to replicate, to a high degree of accuracy, the performance of the swap during arbitrary yield curve tilts and flexes. Note that in this example, the forward nudge used in each bin is 10bp.

It should also be remembered that the gamma of the futures and the swap are not identical. This means that some small – relative to a typical option replication – rebalancing of the futures strip may be required through time.

The smile effect and basis equilibrium

The smile effect noticed in *exercise 10a* is worth analysing further. It seems to indicate a distinct advantage in using futures when replicating a fixed-to-floating swap – receiving fixed rate, and a disadvantage when paying fixed rate. However, in efficient markets such free lunches are not expected to prevail very long. In the example above, replicating a receive fixed rate swap, either the futures index should be expected to drift upwards through time – rate drifting down – or the futures yield curve is displaced upwards relative to the swap yield curve at the outset. The equilibrium value of this displacement or basis shift between the forward and futures curve will be a function of the volatility of the forward/future rates and the expected profit from the smile effect should be balanced by the yield basis shift. In this sense there is no expected advantage between an actual swap or a futures strip replicating the swap even though their payoffs are not identical.

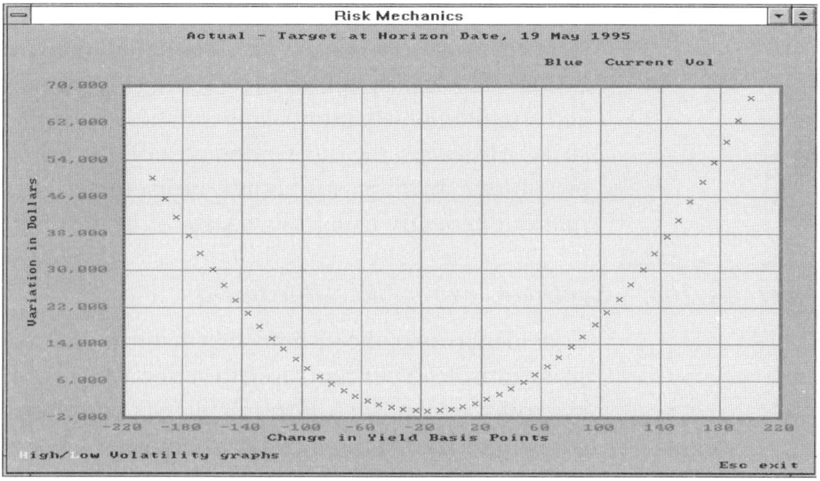

Window 10.3
Tracking error for futures strip replicating a fixed-to-floating swap under instantaneous uniform yield shifts

Risk Mechanics

URM Ver 3.073 DOS — Ristek

Today's date 19 May 1997 — Assumed date 19 May 1995

Bin Analysis
Number of Bins 8

No	Bin Months	Width Months	$ Change Hedge Parcel Up 10bp	Down 10bp	$ Error Actual - Target Up 10bp	Down 10bp	$ Error Act.-Trg.+ Hdg.Par. Up 10bp	Down 10bp
1	0.00	3.76	24,674	-24,692	-24,667	24,685	7	-7
2	3.76	3.10	24,182	-24,199	-24,188	24,206	-6	7
3	6.85	2.99	22,982	-22,999	-22,866	22,883	116	-116
4	9.85	2.99	22,493	-22,509	-22,390	22,406	103	-103
5	12.84	2.99	22,013	-22,029	-21,928	21,944	85	-85
6	15.83	2.99	21,534	-21,550	-21,481	21,498	53	-52
7	18.82	2.98	21,060	-21,075	-20,985	21,001	75	-74
8	21.81	2.98	15,495	-15,506	-15,417	15,428	78	-78
	Total		174,433	-174,559	-173,922	174,051	511	-508

Tagged only No

ETOs FRAs Swaps CFCs Phys Bills Bonds Cashflows Target
^Quit F1 help ? menu F11 flip screen file name RMW10A

Window 10.4
Bin tracking errors for futures strip replicating a fixed-to-floating swap

Synthetic adjustment of cap/floor strike rate

It is not uncommon for users of over-the-counter caps and floors to want to adjust strike rates before these instruments mature. This can be achieved by selling the existing cap/floor and simultaneously purchasing another cap/floor at the new strike. However, the transaction cost of this exercise may be prohibitive. In this case, it is may be useful to adjust the strike rate synthetically using say, a strip of futures for forwards.

Exercise 10b – Synthetic cap strike adjustment

Consider an over-the-counter cap maturing in two years with strike rate of 7.5 per cent, used to hedge a $100 million 90 day bill rollover exposure. Formulate a 90 day futures strip that adjusts, synthetically, the cap strike from 7.5 per cent to 9.0 per cent and, determine the expected saving in cap premium. The existing cap, in exploded form, is illustrated in *window 10.5*.

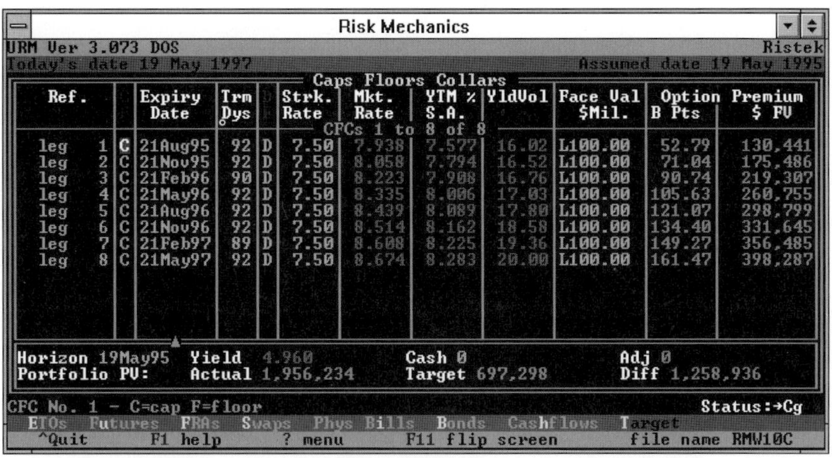
Risk Mechanics
URM Ver 3.073 DOS Ristek
Today's date 19 May 1997 Assumed date 19 May 1995
Caps Floors Collars

Ref.		Expiry Date	Trm Dys		Strk. Rate	Mkt. Rate	YTM % S.A.	YldVol	Face Val $Mil.	Option B Pts	Premium $ FV
leg 1	C	21Aug95	92	D	7.50	7.938	7.577	16.02	L100.00	52.79	130,441
leg 2	C	21Nov95	92	D	7.50	8.058	7.794	16.52	L100.00	71.04	175,486
leg 3	C	21Feb96	90	D	7.50	8.223	7.908	16.76	L100.00	90.74	219,307
leg 4	C	21May96	92	D	7.50	8.335	8.006	17.03	L100.00	105.63	260,755
leg 5	C	21Aug96	92	D	7.50	8.439	8.089	17.80	L100.00	121.07	298,799
leg 6	C	21Nov96	92	D	7.50	8.514	8.162	18.58	L100.00	134.40	331,645
leg 7	C	21Feb97	89	D	7.50	8.608	8.225	19.36	L100.00	149.27	356,485
leg 8	C	21May97	92	D	7.50	8.674	8.283	20.00	L100.00	161.47	398,287

CFCs 1 to 8 of 8
Horizon 19May95 Yield 4.960 Cash 0 Adj 0
Portfolio PV: Actual 1,956,234 Target 697,298 Diff 1,258,936
CFC No. 1 - C=cap F=floor Status:→Cg
ETOs Futures FRAs Swaps Phys Bills Bonds Cashflows Target
^Quit F1 help ? menu F11 flip screen file name RMW10C

Window 10.5
Exploded view of a two year cap, face value $100 million and 7.5 per cent strike rate

The different payoffs of the existing 7.5 per cent cap and the preferred 9.0 per cent cap are illustrated in *window 10.6* – assuming instantaneous uniform yield shifts. A bin-by-bin delta replication of the target 9 per cent cap is performed, where the replicating portfolio comprises the existing 7.5 per cent cap and a 90 day futures strip. The futures strip, produced by bin-by-bin delta matching, is illustrated in *window 10.7.* The bin-by-bin sensitivity analysis, illustrated in *window 10.8,* indicates that the futures strip is quite well balanced. Notice the zero delta, positive gamma effect in the first three bins – profits from yield shifts in both directions.

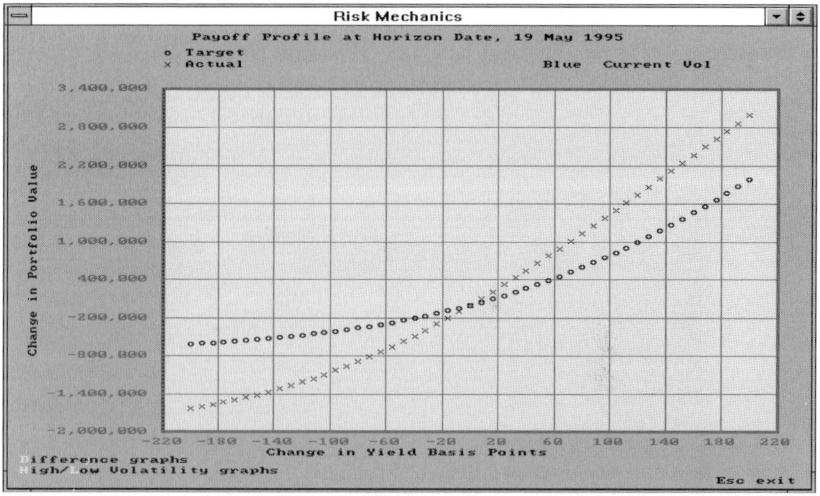

Window 10.6
Payoffs of existing 7.5 per cent cap and preferred 9.0 per cent cap using instantaneous uniform yield shifts

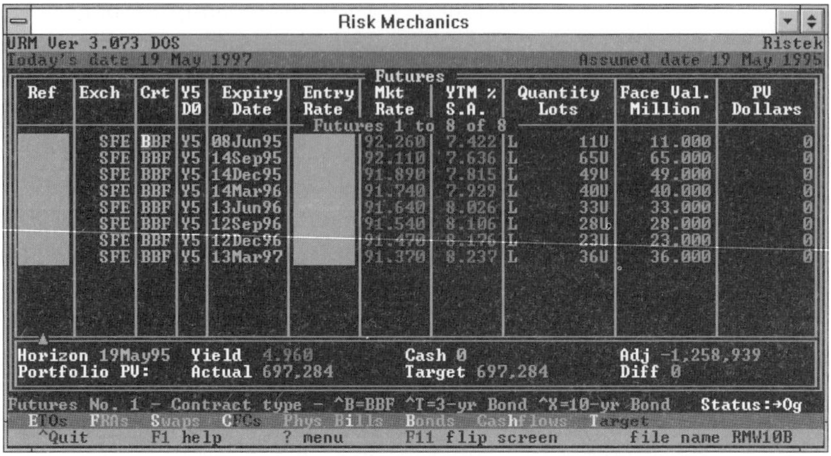

Risk Mechanics
URM Ver 3.073 DOS Ristek
Today's date 19 May 1997 Assumed date 19 May 1995
Futures
Futures 1 to 8 of 8

Ref	Exch	Crt	Y5 D0	Expiry Date	Entry Rate	Mkt Rate	YTM % S.A.	Quantity Lots	Face Val. Million	PV Dollars
	SFE	BBF	Y5	08Jun95		92.260	7.422	L 11U	11.000	0
	SFE	BBF	Y5	14Sep95		92.110	7.636	L 65U	65.000	0
	SFE	BBF	Y5	14Dec95		91.890	7.815	L 49U	49.000	0
	SFE	BBF	Y5	14Mar96		91.740	7.929	L 40U	40.000	0
	SFE	BBF	Y5	13Jun96		91.640	8.026	L 33U	33.000	0
	SFE	BBF	Y5	12Sep96		91.540	8.106	L 28U	28.000	0
	SFE	BBF	Y5	12Dec96		91.470	8.176	L 23U	23.000	0
	SFE	BBF	Y5	13Mar97		91.370	8.237	L 36U	36.000	0

Horizon 19May95 Yield 4.960 Cash 0 Adj -1,258,939
Portfolio PV: Actual 697,284 Target 697,284 Diff 0
Futures No. 1 - Contract type - ^B=BBF ^T=3-yr Bond ^X=10-yr Bond Status:→Og
ETOs FRAs Swaps CFCs Phys Bills Bonds Cashflows Target
^Quit F1 help ? menu F11 flip screen file name RMW10B

Window 10.7
Futures strip synthetically adjusting 7.5 per cent cap into a 9.0 per cent cap

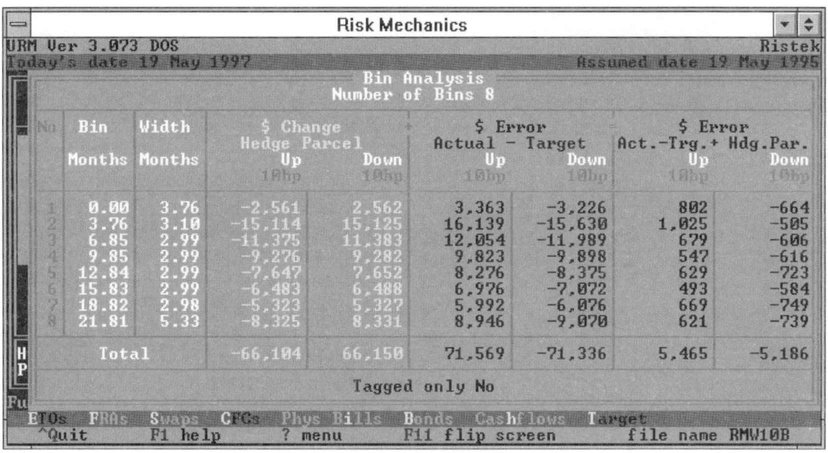

Risk Mechanics
URM Ver 3.073 DOS Ristek
Today's date 19 May 1997 Assumed date 19 May 1995
Bin Analysis
Number of Bins 8

No	Bin Months	Width Months	$ Change Hedge Parcel Up 10bp	Down 10bp	$ Error Actual - Target Up 10bp	Down 10bp	$ Error Act.-Trg.+ Hdg.Par. Up 10bp	Down 10bp
1	0.00	3.76	-2,561	2,562	3,363	-3,226	802	-664
2	3.76	3.10	-15,114	15,125	16,139	-15,630	1,025	-505
3	6.85	2.99	-11,375	11,383	12,054	-11,989	679	-606
4	9.85	2.99	-9,276	9,282	9,823	-9,898	547	-616
5	12.84	2.99	-7,647	7,652	8,276	-8,375	629	-723
6	15.83	2.99	-6,483	6,488	6,976	-7,072	493	-584
7	18.82	2.98	-5,323	5,327	5,992	-6,076	669	-749
8	21.81	5.33	-8,325	8,331	8,946	-9,070	621	-739
	Total		-66,104	66,150	71,569	-71,336	5,465	-5,186

Tagged only No
ETOs FRAs Swaps CFCs Phys Bills Bonds Cashflows Target
^Quit F1 help ? menu F11 flip screen file name RMW10B

Window 10.8
Bin analysis of futures strip synthetically adjusting 7.5 per cent cap into a 9.0 per cent cap

Window 10.9 illustrates the payoff of the 7.5 per cent cap with the futures strip – the synthetic cap – and the target 9.0 per cent cap, over a 400bp range of instantaneous uniform yield shifts. Notice the synthetic cap shows an unexpected increase in value when rates fall more than 1 per cent. This improved performance has a down side. A sensitivity analysis reveals that the synthetic cap loses value, with time lapse, faster than the target 9.0 per cent cap.

The fair market present value is for the 7.5 per cent cap is $1,956,234 and for the target 9.0 per cent cap it is $697,298. Therefore, the expected saving in cap premium is $1,258,936 in present value terms.

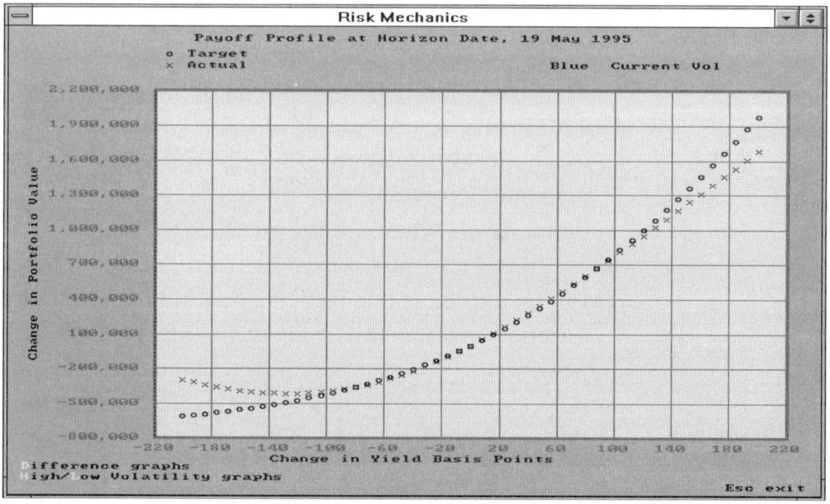

Window 10.9
Payoff graphs showing futures adjusted 7.5 per cent cap and target 9.0 per cent cap

Manufacturing catastrophe insurance

Financial markets tend to experience occasional, sudden, large, unexpected shifts. It appears that the frequency and size of these abnormal shifts is greater than would be expected from a normal or bell shaped distribution.

Catastrophe "insurance", in the form of deep-out-of-the-money options, provides protection against the unlikely or unexpected. It is cheap relative to more protective options and is used when protection against "normal" market shifts is not essential, but open-ended loss potential is deemed unacceptable. Most of the time catastrophe insurance is not exercised and the cost of the protection is not recovered but when used, its payoff is likely to be substantial.

True catastrophe insurance protects against large price shifts as well as gaps. Gap protection is not exactly the same as large shift protection. Large shifts usually occur through a number of smaller shifts. Less rigorous hedge techniques may provide reasonable protection against gradual large market shifts but break down when a large market gap occurs.

For example, in the case of a market experiencing a number of smaller price shifts, all in the same direction, it may be possible to execute several rebalancing transactions – in response to each smaller shift. This may enable some dynamic replication techniques to be effective. A market price gap, however, provides no opportunity to initiate a hedge or adjust an existing hedge. Further, the credit risk of the counter party may be especially important in times of high volatility.

How can catastrophe insurance be obtained? Over-the-counter options may be available. In this case, the counterparty credit risk will be a very important consideration. Can the counterparty manage the risk transferred to it if a catastrophic event occurs? Is the counterparty likely to accept the underwriting risk unhedged – perhaps expecting the options will expire out-of-the-money? And, of course, it may not be possible to obtain tailored, deep, out-of-the-money options at prices close to fair market values.

These are some of the reasons why it may be prudent for buyers of catastrophe insurance to self-manufacture the insurance using exchange traded options and futures, perhaps combined with more liquid closer-to-the-money, over-the-counter options.

Exercise 10c – Manufacturing catastrophe insurance

Use exchange traded instruments to manufacture a deep out-of-the-money cap with 12 per cent strike to protect the 90 day rollover rates on a three-year $100 million debt. We will assume the first strike is in one month and the first term is shortened. The current swap rate is 8.18 per cent per annum.

The required cap is illustrated, in exploded form, in *window 10.10.* Its present value is $48,770 – quite a low price compared with an at-the-money cap with strike 8.18 per cent with fair market price of $961,013.

At first, we might try using exchange-traded options (ETOs) to replicate the cap, rather than a futures strip, since we know that straight futures will not track an option well over large gaps. Because we are attempting to manufacture catastrophe insurance to protect against a sudden increase in yields, we must perform a delta-matching over a very wide range of yield shifts – say 400bp increase. Perhaps, we are not so concerned about a sudden fall in yields. However, a poorly constructed hedge may loss much more than expected when yields fall and thereby eliminate the expected payoff advantage of the cheap insurance.

We might, for example, try September 1995 ETOs at 92 strike – expiring in 105 days. This ETO is trading at 25bp while the underlying futures is trading at 92.11 as an index yield quote.

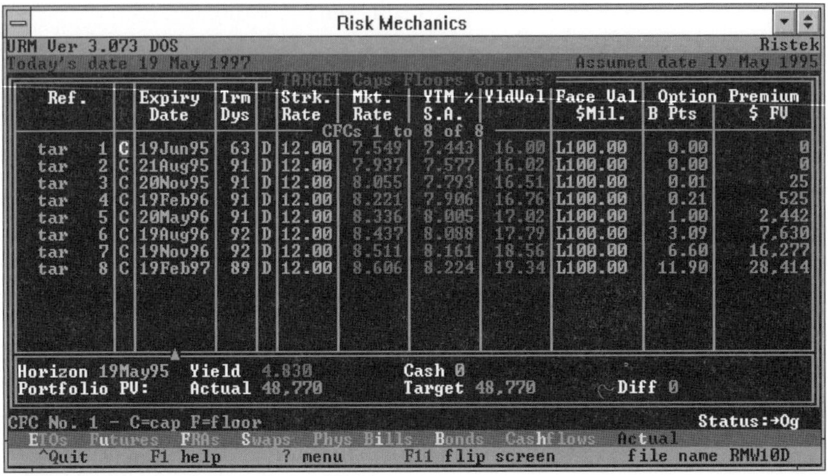

Ref.		Expiry Date	Trm Dys		Strk. Rate	Mkt. Rate	YTM % S.A.	YldVol	Face Val $Mil.	Option B Pts	Premium $ FV
tar 1	C	19Jun95	63	D	12.00	7.549	7.443	16.00	L100.00	0.00	0
tar 2	C	21Aug95	91	D	12.00	7.937	7.577	16.02	L100.00	0.00	0
tar 3	C	20Nov95	91	D	12.00	8.055	7.793	16.51	L100.00	0.01	25
tar 4	C	19Feb96	91	D	12.00	8.221	7.906	16.76	L100.00	0.21	525
tar 5	C	20May96	91	D	12.00	8.336	8.005	17.02	L100.00	1.00	2,442
tar 6	C	19Aug96	92	D	12.00	8.437	8.088	17.79	L100.00	3.09	7,630
tar 7	C	19Nov96	92	D	12.00	8.511	8.161	18.56	L100.00	6.60	16,277
tar 8	C	19Feb97	89	D	12.00	8.606	8.224	19.34	L100.00	11.90	28,414

Window 10.10
Exploded view of 12 per cent two year cap – catastrophe insurance

A long range delta-matching produces 125 September 1995 ETOs. The payoff is illustrated in *window 10.11*. Notice the tracking error is positive for the first 300bp yield increase, then it quickly becomes negative. The problem is that, as yields increase, the ETO portfolio payoff profile becomes linear too quickly. This indicates we need to use ETOs with lower gamma. Longer dated, further, out-of-the-money options tend to have lower gamma. Therefore we try adding a December 1995 ETO – expiring in 196 days – at strike 90.00. The December ETO is trading at 2bp while its underlying futures is trading at 91.89. We will assume that liquidity restrictions inhibit the use of ETOs longer dated than the December 1995 contract month.

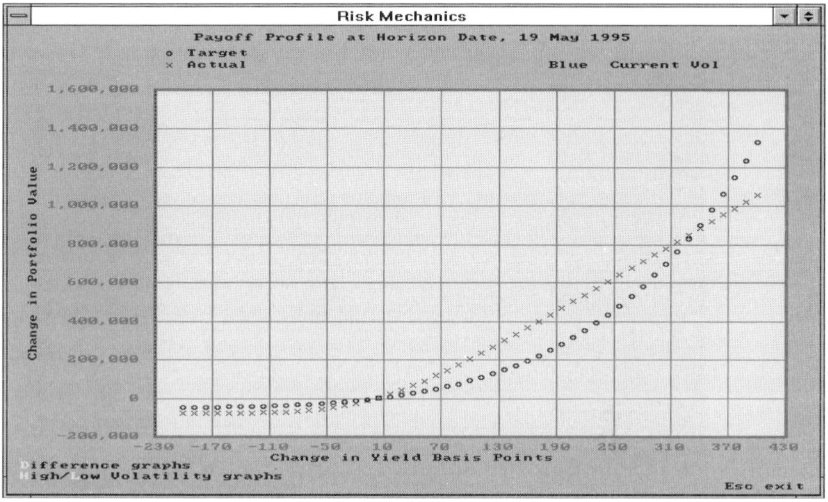

Window 10.11
Payoffs of 125 short term ETOs and the target 12 per cent two year cap

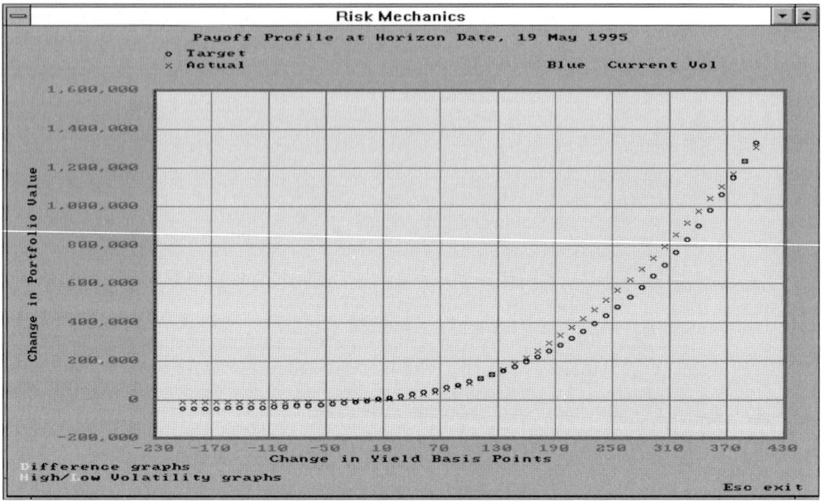

Window 10.12
Short and medium term ETO portfolio and the target 12 per cent two year cap

This time the long-range delta-matching produces a portfolio of short 5 September ETOs and long 273 December ETOs. The payoff graph is illustrated in *window 10.12*.

Should we be happy with this analysis? No! We need to check the time decay and tilt matching. With all the ETO delta concentrated at the near end of the curve, we should expect a large tilt risk. The one day pure time lapse error is $46 in our favour, so this is not a problem. However, the 0 – 100bp two year tilt risk is $141,217 adverse. See *window 10.12a*. How can this tilt risk be managed?

We need to include instruments that are sensitive to forward rates out to two years. Therefore we try including the first eight 90 day futures contracts in the hedge parcel. The futures provide sensitivity to all yields affecting the target cap, enabling tilt risk to be managed. And, the ETOs provide gamma risk, enabling an asymmetric payoff to be achieved.

The futures strip illustrated in *window 10.13* was combined with zero September ETOs and 238 long December ETOs. The first three futures are long because some of the ETO delta in the near bins needs to be neutralised. The payoff of this portfolio is illustrated in *window 10.14*. This time the one day time lapse is $54 in our favour and the 0 – 100 two year tilt risk is now $33,349 adverse.

A perfect result is not possible using short term ETOs. This is another "bumps in the risk carpet" type problem. Also volatility risk should be considered. However, as a form of insurance against major shifts, it provides significant protection using secure liquid instruments.

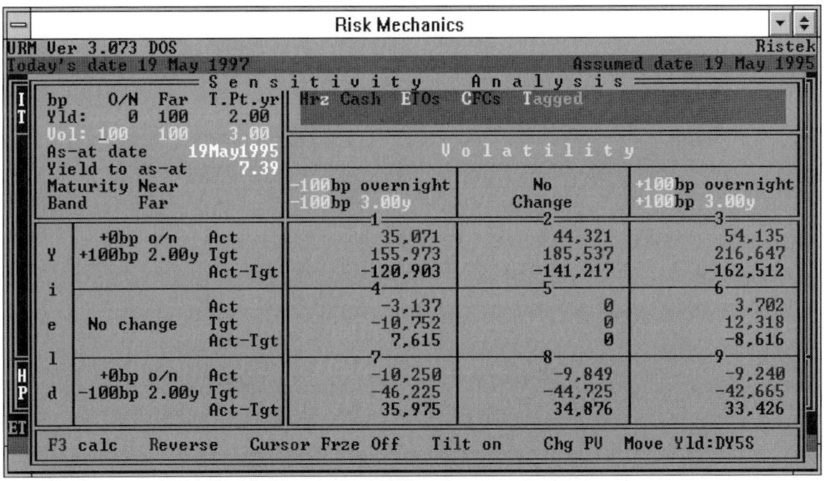

Window 10.12a
Short and medium term ETO portfolio and the target 12 per cent two year cap – illustrating tilt risk

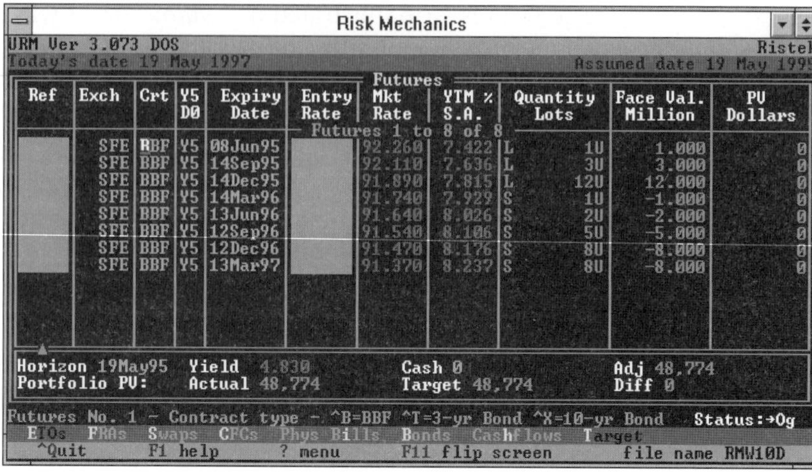

Window 10.13
Futures strip combined with ETOs

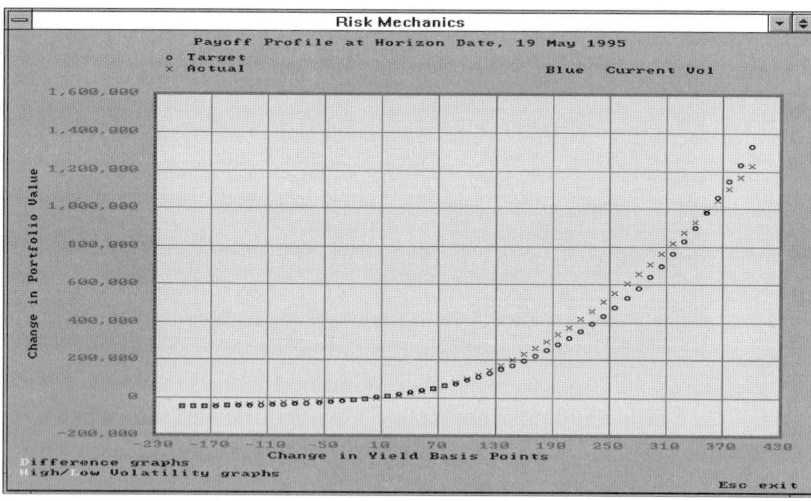

Window 10.14
Futures strip with ETOs and the target 12 per cent two year cap

Check using URM – Exercise 10a

Load file RMW10A. Go to the target floating swap window <T> <S>. The exploded view of the swap appears. Calculate <F3>. Press <S> to see the fixed legs. Press <S> again to see the combined fixed/ floating window. Press <S> again to see the collapsed swap. *See window 10.1.*

Go to the futures (actual) window <T> <U>. Access the futures add menu <A>. Move the cursor to the last field and select the first eight contracts <8 Enter>. Create the futures strip in the futures window <Ctrl A>. Update the market data <Alt U>. Calculate <F3>. The futures strip in *window 10.2* appears.

Observe the payoff difference graph <F8> <F8> <D>. See *window 10.3*. Observe the bin analysis <F7>. See *window 10.4*. Use the sensitivity analysis <F6> to confirm that the replication of the swap using futures is effective when the yield curve tilts.

Check using URM – Exercise 10b

Load file RMW10B. The existing two-year cap with 7.5 per cent strike appears in the cap/floor window <C> in exploded form. The required cap with strike of 9.0 per cent appears in the target cap/floor window <T>. Calculate <F3>. The value of the existing and target caps both appear in the lower fields labelled Portfolio PV. The present values also appear in the summary window <F5>. The fair market value is $1,965,234 for the existing 7.5 per cent cap and $697,298 for the target 9.0 per cent cap.

View the payoff graph <F8> <F8>. Notice the mismatch – see *window 10.6*. Go to the futures (actual) window <U>. If the *target portfolio* window appears instead of the *actual*, press <T>. Add the 90 day futures strip through the add menu

<A> and <8 Enter> in the *Number of Futures* field followed by <Ctrl A> to create the strip. The eight nearest contract months appear in the futures window. Update the market date <Alt U>. Calculate <F3>.

The bin-by-bin delta-matched futures quantities are produced. See *window 10.7*. Observe the bin analysis <F7> – see *window 10.8* – and payoff graph <F8> <F8> – see *window 10.9*. Also study the sensitivity analysis <F6>. Notice a time lapse tracking loss occurs.

Check using URM – Exercise 10c

Load file RMW10D. The required cap appears in the target cap/floor window <T> <C>. Calculate <F3>. See *window 10.10*. A September 1995 ETO with 92 strike appears in the (actual portfolio) ETO window <T><E>. Calculate <F3>. Notice the cap value is $48,770. Also notice the number of ETO contracts is 127. The upward yield shift is matched over the very wide range of 400bp – see the risk control window <F2>.

Study the sensitivity analysis <F6> and payoff graph <F8><F8> – see *window 10.11*. The tracking error is positive for the first 300bp shift, then it quickly becomes negative. We need to use ETOs with lower gamma. Therefore try adding a December 1995 ETO with 90.00 strike. Go to the ETO portfolio window <Esc> <E>. The December ETO is already present but the face value is set to zero. Unfix the face value field using <Delete>. Press <F3> to calculate.

This time the automated delta matching produces a matching portfolio with 5 September 1995 ETOs and 277 December 1995 ETOs. View the payoff graph <F8> <F8> – see *window 10.12*. View the sensitivity analysis <F6>.

Test the tilt risk by activating tilt <L>, entering <0> for the O/N (overnight) yield shift and <2> for the tilt point (in years). Notice the tracking error in cell 2 is $141,217. See *window 10.12a*. Test the one-day pure time lapse tracking error by entering <1> into the as-at date field and observing the middle cell (cell 5). Notice the error is $46 favourable.

Next we try including the first eight 90 day futures contracts, along with the two ETOs, in the hedge parcel.

Go to the futures window <U>. Access the add menu <A>, move the cursor to the last field and select the first eight contracts <8 Enter>. Create the futures strip <Ctrl A>. Update market data <Alt U>. Calculate <F3>. Notice that all eight futures used and that the first three contracts are long and all the other contracts are short. See *window 10.13*. View the ETO window <E>. Notice that zero September ETOs and 238 long December ETOs are used in combination with the futures strip.

The first three futures are long positions because some of the ETO delta, which is concentrated at the near end, needs to be neutralised. View the payoff graph <F8><F8> – see *window 10.14*. Use the sensitivity analysis to confirm that the one-day time lapse is $54 in our favour and the 0 – 100 two year tilt risk is now $33,349 adverse.

Summary

- Futures can be used to replicate/hedge swaps but some gamma risk remains.

- Volatility risk in caps and floors cannot be hedged with futures/forwards alone.

- Strongly asymmetric instruments, such as exchange traded options, can be used in combination with futures and forwards to improve volatility and gap risk protection.

- The bin technique is an effective way to formulate risk reshaping hedge parcels.

- The market value of any instrument can be manufactured using a different instrument type, or combination of instruments, provided the market value of the instrument is replicated through time.

- Effective catastrophe insurance must perform under extreme market gaps.

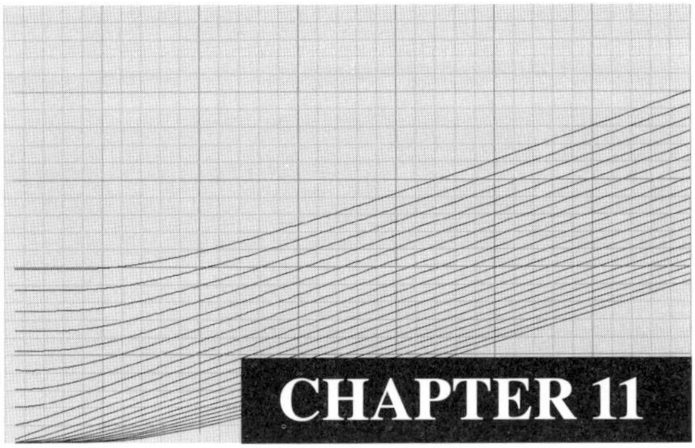

Benchmarks and Riskmarks

In this chapter we discuss:

- payoff benchmarks;
- the need to specify the benchmark correctly;
- the reshaping process;
- flat benchmarks;
- asymmetric benchmarks, and
- measuring performance.

Payoff benchmarks

Reshaping risk in line with a pre-set target or benchmark may be seen as the objective of risk management.

The target risk must be specified. If the benchmark is not specified as a payoff profile at each point in time, or is not capable of being recast in this form, *risk holes* will exist. Obviously market linked benchmarks do not satisfy this test. The benchmark payoff should encompass expected as well as unexpected market changes. Without the foundation of a payoff related benchmark, reliable arbitrage based techniques cannot be used to determine the expected hedge cost or the composition of the hedge portfolio through time, and it will be difficult to produce a meaningful performance measure.

Risk reshaping

The benchmark can be viewed as a virtual financial instrument and expressed as risk components in the same manner as a real instrument. The native risk can then be reshaped to match the benchmark risk measures by matching its risk measures through time using hedge instruments.

Flat benchmarks

A common form of benchmark is the fully hedged exposure designed to reshape all native risk to zero. However, it should be remembered that the flat benchmark does not necessarily eliminate exposure to market movements. For example, if the market moves favourably relative to the native exposure, the hedging portfolio incurs an offsetting loss. This is, in fact, a high risk hedge if there is a possibility that the native exposure can change or, worse, vanish before the hedge matures – a large uncovered hedge loss could be incurred.

Hence, the flat benchmark does not necessarily result in the hedge with lowest market risk exposure – it may not be the most conservative or safest benchmark. Also, the flat benchmark eliminates any possibility of gains from favourable market movements. For these reasons the asymmetric benchmark often produces a lower risk, more appealing hedge.

Asymmetric benchmarks

Frequently it is desirable to adopt a benchmark that limits hedging losses to a pre-set level, but which allows for the possibility of capturing some of the gains from favourable market movements. This is an asymmetric benchmark.

As with asymmetric derivatives, the natural advantage of asymmetric benchmarks must be paid for in the form of an upfront premium or implied hedging cost. Also, asymmetric benchmarks are sensitive to volatility shifts.

Arbitrage pricing techniques can be used to determine the fair market cost of virtually any form of asymmetric benchmark.

This costing can be compared with that of any asymmetric derivatives available in the market that match the hedge instrument implied in the benchmark.

Alternatively, the benchmark payoff can be manufactured from more elementary liquid derivatives using dynamic replication techniques – delta and *multirisk* hedging. As with all replication techniques, accuracy depends on the robustness or stability of the risk measure matching as well as the number of risk measures matched.

Asymmetric benchmarks are very common. For example, any actively managed hedging program which attempts to limit hedging losses and capture gains from favourable market movements using a partial hedge adjusted through time, is an attempt to produce an asymmetric payoff – whether recognised or not. Frequently, these hedge adjustments are based on market forecasts. However, a more rigorous and predictable outcome is achieved by manufacturing the benchmark payoff using arbitrage based replication principles.

Performance measurement

Should risk managers attempt to beat their benchmarks?

Attempts to beat benchmarks create *risk holes*. The only benchmark that can be beaten without creating a speculative based *risk hole* is one that is incorrectly formulated – that is, its estimated cost is too high.

Viewed this way, the professional risk manager should never attempt to beat an arbitrage based benchmark.

Rather, the objective should be to achieve a trading result as close as possible to the benchmark. It follows that if *risk holes* are to be avoided, outcomes significantly better than an arbitrage based benchmark should be cause for concern.

Risk management is a process of reshaping the distribution of returns, in line with a pre-set target, as accurately as possible.

Summary

- Benchmarks based on payoff profiles can be manufactured from derivatives using arbitrage based replication techniques.
- Risk management is also a process of reshaping the distribution of returns in line with a pre-set target.
- The reshaping cost is influenced by the degree of asymmetry of the target payoff or benchmark and market parameters such as yields and yield volatility.
- Flat benchmarks can be high risk if there is a possibility that the native exposures can change.
- Asymmetric benchmarks limit hedging losses.
- Any hedging program that attempts to limit hedge losses and capture favourable market movements is a form of asymmetric hedge.
- Attempts to beat benchmarks create *risk holes*.

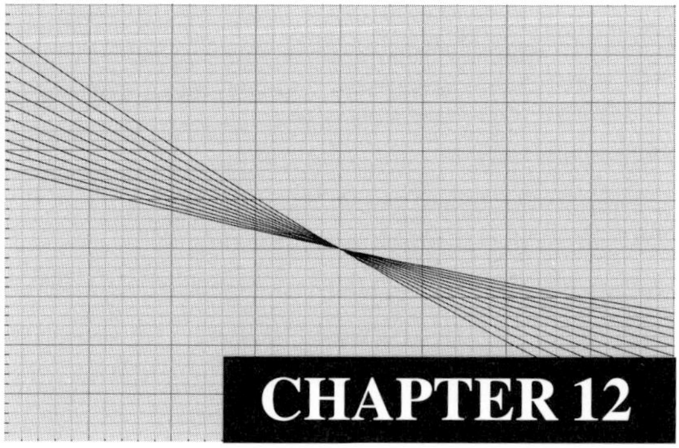

CHAPTER 12

Pricing Formula – Summary

This chapter lists, with brief explanation, the most commonly used formulae in this publication.

Cashflow present value

The present value of a cashflow is determined by multiplying its face value by its discount factor. The discount factor is a function of both the cashflow duration and the relevant interest (zero) rate. Although there is only one discount factor, the formula for the discount factor depends of the form of interest rate quoted. Interest may be paid in advance or arrears – that is, the discount or yield method. Also, the compounding frequency may be continuous or discrete and the day count basis can vary.

Continuously compounded

$$PV = FV\ e^{-rt}$$

Simple interest in arrears, yield quote

$$PV = FV/(1 + rt)$$

Simple interest in advance, discount quote

$$PV = FV(1 - rt)$$

Discrete compounding interest, yield quote

$$PV = FV/(1 + r/n)^{nt}$$

Discrete compounding interest, discount quote

$$PV = FV(1 - r/n)^{nt}$$

where:

n = compounding frequency
t = projection term in days/(d_y)
d_y = day count, 365 or 360 depending on convention

The two simple interest formulae are used for pricing discount instruments such as bank bills, treasury notes, deposits and promissory notes, futures as well as forwards such as FRAs and swap legs. However, in the case of forwards future values must be discounted to present value.

FRA valuation

The present value of a FRA is:

Yield quote:

$$\Delta PV_{FRA.\Delta r} = d_{f\Delta}FV[1/(1+r_1t) - (1/(1+r+\Delta r)t)] - d_fFV[1/(1+r_1t) - 1/(1+rt)]$$

and

Discount quote:

$$\Delta PV_{FRA.\Delta r} = FVt[d_{f\Delta}(r-r_1+\Delta r) - d_f(r-r_1)]$$

where:

PV = present value of the underlying instrument
FV = future value of the underlying instrument
r = current or market FRA rate
t = FRA term in days divided by 360 or 365
r_1 = contract or FRA entry rate
d_f = current discount factor from the FRA cashflow settlement date to today.
$d_{f\Delta}$ = discount factor after the market nudge.
Δr = nudge in the FRA rate

Macaulay's duration

The Macaulay duration is a present value weighted average of the terms of the payment stream. Its dimension is time, in years.

$$dur_{mac} = \frac{\sum_{i=1}^{n} PV_i t_i}{\sum_{i=1}^{n} PV_i}$$

Cashflow portfolio sensitivity

The change in the present value of a portfolio of cashflows for small yield shifts is:

$$\Delta PV_T \approx -dur_{mod} \times PV_T \times \Delta r$$

where:

$$dur_{mod} \approx \frac{dur_{mac}}{1+r/n}$$

r	=	internal rate of return
Δr	=	change in internal rate of return
PV_T	=	total present value
ΔPV_T	=	change in present value
n	=	compounding frequency

European option pricing

A convenient variant of the Black-Scholes European option pricing formula is provided. It is known as the Garman-Kohlhagen or Grabbe formula. This formula can be used to determine the arbitrage based price of foreign exchange options. It can also be used to estimate the price of interest rate options by setting r_f equal to r_d.

$$C = e^{-r_f T} S N(x+\sigma\sqrt{T}) - e^{-r_d T} K N(x) \geq 0$$

$$P = e^{-r_f T} S[N(x+\sigma\sqrt{T}) - 1] - e^{-r_d T} K[N(x) - 1] \geq 0$$

where:

$$x = \frac{\ln(S/K) + r_d T - r_f T - \sigma^2 T/2}{\sigma\sqrt{T}}$$

C = call price
P = put price
S = spot rate
K = strike
σ = annualised standard deviation of daily returns
T = years to maturity
r_d = base currency risk free continuous interest rate
r_f = dividend yield of underlying asset, or foreign currency risk free continuous interest rate
N = cumulative standard normal distribution function.

Bond price

The unit price of a fixed interest rate bond, assuming all coupon payments are received is:

$$P = C/F\,[Y^{N(1/F - T)} - Y^{-NT}]/[Y^{N/F} - 1] + Y^{-NT}$$

where:

Y = $1+R/N$
R = average bond yield
C = coupon rate
F = coupon frequency
N = yield conversion frequency
T_1 = duration of first coupon in years
T = duration of principal payment in years.

The following formulae are not used in this edition but are included here as a convenient reference.

Volatility estimation[1]

Suppose that we have a two time series $A_0, A_1, \ldots, A_n$ and $B_0, B_1, \ldots, B_n$ at n+1 equally spaced time steps such as daily closing prices. Denote the time step between data by Δt. This time step is to be measured in years. For example, if the data is taken daily, since there are approximately 250 trading days in a year, $\Delta t = 1/250 = 0.004$. There are two common methods for estimating volatilities and instantaneous correlations between these series – linear differences and the logarithmic method.

Linear Differences:
The first unbiased estimator for the volatility σ_A for the process A is calculated as follows.

Define m_A by:

$$m_A = \frac{1}{n}\sum_{j=0}^{n}\frac{A_{j+1}-A_j}{A_j}$$

Then

$$\sigma_A^{\;2} = \frac{1}{n\Delta t}\sum_{j=0}^{n-1}\left[\frac{A_{j+1}-A_j}{A_j} - m_A\right]^2$$

The volatility σ_B for the process B is similarly estimated. The correlation ρ is estimated by:

$$\rho = \frac{\frac{1}{n\Delta t}\sum_{j=0}^{n-1}\left[\frac{A_{j+1}-A_j}{A_j}-m_A\right]^2\left[\frac{B_{j+1}-B_j}{B_j}-m_B\right]^2}{\sigma_A\sigma_B}$$

Logarithmic Method:

This method is the same except that $\frac{A_{j+1}-A_j}{A_j}$ and $\frac{B_{j+1}-B_j}{B_j}$ are replaced with $\log(A_{j+1}/A_j)$ and $\log(B_{j+1}/B_j)$ respectively.

Interest rate parity

The interest rate parity formulae expresses a currency forward price in terms the spot rate of exchange and the domestic and foreign interest rates:

$$F = Se^{(r_d - r_f)T} \geq 0$$

where:

F = forward rate – direct quote
S = spot rate – direct quote
r_d = domestic interest rate – from spot date
r_f = foreign interest rate – from spot date
T = duration in years

Notes

1 Extract from R. McKay and J. Price. Optimal Cross Hedging of Forwards. Unpublished paper, 1996.

First Risk Olympics – Heat I

First Risk Olympics is a worldwide competition for derivatives professionals. It consists of multiple choice questions designed to test and develop risk intuition. All questions can be answered intuitively; you don't need to be a rocket scientist to win. Heat I is the first of several heats and was transmitted to thousands of derivatives professional around the world on 16 July 1996, simultaneously. Names of the highest scoring individuals appear on the ***First Risk Olympics*** Internet site honour list http://www.ristek.com/~ristek/winners.html. Also, the game can be played directly from the Internet http://www.ristek.com/~ristek/heat1.html.

Only one answer is considered correct for each question.

Question 1 **The humble cashflow**

A positive cashflow has a fixed face value. A sensitivity analysis is performed to measure the increase in its present value from a sudden 1per cent decrease in yields. The same analysis is performed on a second cashflow, which is identical in all respects, except it has a longer duration. Assume a flat yield curve at say, 10 per cent semi-annual. The change in present value of the longer term cashflow:

A Is necessarily greater than for the shorter term cashflow.
B Is necessarily less than for the shorter term cashflow.
C May be greater or less than the shorter term cashflow.
D The present values actually decrease, not increase.

Question 2 **The age of VaR**

A risk manager is presented with a Value at Risk (VaR) measure of a complex diversified derivatives portfolio. The

VaR is a single statistic intended to express the maximum one day loss within a 99 per cent confidence limit. The VaR indicates the potential for loss is too high. The risk manager must formulate directly an effective hedge or hedges to reduce the portfolio's market risk exposure.

A The risk manager can do this simply by knowing the VaR.
B The asset types – not specific instrument details – in the portfolio must also be known.
C The asset types, spot and forward market rates must also be known.
D The risk manager cannot determine the required hedge(s) given only the VaR, the relevant asset types and market data.

Question 3 **Exposed to what?**

A corporate enters into a long term FX forward to hedge a contingent liability. The hedge may need to be closed and settled at any time. The present value of the profit or loss on the hedge is, in general, exposed to:

A Changes in the spot (exchange) rate only.
B Changes in the spot rate and the domestic interest rate only.
C Changes in the spot rate and the interest rates of both currencies only.
D Changes in the spot rate, both interest rates as well as time lapse.
E No market rates once a reverse FX forward with equal face value and maturity is entered into.

Question 4 **Is this real?**

A trader performs a stress test on an interest rate related derivatives portfolio using uniform yield shifts with time and all other economic parameters unchanged. The portfolio appears to profit when yields increase. It also appears to profit when yields decrease.

A This suggests the net delta is zero and gamma is zero or positive.
B This suggests the stress analysis software is defective – this result violates arbitrage theory.
C This suggests the portfolio will tend to gain value as time lapses.
D This effect can occur only if options are present in the portfolio.

Question 5 **Does it matter?**

An exporter can use either FX futures or forwards to hedge a long dated FX exposure. Both futures and forwards are available with expiries coinciding with the payment date. Domestic and foreign currency interest rates exceed 10 per cent. To achieve near risk equivalence, the face value of the futures contracts:

A Should be greater than an equivalent forward contract.
B Should be less than a forward contract.
C Should be the same as a forward contract.
D May be greater or less than a forward, depending on which currency has the higher interest rate.

Question 6 **A fundamental thing**

The critical dimension, that is the fundamental unit of measure, of a simple interest rate is:

A A unit of the currency of the underlying instrument eg. dollars for US dollar based instruments.
B It has no dimension – interest rates are dimensionless numbers.

C 1/time.
D time.
E per cent

Question 7 **The business of banking**

A banker uses interest rate derivatives to manage a fixed rate mortgage portfolio. The bank's board views exposure management based on rate forecasts as speculative and prohibits it. A careful stress analysis indicates that the portfolio contains *risk holes* – it is exposed to yield curve changes. The risk manager then formulates and executes a hedge parcel that reduces significantly market risk exposure. With less market risk the expected or average profit to the bank:

A Increases.
B Decreases – but only by the amount of the hedge parcel transaction costs.
C Decreases significantly since less risk means less return.
D Stays the same.
E May increase or decrease.

that's it...

Answers: 1☐ 2☐ 3☐ 4☐ 5☐ 6☐ 7☐

First Risk Olympics – Heat I results

The competition produced a wide variation in scores.

8 per cent scored	7 out of 7 correct
3 per cent scored	6
7 per cent scored	5
11 per cent scored	4
24 per cent scored	3
21 per cent scored	2
18 per cent scored	1
8 per cent scored	0

The average score of all players was 2.92 questions correct out of 7.

The probability of a perfect score through random selection is (1/32,000) and the probability of a zero score selection is (1/6.17).

Qn 1.	23 per cent gave the correct answer
Qn 2.	58 per cent
Qn 3.	61 per cent
Qn 4.	45 per cent
Qn 5.	36 per cent
Qn 6.	41 per cent
Qn 7.	38 per cent

The majority of players answered questions 2 and 3 correctly and all other questions incorrectly. However, for all questions except question 1 the correct answer was the most popular choice. Question 1 *The humble cashflow* produced an unusual result – 63 per cent selected the same incorrect answer and only 23 per cent selected the correct answer.

Countries represented by players include Australia, Belgium, Bermuda, Germany, Italy, Hong Kong, Japan, New Zealand,

South Africa, Taiwan, UK and USA. Altogether, 23 per cent of players were bankers, 18 per cent traders, 11 per cent risk consultants, 8 per cent mathematicians, 6 per cent brokers and 3 per cent fund managers.

Exercises

Equations

Windows

Tables

Charts

Figures

CDDABCB